PHILOSOPHY

D1075981

 TEACH YOURSELF®

For UK orders: please contact Bookpoint Ltd, 78 Milton Park, Abingdon, Oxon OX14 4TD. Telephone: (44) 01235 400414, Fax: (44) 01235 400454. Lines are open 9.00–6.00, Monday to Saturday, with a 24-hour message answering service. E-mail address: orders@bookpoint.co.uk

For USA and Canada orders: please contact NTC/Contemporary Publishing, 4255 West Touhy Avenue, Lincolnwood, Illinois 60646-1975, USA. Telephone: (847) 679 5500, Fax: (847) 679 2494.

Long renowned as the authoritative source for self-guided learning – with more than 40 million copies sold worldwide – the *Teach Yourself* series includes over 200 titles in the fields of languages, crafts, hobbies, business, computing and education.

British Library Cataloguing in Publication Data
A catalogue record for this title is available from the British Library.

Library of Congress Catalog Card Number: On file

First published in UK 2000 by Hodder Headline Plc, 338 Euston Road, London NW1 3BH.

First published in US by NTC/Contemporary Publishing, 4255 West Touhy Avenue, Lincolnwood (Chicago), Illinois 60646-1975, USA.

The 'Teach Yourself' name and logo are registered trademarks of Hodder & Stoughton.

Picture credits: Ann Ronan Picture Library 13, 15, 18, 19, 27, 32, 46, 49, 65, 68, 79, 94, 109, 124, 125, 132, 143, 154, 163, 167, 177; Ann Ronan at Image Select 30, 56, 61, 77, 92, 97, 107, 129, 144, 173, 185, 201; Image Select 37, 48, 71, 116, 190, 209.

Text editor: Ian Crofton
Typeset by TechType, Abingdon, Oxon
Printed in Great Britain for Hodder & Stoughton Educational, a division of Hodder Headline Plc, 338 Euston Road, London NW1 3BH, by Cox & Wyman, Reading, Berkshire

Impression number   10 9 8 7 6 5 4 3 2
Year   2006   2005   2004   2003   2002   2001   2000

Contents

Bold type in the text indicates a cross reference. A plural, or possessive, is given as the cross reference, i.e. is in bold type, even if the entry to which it refers is singular.

abduction

A form of probable **inference**, reaching a probable conclusion on the basis of available evidence. Aristotle uses the term to refer to a weak **syllogism** that fails to carry certainty. For C S **Peirce**, it is the process of generating a **hypothesis**.

Abelard, Peter (1079–1142)

French philosopher, one of the leading figures of **scholasticism**. Abelard opposed **realism** in the debate over universals, and propounded 'conceptualism', whereby universal terms have only a mental existence. He asserted the importance of reason in religious belief, and his skilful application of logic and dialectic to such doctrines as the Trinity and atonement, though controversial, gave theology a new breadth.

> ❝ Insofar as reason is hidden, let us be content with authority. ❞
>
> **Peter Abelard**, quoted in Gordon Leff, *Medieval Thought: St Augustine to Ockham*

HÉLOÏSE AND ABELARD

Abelard was canon of Notre Dame in Paris and master of the cathedral school. His romantic liaison with his pupil Héloïse caused a scandal. When his secret marriage to her (shortly after the birth of a son) became known, she entered a convent. He was castrated at the instigation of her uncle Canon Fulbert, and became a monk. After her death in 1164, Héloïse was buried beside him.

---

abortion

The ethical issues arising from the deliberate termination of pregnancy are difficult, and arouse strong emotions. At one extreme of the argument are the most radical advocates of a woman's right to choose to have an abortion, whatever the circumstances. These 'pro-choice' advocates argue from the point of view of individual **freedom** and **human rights** that a woman should have complete control over her own body. At the other extreme are those who argue, usually but not exclusively on religious grounds, that the fetus, from the moment of conception, is an innocent human being, and thus that abortion in all circumstances is murder.

It is unlikely that these two positions will ever be reconciled. However, moving in from the extremes, the question arises as to the stage at which a fetus becomes a human being. Consider the following three statements:

1. The fetus (or embryo) immediately after conception (being simply a fusion of a sperm cell and an egg cell) is not a human being.

2. The fetus immediately prior to birth is a human being.

3. There is no identifiable point at which the developing fetus becomes a human being.

Probably most people would agree with all three statements. Yet, logically, all three cannot be true. Nevertheless, many countries have based their laws on abortion on the acceptance of the first and third, and have established 'viability' – the point at which the fetus is capable of independent life outside of the womb – as the stage after which abortion is considered as the killing of a human being. This is inevitably relativistic, given that the viability of the fetus is dependent on the state of the medical technology available.

absolute

The opposite of relative, dependent, or conditioned. The underlying view that underlies the idea of the absolute is that any particular thing is incomplete and therefore not fully real: it is only the totality, the universe as a whole, beyond which nothing is, that has unrestricted reality. Ultimately it is this whole or absolute that is the only object of genuine knowledge.

The notion goes back to the Greek pre-Socratic philosopher **Parmenides**. **Plato** regarded the absolute as the source and principle of all reality, as did such later rationalist thinkers as **Descartes, Spinoza**, and the absolute idealist philosophers **Schelling** and **Hegel**.

Philosophers of a more empirical temper have rejected this whole approach and deny that there is an absolute, or that knowledge of a part (as against the whole) is not genuine. Indeed they argue that all knowledge is of this partial kind, since in order to know we must be able to distinguish different features; and, moreover, we must recognize a contrast between knower and known.

❞ Absolute truth belongs to Thee alone. ❟
Gotthold Ephraim Lessing, Wolfenbüttler Fragmente

absolutism

A term that in philosophy has been used to convey two quite separate and distinct ideas:

- The first, which is associated with **Hegel**, refers to the ideal and evolving nature of ultimate reality that Hegel called the **absolute**.

- The second theory asserts the existence and authority of absolute truth, and could be summarized by the assertion that it is in principle possible to say of any statement that it is either true or false, although people do not necessarily possess the means to decide which of these two alternatives it may be. Compare **pragmatism** and **instrumentalism**.

abstraction

In philosophy, the process by which **universals** and **concepts** are formed in our minds, or by which we acquire general words.

- Many modern philosophers, following **Wittgenstein**, hold that no concepts are acquired by abstraction, because the **meaning** of a word is its public use, not a private idea.

- **Aristotle** held that circularity, for example, does not exist apart from circular things, and that we acquire the abstraction of circularity by **induction** – that is, by generalizing from such objects as coins, hoops, and wheels.

- **Locke** thought that the meaning of a general word, such as 'triangle', is an idea in the mind, but that the idea is formed by abstraction from experience.

absurd, the

A term used in existentialism to denote the meaninglessness and irrationality of the universe in which human beings have to make their choices, regardless of rationality or morality. The term is also applied to a related literary movement that emerged in the 1950s, especially to the plays of Samuel Beckett, Eugène Ionesco, Jean Genet, and Harold Pinter.

Academy, the

The name (Greek *Akademeia*) that was originally applied to the Greek school of philosophy founded in around 387 BC by **Plato** in the gardens of Academe, northwest of Athens. After Plato's death (347 BC) the Academy continued in a number of different guises until 79 BC. It was revived in the 4th century AD, but closed by the Byzantine emperor Justinian I, with the other pagan schools, in AD 529. There was also a **Platonic Academy** in 15th-century Florence.

Achilles paradox, the

A paradox of motion, devised in the 5th century BC by **Zeno of Elea**. The great warrior Achilles races the slow tortoise, but the tortoise is given a head start. By the time Achilles has closed the gap, the tortoise has moved on, creating a new, albeit smaller, gap, and so on, so Achilles can never win the race.

Adorno, Theodor (1903–1969)

German philosopher, social theorist, and musicologist. Deeply influenced by the thought of **Karl Marx**, Adorno joined the **Frankfurt School** in 1931. With the rise of Fascism he fled to England and then the USA, returning to Frankfurt in 1949.

- In *Dialectic of Enlightenment* (1947, with Max Horkheimer), Adorno argued that rationality had not been an emancipatory force, but that modern science was an instrument of dehumanization.

- Adorno was the main contributor to *The Authoritarian Personality* (1950), which analysed the psychological origins of fascism within a broadly Freudian framework.

- In *Negative Dialects* (1966) Adorno was critical of all philosophers because they believed in some nonexistent absolute or ultimate entity that would explain everything else. This was dangerous, he argued, because it led to totalitarian and oppressive thinking that turned the individual into an object to be manipulated.

Adorno also wrote extensively on the aesthetics and sociology of music and art, including *The Philosophy of Modern Music* (1947).

aesthetics

The branch of philosophy that deals with the nature of beauty, especially in art. The subject of aesthetics was introduced by **Plato** and enlarged upon by **Aristotle**, but it did not emerge as a distinct branch of enquiry until the mid-18th century. **See** *beauty.*

agnosticism

The belief that the existence of God cannot be proven, and that in the nature of things the individual cannot know anything of what lies behind or beyond the world of natural phenomena. Whereas **atheism** denies the existence of God or gods, an agnostic asserts that God or a **first cause** is one of those concepts (others include the absolute, infinity, eternity, and immortality) that lie beyond the reach of human intelligence, and therefore can be neither confirmed nor denied.

The word 'agnostic' was coined in 1869 by T H Huxley, the renowned biologist who became known as 'Darwin's bulldog' for his defence of the theory of natural selection.

Albertus Magnus, St (1200–1280)
German theologian, philosopher, and scientist. He was known as *Doctor Universalis* because of the breadth of his knowledge. He tried to reconcile the thought of **Aristotle** with Christian teachings, and numbered St Thomas **Aquinas** among his pupils.

al-Farabi, Abu Nasr (*c.* 870–950)
Arab philosopher of Turkish origin, who is best known as having introduced **Aristotle** to the Islamic world. A diligent commentator on Aristotle's works from the **neo-Platonist** standpoint, he applied Plato's political theories to the problems of his day. He exercised considerable influence upon **Avicenna** and **Averroës**, and was known to the medieval schoolmen (see **scholasticism**).

algorithm
A procedure or series of steps that can be used to solve a problem. In computer science, it describes the logical sequence of operations to be performed by a program (compare **heuristics**).

The word algorithm derives from the name of 9th-century Arab mathematician Muhammad ibn-Musa al-Khwarizmi.

alienation
A sense of isolation, powerlessness, and therefore frustration; a feeling of loss of control over one's life; a sense of estrangement from society or even from oneself. As a concept it was developed by **Hegel** and **Marx**. The latter used it as a description and criticism of the condition that developed among workers in capitalist society. The term has also been used by non-Marxist thinkers such as Emile **Durkheim**.

al-Kindi (lived 9th century)
Arab philosopher, who introduced into the Islamic world a system that combined **Aristotelianism** and **neo-Platonism**. His outlook was fundamentally religious, and he considered philosophy as the 'handmaiden of revelation'.

Althusser, Louis (1918–1990)
French philosopher and Marxist, born in Algeria, who argued that the idea that economic systems determine family and political systems is too simple. He attempted to show how the ruling-class ideology of a particular era is a crucial form of class control. His **structuralist** analysis of capitalism sees individuals and groups as agents or bearers of the structures of social relations, rather than as independent influences on history.

Althusser murdered his wife in 1980, and spent the next few years in mental hospitals.

altruism

A term, briefly defined as 'living for others', coined by the French positivist philosopher Auguste **Comte**. He believed that altruism is a social instinct or impulse, and is evidenced in kindness, veneration, and affection. It was this instinct or tendency in human beings that Comte wished to raise to a conscious principle, or an ethical ideal, making it the chief aim of human action to seek the welfare of others. Herbert **Spencer** in his *Data of Ethics* (1879) sought to show that in the course of social evolution egoism and altruism would be reconciled. Altruism is not the exclusive possession of humanity, but is seen among some other animals.

amorality and immorality

Amorality is often mistakenly assumed to mean extreme immorality or wickedness, whereas its correct meaning is the absence of any knowledge of moral values. Amorality is thus universally found in babies and young children, and the laws of most countries set an age under which an individual is not regarded as accountable for actions that would otherwise be regarded as criminal. Immorality, by contrast, involves the conscious and deliberate breaking of moral principles. In the past, European observers often interpreted certain non-Western societies as amoral (for example, if they had a more permissive approach to sex), whereas in fact such societies usually have highly evolved – but different – systems of moral values.

analytic

A term derived from **Kant**: the converse of **synthetic**. In an analytic judgement, the judgement provides no new knowledge; for example: 'All bachelors are unmarried.'

analytic philosophy

Term applied to much of 20th-century British and American philosophy by its practitioners. Analytic philosophy is more of an approach than a coherent body of beliefs. It emphasizes the values of rigour, precision, logic, and a close attention to language, regards **metaphysics** as an inappropriate subject for philosophers, and is generally hostile to the system-building of **continental philosophy**. It derives from the **empiricism** of *Locke* and *Hume*, and its first important practitioners, at the beginning of the 20th century, were Bertrand **Russell** and G E **Moore**.

anarchism

Political philosophy that society should have no government, laws, police, or other authority, but should be a free association of all its members. It opposes both **capitalism** and **communism**. Anarchism does not mean 'without order'; most theories of anarchism imply an order of a very strict and symmetrical kind, but they maintain that such order can be achieved by cooperation and education. Anarchism must not be confused with **nihilism** (a purely negative and destructive activity directed against society).

Anarchism was an influential ideology in the 19th and early 20th centuries. It was revived by young radicals in the 1960s, and is still important among followers of alternative life-styles. Notable anarchist thinkers include William **Godwin**, P J **Proudhon**, Mikhail **Bakunin**, Peter **Kropotkin**, and Mahatma **Gandhi**.

Anaxagoras (*c.* 500–428 BC)

Greek cosmologist and pre-Socratic philosopher. He speculated that everything consisted of 'seeds', which contained a little of every natural substance. Changes in things occurred by the exchange of portions of seeds. In the beginning, all natural substances were mixed together and Mind ('finest of all things and purest') started a rotation that formed the Earth by vortex action. Anaxagoras studied under **Anaximenes**, and his pupils included the politician Pericles, the playwright Euripides, and possibly the philosopher **Socrates**. **See also:** *logos.*

THE IMPIOUS PHILOSOPHER

Anaximander was prosecuted for impiety and banished from Athens because he described the Sun as a white-hot lump of stone.

Anaximander (*c.* 610–*c.* 546 BC)

Greek astronomer and pre-Socratic philosopher. A pupil of **Thales**, he shared the early Greek philosophical urge to explain the universe with a tiny number of general laws. Among his beliefs was the idea that the universe originated as a formless mass containing within itself the contraries of hot and cold, and wet and dry, from which land, sea, and air were formed out of the union and separation of these opposites. He is thought to have been the first to determine solstices and equinoxes, and he credited with drawing the first geographical map of the whole known world.

Anaximenes (died *c.* 528 BC)

Greek cosmologist and pre-Socratic philosopher. He was the teacher of **Anaxagoras**. He originated the important idea of monism: that one substance could account for the diversity of the world. This substance was air or mist. Rarefied, it became fire; condensed, water and earth. He seems to have chosen air or mist as the basic substance because of its apparent connections with fire, rain, and breath in living creatures.

anguish (English), **Angst** (German), **angoisse** (French)
In existentialism, the general human anxiety at having free will, that is, of being responsible for one's actions.

animals
For many centuries questions regarding the moral status and rights of animals did not greatly concern Western philosophers and theologians. The account in Genesis of God giving humans dominion over the animals set the tone, and in Christian theology only human beings were accorded a soul. (Such views are in sharp contrast to the beliefs of many non-Western cultures.) A few thinkers, such as Thomas **Aquinas** and Immanuel **Kant**, thought that the only reason not to be cruel to animals was that such actions were likely to lead us to be cruel to our fellow humans. Jeremy **Bentham** was perhaps the first Western philosopher to extend his ethical thinking to animals, and the 19th century witnessed the first legislation against cruel treatment of animals.

The advent of **Darwinism** in the middle of the 19th century profoundly undermined the traditional distinctions between humans and animals. However, despite this intellectual revolution, the concept of animal rights – the extension of **human rights** to animals – did not become established until the publication in 1976 of *Animal Liberation* by the Australian philosopher Peter Singer (1946–). Since then, human responsibility to other animals has become a major concern of moral philosophers. **See also:** *consciousness; soul.*

> ❦ Brutes never meet in bloody fray,
> Nor cut each other's throats, for pay. ❦
>
> **Oliver Goldsmith**, 'Logicians Refuted'

Anselm, St (*c.* 1033–1109)
Italian priest and philosopher, who became archbishop of Canterbury in 1093. He holds an important place in the development of **scholasticism**. In his *Proslogion*, Anselm developed the **ontological argument**, which infers God's existence from our capacity to conceive of a perfect being.

anthropology
The study of humankind. It investigates the cultural, social, and physical diversity of the human species, both past and present. It is divided into two broad categories:

- Biological or physical anthropology, which attempts to explain human biological variation from an evolutionary perspective.

- The larger field of social or cultural anthropology, which attempts to explain the variety of human cultures.

In the 19th century, Ludwig **Feuerbach** argued that philosophy should become anthropology, in the sense of a scientific study of the human being as a whole. The German philosopher Max Scheler (1874–1928) suggested the term 'philosophical anthropology' to describe the study of different conceptions of humanity.

See also: *human nature; Lévi-Strauss.*

Antisthenes (*c.* 444–*c.* 366 BC)

Greek philosopher, a pupil of **Socrates**, at whose death he was present. He is sometimes regarded as the founder of the **Cynic** school, but he also influenced **Stoicism** with his practical ethics. He believed that virtue could be taught, and that virtue with physical exercise was the way to happiness. He disapproved of all speculation, and so was opposed to **Plato**. Although not an adherent of **asceticism**, he held that wealth and luxury were unimportant, as were established laws and conventions, birth, sex, and race. Among his pupils was **Diogenes the Cynic**.

Apollonian and Dionysiac

Two terms used by **Nietzsche** in *The Birth of Tragedy* (1872), his study of the origins of ancient Greek drama. In this work he contrasted the Apollonian principle – incorporating the individuating, rationalizing, and conscious principle in human society – with the Dionysiac, which he saw as collective, irrational, and lyrical.

APOLLO AND DIONYSUS

In the Greek pantheon of gods, Apollo was the god of sun, music, poetry, prophecy, agriculture, and pastoral life. Dionysus was the god of wine, orgiastic excess, and mystic ecstasy.

---

a posteriori

A Latin term (literally 'from the latter') that is applied to arguments that derive causes from their effects, or a general principle from particular facts. Thus an a posteriori argument involves **induction**, and a posteriori knowledge depends on experience. A posteriori is the converse of **a priori**.

appearance

In philosophy, what is visible, or manifest to the senses, but is ultimately illusory. Hence, appearance is usually contrasted with reality, and so the term often occurs in **idealism** and **scepticism**.

apperception

A term introduced by **Leibniz** to denote the process by which the mind gets hold of the 'perceptions' of sense and turns them into conscious knowledge. **Kant** went on to speak of the transcendental and synthetic unity of apperception: the former is tantamount to self-consciousness, the very thing that gives meaning to a set of empirical experiences as belonging jointly to one experiencing self; the latter to the process of that self as consciously combining its perceptions.

a priori

A Latin term (literally 'from what comes before') applied to an argument or knowledge that is known to be true, or false, without reference to experience. Thus an a priori argument involves **deduction** from a general principle to particular facts or effects. A priori is the converse of a **posteriori**. **See also:** *contingent and necessary*.

KANT AND A PRIORI KNOWLEDGE

Immanuel Kant asserted that we do not derive such concepts as space, time, reality, and negation from experience, and so arguments from these are a priori. It is through the application of these concepts that we acquire experience. In morality he declares that the ideas implied in the words 'good' and 'bad' are innate and imperative in every mind, independently of actual observation.

Aquinas, St Thomas (1225–1274)

Italian philosopher and theologian, the greatest figure of **scholasticism**. A *Dominican monk*, he was known as the Doctor Angelicus ('Angelic Doctor'). Aquinas argued that reason and faith are compatible, and assimilated the philosophy of **Aristotle** into Christian doctrine. He also drew on the works of St **Augustine, Avicenna, Averroës**, and the **neo-Platonists**, and was a pupil of **Albertus Magnus**. His works, such as *Summa contra Gentiles* and *Summa Theologica*, embody the world view taught in universities until the mid-17th century. In 1879 his works were recognized as the basis of Catholic theology.

In metaphysics, Aquinas contrasts a thing's **essence** (that is, what makes it what it is) with its existence, though in God they coincide. He argued that the soul is immortal but cannot be permanently disembodied; therefore, physical resurrection is required. He developed five ways of demonstrating the existence of God. His theory of meaning relies on analogy; for example, the term 'God's wisdom' is to be understood by analogy with human wisdom. **See also:** *neo-Thomism*.

❝ Grace does not abolish nature, but perfects it. ❞

St Thomas Aquinas, quoted in Gordon Leff, *Medieval Thought*:
St Augustine to Ockham

Arendt, Hannah (1906–1975)

German-born US political philosopher. Her concerns included totalitarianism, the nature of evil, and the erosion of public participation in the political process. Arendt studied at Heidelberg under **Husserl** and **Jaspers**, but with the rise of the Nazis she moved to France, then emigrated to the USA in 1940. In her report of the trial of a leading Nazi war criminal, *Eichmann in Jerusalem* (1963), she coined the phrase 'the banality of evil' to describe how bureaucratic efficiency can facilitate the acceptance of the most terrible deeds. Other works include *The Origins of Modern Totalitarianism* (1951), *The Human Condition* (1958), *On Revolution* (1963), and *On Violence* (1972).

❝ Under conditions of tyranny it is far
easier to act than to think. ❞

Hannah Arendt, quoted in W H Auden *A Certain World*

argument

In logic, the middle term in a **syllogism**. More commonly, the word 'argument' denotes a connected series of propositional steps leading from a given premise to a conclusion.

See also: *a posteriori; a priori; deduction; induction.*

argument from design

One of four traditional arguments for the existence of God, the others being the **cosmological argument**, the **moral argument**, and the **ontological argument**. The argument from design (also known as the teleological argument; see **teleology**) states that the universe is so complex that it can only have been designed by a superhuman power (God). The argument became popular with Protestant theologians in the 18th century as a means of accommodating the science of Isaac **Newton**. It was attacked by the Scottish philosopher David **Hume**, among others. An alleged weakness in the argument is that it attempts a causal inference from the universe to God, when it only makes sense to speak of causal relations as holding between observable states of affairs. **See also:** *first cause.*

Aristippus (c. 435–356 BC)

Greek philosopher. He was the founder of the **Cyrenaic** or hedonist school. A pupil of **Socrates**, he developed the doctrine that pleasure is the highest good in life.

THE HEDONIST AND THE COURTESAN

Aristippus believed that self-control was the key to pleasure, the highest good. When criticized for consorting with a courtesan, he is reported to have responded: 'I possess her, but am not possessed by her; for to control pleasures without being mastered by them is better than not to control them at all.'

Aristotelianism

A tradition of ways of thinking based on the writings of the Greek philosopher **Aristotle**. Aristotelianism was the dominant philosophical influence in the early Middle Ages in Europe (see **scholasticism**), culminating in the work of St Thomas **Aquinas**, but was based on only a partial knowledge of Aristotle. Aristotelianism survives today in **neo-Thomism**.

Aristotle (384–322 BC)

Enormously influential Greek philosopher and scientist. He had an astonishingly wide range of interests, and his works that survive deal with logic, ethics, politics, metaphysics, physics, astronomy, meteorology, biology, psychology, and aesthetics. Aristotle was at first a follower of **Plato**, but, contrary to Plato's teaching, he came to maintain that sense experience is our only source of knowledge, and that by reasoning we can discover the essences of things, that is, their distinguishing qualities.

- Aristotle held that all matter consisted of a single 'prime matter', which was always determined by some form.
- The principle of life he termed a soul, which he regarded as the form of the living creature, not as a substance separable from it.
- The intellect, he believed, can discover in sense impressions the universal, and since the soul thus transcends matter, it must be immortal.
- He held that art embodies nature, but in a more perfect fashion, its end being the purifying and ennobling of the affections. He maintained that the essence of beauty is order and symmetry.
- In his works on ethics and politics, he suggested that human happiness consists in living in conformity with nature, and derived his political theory from the recognition that mutual aid is natural to humankind.
- He made the first systematic attempt to distinguish between different forms of government.

An artist's impression of Aristotle teaching Alexander the Great.

In the early Middle Ages, Aristotle's philosophy became the foundation of Islamic philosophy, and was then incorporated into Christian theology (see **Aristotelianism; scholasticism**). However, medieval scholars tended to accept his vast output without question, and many of his mistaken scientific theories held sway until the Scientific Revolution of the 16th and 17th centuries.

❦ This man [Aristotle] is ... an example which nature has devised to demonstrate supreme human perfection. ❧

Averroës, quoted in Gordon Leff, *Medieval Thought: St Augustine to Ockham*

artificial intelligence (AI)
The branch of **computer science** concerned with creating programs that can perform actions comparable with those of an intelligent human. The possibility of artificial intelligence was first proposed by Alan **Turing** in 1950. His test for distinguishing between real (human) and simulated (computer) thought is known as the 'Turing test': with a person in one room and the machine in another, an interrogator in a third room asks questions of both to try to identify them. When the interrogator cannot distinguish between them by questioning, the machine will have reached a state of humanlike intelligence.

asceticism
The renunciation of physical pleasures such as those found in eating, drinking, sex, and human company. The term comes from the Greek *askesis* 'practice or training for an ideal', and was defended by some of the Greek

THE CHINESE ROOM

Although those who argue strongly in favour of the possibility of true AI suggest that a machine that passes the Turing test would be experiencing a mental state, comparable to human consciousness, others have been more sceptical. The sceptics cite the 'Chinese room' thought experiment, in which a human is placed in a room with two windows. Through one window come inputs written in Chinese characters. The human has a set of instructions (analogous to a computer program) by which he or she can match the inputs with the appropriate outputs, also written in Chinese characters, which go out of the second window. The human does not need to understand Chinese to carry out the operations successfully, although those on the outside might assume that he or she did.

Cynic philosophers, while being opposed by the **Cyrenaic** or hedonist school. Practitioners of a number of religions use asceticism – to varying degrees – as a way of coming closer to God or enlightenment.

atheism

Nonbelief in, or the positive denial of, the existence of a God or gods. Like **theism**, its opposite, atheism cannot be proved or disproved conclusively. Perhaps the strongest atheistic argument concerns the existence of **evil**, which is hard to reconcile with the notion (in Christianity and other religions) that the world was created by an omnipotent, all-loving God. Theologians have responded with a variety of justifications for the existence of evil (see **theodicy**). Compare **agnosticism**.

VARIETIES OF ATHEISM
- Dogmatic atheism asserts that there is no God.
- Sceptical atheism maintains that the finite human mind is so constituted as to be incapable of discovering that there is or is not a God.
- Critical atheism holds that the evidence for theism is inadequate. This is akin to …
- Philosophical atheism, which fails to find evidence of a God manifest in the universe.
- Speculative atheism comprises the beliefs of those who, like **Kant**, find it impossible to demonstrate the existence of God.

❝ A little philosophy inclineth man's mind to atheism, but depth in philosophy bringeth men's minds about to religion. ❞

Francis Bacon, *Essays*, 'Atheism'

Augustine of Hippo, St
(354–430)

Early Christian leader and writer. After prolonged study of **neo-Platonism** he was converted to Christianity and became bishop of Hippo (modern Annaba, Algeria). Among Augustine's many writings are his *Confessions*, a spiritual autobiography, and *De Civitate Dei/The City of God*, vindicating the Christian church and divine providence. He attacked **Manichaeism** and the teachings of **Pelagius**, maintaining the doctrine of original sin and the necessity of divine grace.

St Augustine of Hippo.

❝ Give me chastity and continence, but do not give it yet. ❞

St Augustine, *Confessions*

Aurelius, Marcus
See *Marcus Aurelius*.

Austin, J(ohn) L(angshaw) (1911–1960)
British philosopher, a pioneer in the investigation of the way words are used in everyday speech. His later work was influential on the philosophy of **language**. His lectures *Sense and Sensibilia* and *How to do Things with Words* were published posthumously in 1962.

authenticity
A term used in **existentialism** to denote the condition of those who accept that they have **free will**, who take responsibility for their own lives, and who

---

AUSTIN'S SPEECH ACTS

According to Austin, there are three kinds of speech act:
- Locutions, or the uttering of meaningful sentences.
- Illocutions, or what one does in saying things, such as stating, promising, urging.
- Perlocutions, or what one does by saying things, such as persuading, frightening, embarrassing.

---

create their own identity, rather than allowing others to create it for them. The term in this sense was coined by Martin **Heidegger**. Compare **bad faith**.

Averroës (1126–1198)

Arab philosopher, also known as Ibn Rushd, who was born in Spain and spent much of his life there. His philosophical writings include commentaries on **Aristotle** and on **Plato's** *Republic*. He argued for the eternity of matter and against the immortality of the individual soul. He influenced Christian and Jewish writers into the Renaissance, and reconciled Islamic and Greek thought in asserting that philosophic truth comes through reason. Thomas **Aquinas** opposed this position. However, his European followers defended a distinction between philosophical truth and revealed religion.

> ❝ Philosophy is the friend and milk-sister of the Law. ❞
>
> **Averroës**, *The Decisive Treatise*

Avicenna (979–1037)

Iranian philosopher and physician, also known as Ibn Sina, the most renowned philosopher of medieval Islam. His philosophical writings were influenced by a**l-Farabi, Aristotle**, and **neo-Platonistm,** and in turn influenced 13th-century European **scholasticism**. His concept of God as the being in which **essence** and **existence** are identical gained wide currency, influencing Moses **Maimonides** and Thomas **Aquinas**.

axiom

In mathematics, a statement that is assumed to be true and upon which **theorems** are proved by using logical deduction; for example, two straight lines cannot enclose a space. The Greek mathematician Euclid used a series of axioms that he considered could not be demonstrated in terms of simpler concepts to prove his geometrical theorems.

Ayer, A(lfred) J(ules) (1910–1989)

English philosopher. His *Language, Truth and Logic* (1936) is an exposition of the theory of **logical positivism**, presenting a criterion by which meaningful statements (essentially truths of logic, as well as statements derived from experience) could be distinguished from meaningless metaphysical utterances (for example, claims that there is a God or that the world external to our own minds is illusory).

> ❦ No morality can be founded on authority, even if the authority were divine. ❧
>
> **A J Ayer**, Essay on Humanism

Bachelard, Gaston (1884–1962)

French philosopher and scientist who argued for a creative interplay between reason and experience. He attacked both Cartesian **rationalism** and **empiricism**, insisting that science was derived neither from first principles nor directly from experience.

> 6 There is no original truth, only original error. 9
>
> **Gaston Bachelard**, *Fragments of a Poetics of Fire*

Bacon, Francis (1561–1626)

English philosopher, politician, and writer, a founder of modern scientific research. He claimed to have 'taken all knowledge to be my province'. His works include:

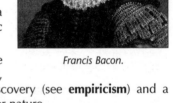

Francis Bacon.

- *Essays* (1597, revised and augmented 1612 and 1625)

- *The Advancement of Learning* (1605), a seminal work discussing **scientific method**

- *Novum Organum* (1620), in which he redefined the task of natural science, seeing it as a means of empirical discovery (see **empiricism**) and a method of increasing human power over nature

- *The New Atlantis* (1626), describing a utopian state in which scientific knowledge is systematically sought and exploited.

A CHILLY DEATH

Bacon was probably the first person whose death was caused by frozen food. Experimenting with the idea of preserving meat by freezing, he stuffed a chicken with snow. Unfortunately the experiment resulted in his catching a chill, then bronchitis, which led to his death.

Knighted on the accession of James I in 1603, he became Baron Verulam in 1618 and Viscount St Albans in 1621. He was briefly Lord Chancellor in 1618 but lost his post through corruption.

❝ If a man will begin with certainties, he shall end in doubts; but if he will be content to begin with doubts, he shall end in certainties. ❞

Francis Bacon, *The Advancement of Learning*

Bacon, Roger (*c.* 1214–1294)

English philosopher, scientist, and inventor, a pioneer of **scientific method**, summed up in his dictum, 'Without experience nothing can be known sufficiently.' He was a Franciscan friar, known as *Doctor Mirabilis* ('wonderful teacher'), who followed the maxim 'Cease to be ruled by dogmas and authorities; look at the world!' In 1277 he was condemned and imprisoned by the church for 'certain novelties' (heresy) and not released until 1292. His *Opus majus* ('great work') is a compendium of all branches of knowledge.

Roger Bacon, imprisoned in the Franciscan monastery at Paris, sent the manuscript of his Opus Majus *and his instruments to the Pope, using a brother monk as his messenger.*

SPECULATION AND INVENTION

Roger Bacon was interested in alchemy, the biological and physical sciences, and magic. Many discoveries have been credited to him, including the magnifying lens, and he foresaw the extensive use of gunpowder and mechanical cars, boats, and planes.

bad faith or mauvaise foi

In the **existentialism** of **Sartre**, a type of moral self-deception, involving our behaving as a mere thing rather than choosing authentically (see **authenticity**). In bad faith, we evade responsibility and **anguish** (*angoisse*) by not noticing possibilities of choice, or by behaving in a role others expect of us.

Sartre derives the concept from his metaphysical analysis of being. Humans must strive to escape mere being-in-itself, and try to achieve their true *being*, being-for-itself.

Bakunin, Mikhail (1814–1876)
Russian revolutionary and theorist of **anarchism**. He was critical of all forms of political power, whether wielded by a capitalist bourgeoisie or a communist proletariat. Stormy conflicts with **Marx** led to his expulsion in 1872 from the First International (a coordinating socialist body). He had a large following, mainly in the Latin American countries.

REVOLUTION AND EXILE

Bakunin participated in the European Revolutions of 1848. He was arrested in 1849 in Dresden, handed over to the Russians, and sent to Siberia in 1855. He escaped to Switzerland in 1861.

Barth, Karl (1886–1968)
Swiss Protestant theologian. He rejected liberal theology and **Enlightenment** rationalism, stressing instead the teachings of Scripture and the infinite gulf that separates God from humanity, which can be overcome only by the grace of God. Barth's theology has been described as neo-**Calvinism**. A socialist in his political views, Barth spoke out against the Nazis.

Barthes, Roland (1915–1980)
French philosopher, critic, theorist of **semiology**, and a leading exponent of **structuralism**. He attacked traditional literary criticism in *Writing Degree Zero* (1953). Barthes's main aim was to expose the bourgeois values and ideology he saw as implicit in the seemingly 'natural' and innocent language of French literature.

For Barthes, a text was not a depiction of the world or the expression of an author's personality, but a system of signs in which meanings are generated solely by the interplay of these signs. In *Mythologies* (1957) he applied this structuralist approach to the study of signs in everyday life, looking at such things as toys, advertisements, and wrestling. This and similar studies had a profound influence on the study of popular culture. His later work became more subjective and unorthodox. **See also:** *deconstruction*.

Baudrillard, Jean (1929–)
French cultural theorist. Originally influenced by **Marxism** and **structuralism**, Baudrillard evolved a critique of consumer society and of an information-world dominated by the reproduction of images, producing a state which he called 'hyper-reality'.

> ❝ Terror is as much a part of the concept of truth as runniness is of the concept of jam ... We wouldn't like truth if it wasn't sticky, if, from time to time, it didn't ooze blood. ❞
>
> **Jean Baudrillard**, *Cool Memories*

Bayle, Pierre (1647–1706)

French critic and philosopher. In *Dictionnaire historique et critique/ Historical and Critical Dictionary* (1696), he wrote learned and highly sceptical articles attacking almost all the contemporary religious, philosophical, moral, scientific, and historical views. For example, he argued that Christianity was irrational, that Old Testament figures such as David were immoral, and that all existing philosophies were inadequate. His scepticism greatly influenced the French **Encyclopédistes** and most **Enlightenment** thinkers.

beauty

The branch of philosophy that deals with beauty is **aesthetics**. There are various philosophical theories about beauty. It may stand for a felt or intuited quality, or for a causal property evoking a special reaction in us, or even for the expression of nonpossessive love.

- Some philosophers, following **Plato**, have regarded beauty as an abstract and eternal 'idea', to which works of art or natural objects may aspire, but never match, being mere shadows of the ideal.
- Others have regarded it as an abstract but real quality somehow possessed by works of art that we regard as beautiful. Such a concept of

---

BEAUTY – THE SUPREME AESTHETIC QUALITY?

The question as to whether beauty, defined as the quality that gives us pleasure and delight, is the supreme aesthetic quality is a difficult one. There are many powerful works of art – for example, the tragic dramas of Shakespeare – that we might hesitate to describe as beautiful in the sense mentioned above. Nevertheless, we describe such works as great works as art. We could use the term 'beauty' to denote this aesthetic greatness, but it begins to become a rather meaningless concept. **Aristotle** defined great tragedy both in terms of its formal qualities, and in terms of its effect upon the audience (the arousal of pity and terror, followed by catharsis, the purgation of these emotions). **See also** *sublime, the.*

beauty can only be described or defined in terms of a description of our response to the work of art, in other words our feeling that the work is beautiful.

• Others again insist that beauty is a mental construct that we ascribe to certain external objects, but that can only be characterized by describing the individual work of art itself, rather than describing a separable quality in the work of art, or our response to it.

❝ Beauty in things exists in the mind which contemplates them. ❞

David Hume, 'Of Tragedy'

Beauvoir, Simone de (1908–1986)

French feminist, philosopher, and writer. The lifelong companion of Jean-Paul **Sartre**, she applied his **existentialism** to her pioneering **feminism**, in which she advocated that women must take responsibility for their own lives. Her book *The Second Sex* (1949) is an encyclopedic study of the role of women in society, drawing on literature, myth, and history. In this work she argues that the subservient position of women is the result of their systematic repression by a male-dominated society that denies their independence, identity, and sexuality. She also published novels and many autobiographical volumes.

❝ One is not born a woman. One becomes one. ❞

Simone de Beauvoir, *The Second Sex*

behaviourism

School of psychology, largely founded by the US psychologist J B Watson (1878–1958). Behaviourists maintain that all human activity can ultimately be explained in terms of conditioned reactions or reflexes and habits formed in consequence. Rejecting **introspection**, they believe that psychology, to be scientifically objective, must restrict itself to observations of behaviour, rather than indulging in speculations about inner mental states.

Although behaviourist methodology has yielded some fruitful results in terms of our understanding of animal behaviour under laboratory conditions, most psychologists and philosophers today regard the approach as excessively reductionist and inadequate to the tasks of explaining complex processes such as emotion, language, and relationships. Behaviourism has generally been superseded by other approaches, such as **cognitive science**.

being
The basic state of **existence** shared by everything and everybody. Being is a fundamental notion in **ontology** and metaphysics generally, but particularly in **idealism** and **existentialism**.

- **Aristotle** insisted that to say something exists adds nothing to its description.
- **Idealist** philosophers tend to believe that there are not only different kinds but also different degrees of being.
- **Sartre** distinguished between being-in-itself and being-for-itself (see **bad faith**).
- **Quine** held that 'to be is to be the value of a variable' in a system of formal logic – that is, that to be or exist is always to have a quality or feature.
- The **ontological argument** for the existence of God turns on whether being can be a **predicate** or **property**.

belief
Assent to the truth of propositions, statements, or facts. In philosophy, belief that something is the case is contrasted with **knowledge**, because we only say we *believe* that something is the case when we are unjustified in claiming to *know* that it is. **Descartes** held that the assent to the truth of a proposition is a matter of will, whereas **Hume** held that it is an emotional condition. **See also:** *certainty.*

In religion, belief is based on acceptance of the reported existence, acts, and teachings of religious figures, not witnessed first-hand but passed down the generations in written form and ritual. **See also:** *faith; fideism.*

Benjamin, Walter (1892–1940)
German philosopher, cultural critic, and essayist. Some of his essays were collected in *Illuminations* (1961). Benjamin's works are a complex and unlikely blend of **Marxism** and Jewish mysticism. Rejecting more orthodox Marxist aesthetic theory, he was a staunch supporter of Modernism, and wrote important essays on the writers Franz Kafka, Bertolt Brecht, and Charles Baudelaire, and on the relationship between technology, the arts, and society.

Bentham, Jeremy (1748–1832)
English philosopher, legal and social reformer, and founder of **utilitarianism**. Bentham declared that the 'utility' of any law is to be measured by the extent to which it promotes the pleasure, good, and happiness of the people concerned. The essence of his moral philosophy is found in the pronouncement of his *Principles of Morals and Legislation* (written in 1780, published in 1789): that the object of all legislation should be 'the greatest happiness for the greatest number'.

Bentham made suggestions for the reform of the poor law in 1798, which formed the basis of the reforms enacted in 1834, and in his *Catechism of Parliamentary Reform*, published in 1817, he proposed annual elections, the secret ballot, and universal male suffrage. He was also a pioneer of prison reform. In economics he was an apostle of *laissez-faire*, and in his *Defence of Usury* (1787) and *Manual of Political Economy* (1798) he contended that his principle of 'utility' was best served by allowing every man (sic) to pursue his own interests unhindered by restrictive legislation. He was made a citizen of the French Republic in 1792.

BENTHAM'S BODY

Pursuing his principle of 'utility' to the end, Bentham requested that after his death his body should be dissected in the presence of his friends. His skeleton was subsequently reconstructed, given a wax head, and dressed in his clothes. This 'auto-icon' and is still on view in a glass case at University College, London.

❝ The arch-philistine Jeremy Bentham was the insipid, pedantic, leather-tongued oracle of the bourgeois intelligence of the nineteenth century. ❞

Karl Marx, *Das Kapital*

Bergson, Henri (1859–1941)

French philosopher. He believed that time, change, and development are the essence of reality, and viewed time as a continuous process in which one period merged imperceptibly into the next. In *Creative Evolution* (1907) he attempted to prove that all evolution and progress are due to the working of the *élan vital*, or life force; this theory is known as 'vitalism'. He won the Nobel Prize for literature in 1928.

Berkeley, George (1685–1753)

Irish philosopher and bishop who believed that nothing exists apart from **perception**, and that the all-seeing mind of God makes possible the continued apparent existence of things. For Berkeley, everyday objects are collections of ideas or sensations, hence the dictum *esse est percipi* ('to exist is to be perceived'). With John **Locke** and David **Hume** he is considered to be one of the British empiricists (see **empiricism**), but his philosophy – that nothing exists except in the mind – is also described as subjective **idealism**.

❝ I do know that I, who am a spirit or thinking substance, exist as certainly as I know my ideas exist. ❞

George Berkeley, *Three Dialogues Between Hylas and Philonous*

THERE WAS ONCE A MAN ...

The English Roman Catholic scholar Ronald Knox wrote the following limerick on Berkeley:

'There was once a man who said 'God
Must think it exceedingly odd
If he finds that this tree
Continues to be
When there's no one about in the Quad.'
To which an anonymous writer responded:
'Dear Sir, Your astonishment's odd:
I am always about in the Quad.
And that's why the tree
Will continue to be,
Since observed by Yours faithfully, God.'

Berlin, Isaiah (1909–1997)

Latvian-born British philosopher and historian of ideas. A pluralist, he was believer in individual freedom. In *The Hedgehog and the Fox* he wrote about Leo Tolstoy's theory of irresistible historical forces; and in *Historical Inevitability* (1954) and *Four Essays on Liberty* (1969), he attacked all forms of historical **determinism**. His other works include *Karl Marx* (1939), *Two Concepts of Liberty* (1957), and *Vico and Herder* (1976). Some of Berlin's finest essays were collected not long before his death in *The Proper Study of Mankind* (1997).

❝ Liberty is liberty, not equality or fairness or justice or human happiness or a quiet conscience. ❞

Isaiah Berlin, *Two Concepts of Liberty*

bivalence

In logic, a principle or law that can be formulated as 'every proposition is either true or false'. If the principle of bivalence is true, then two-valued logic, in which true and false are in practice the two main truth-values of propositions, is the only possible logic. If the principle is false, then many-valued logics are possible, in which propositions can have values such as 'known to be false', 'known to be true', 'necessarily false', and 'necessarily true'. 'Every proposition is either true or false' is also one form of what is known as the law of the excluded middle.

black box

In psychology, computer science, artificial intelligence, and so on, a black box is a system in which the inputs and outputs are described, but whose inner workings do not need to be understood. For example, it is possible (and useful) to study *what* the brain does (the realm of psychology), without understanding *how* it does it (the realm of neurophysiology). Similarly, a designer of a computer system need not understand the microelectronics involved in each circuit, which may remain as 'black boxes'. **See also:** *artificial intelligence* (for the Turing test and the Chinese room).

black philosophy

A movement, originating in the USA, that uses the techniques and concepts of Western philosophy to re-examine and redefine issues relating to black people, such as justice, freedom, racism, and violence. By clarifying these issues, the movement aims to bring about political change.

Bodin, Jean (1530–1596)

French political philosopher, whose six-volume *De la République* (1576) is considered the first work on political economy. His theory of an ideal government emphasized obedience to a sovereign ruler.

Boehme, Jakob (1575–1624)

German mystic who had many followers in Germany, the Netherlands, and England. He claimed divine revelation of the unity of everything and nothing, and found in God's eternal nature a principle to reconcile good and evil. His thinking influenced such philosophers as **Hegel** and **Schelling**, and also the New England Transcendentalists (see **transcendentalism**).

Boethius (AD 480–524)

Roman philosopher. He is best known for *The Consolation of Philosophy*, a dialogue in prose, which he wrote while imprisoned on suspicion of treason by Emperor Theodoric the Great. In it, a lady, Philosophy, responds to Boethius' account of his misfortunes with Stoic, Platonic, and Christian advice. Boethius also translated Aristotle's works on logic, and wrote treatises on Christian philosophy.

English translations of The Consolation of Philosophy were made by Alfred the Great, Geoffrey Chaucer, and Queen Elizabeth I.

6 It is the nature of human affairs to be fraught with anxiety. 9

Boethius, *The Consolation of Philosophy*

Boole, George
(1815–1864)
English mathematician, whose **Boolean algebra** forms the basis of modern computing. He established the basis of modern mathematical **logic**, later built on by Bertrand **Russell** and A E **Whitehead**. Boole stated that logic was more closely allied to mathematics than to philosophy. He argued not only that there was a close analogy between algebraic symbols and those that represented logical forms, but also that symbols of quantity could be separated from symbols of operation.

George Boole.

THE MIRACULOUS AUTODIDACT

Boole received little formal education, but was inspired by the interest of his father, a cobbler, in mathematics. He taught himself five languages, opened his own school at the age of 20, and spent all his spare time studying mathematics and writing papers. He was awarded a medal by the Royal Society in 1844, and in 1849 he was appointed professor of mathematics at Queen's College in Cork, Ireland, a post he held until his death.

Boolean algebra
Set of algebraic rules, named after the mathematician George **Boole**, in which TRUE and FALSE are equated to 0 and 1. Boolean algebra includes a series of operators – AND, OR, NOT, NAND (NOT AND), NOR, and XOR (exclusive OR) – that can be used to manipulate TRUE and FALSE values. It is the basis of computer logic because the truth values can be directly associated with bits. These rules are often used in searching databases either locally or across the Internet.

Bosanquet, Bernard (1848–1923)
English philosopher of the British idealist or neo-Hegelian tradition (see **idealism**; **Hegel**). In his chief metaphysical work, *The Principle of Individuality* (1912), he stressed the concrete nature of logical thought, in opposition to those who saw in it a process of ever more remote abstraction; to Bosanquet, the aim of logic is to capture truth in its totality. He was particularly interested in art and **aesthetics**, which he saw as part of the whole that constitutes the **absolute.**

Bradley, F(rancis) H(erbert) (1846–1924)
British philosopher who argued for absolute **idealism** – the theory, influenced by **Hegel**, that there is only one ultimately real thing, the **absolute**, which is spiritual in nature. In ethics he attacked the utilitarianism of J S **Mill**. Bradley's works include *Ethical Studies* (1876), *Principles of Logic* (1883), *Appearance and Reality* (1893), and *Truth and Reality* (1914).

Brentano, Franz (1838–1916)
German-Austrian philosopher and psychologist. He developed the theory that mental phenomena can be identified as those that have 'intentionality'; that is, have an object within themselves. For example, fear is always fear of something and joy or sorrow are always about something. He has been called 'the grandfather of **phenomenology**', and he influenced many other thinkers, including **Freud, Husserl, Russell,** G E **Moore, Heidegger,** and the founders of **Gestalt** psychology.

Brouwer, L(uitzen) E(gbertus) J(an) (1881–1966)
Dutch mathematician. He worked on the nature and foundation of mathematics, and was the founder of **intuitionism**. He held that the foundation of mathematics is a fundamental intuition of temporal sequence – the counting of moments of time – and that numbers and mathematical entities were constructible from this intuition. He was opposed to the derivation of mathematics from logic (as **Russell** and **Whitehead** had attempted), and from geometry (as in the formalism of **Hilbert**).

Bruno, Giordano (1548–1600)
Italian philosopher. Drawing both on contemporary science (in particular the theories of Copernicus) and on magic and esoteric wisdom, he developed a radical form of **pantheism** in which all things are aspects of a single, infinite reality animated by God as the 'world soul'. His views had a profound influence on **Spinoza** and **Leibniz**.

Buber, Martin (1878–1965)
Austrian-born Israeli philosopher, an advocate of the reappraisal of ancient Jewish thought in contemporary terms. His book *I and Thou* (1923) posited a direct dialogue between the individual and God, and had great impact on

---

A TURBULENT LIFE

Bruno was a Dominican monk, but his sceptical attitude to Catholic doctrines forced him to flee Italy in 1577. After visiting Geneva and Paris, he lived in England (1583–85), where he wrote some of his finest works. During this period he also appears to have been working as an undercover agent attempting to thwart Catholic plots against Queen Elizabeth I. He was not only excommunicated by the Roman Catholic Church, but also by the Lutherans and Calvinists. In 1593, in Venice, he was arrested by the Inquisition and burned at the stake for his adoption of Copernican astronomy and his heretical religious views.

Christian and Jewish theology. When forced by the Nazis to abandon a professorship in comparative religion at Frankfurt, Buber went to Jerusalem and taught social philosophy at the Hebrew University (1937–51).

❝ To the Christian the Jew is the incomprehensibly obdurate man, who declines to see what has happened; and to the Jew the Christian is the incomprehensibly daring man, who affirms in an unredeemed world that its redemption has been accomplished. ❞

Martin Buber, *Paths in Utopia*

Burke, Edmund (1729–1797)

Irish-born British politician and political theorist, regarded as one of the founders of modern **conservatism**. Burke's basic political credo was that liberty is only possible within the strict framework of law and order.

Burke opposed the British government's attempts to coerce the American colonists, and supported the emancipation of Ireland. However, he was a vehement opponent of the French Revolution, which he denounced in *Reflections on the Revolution in France* (1790). Burke's attack was famously countered by Thomas **Paine**. Burke also wrote *A Philosophical Inquiry into the Origin of our Ideas on the Sublime and Beautiful* (1756), on aesthetics.

❝ Rage and frenzy will pull down more in half an hour, than prudence, deliberation, and foresight can build up in a hundred years. ❞

Edmund Burke, *Reflections on the Revolution in France*

---

cabbala
See *kabbala*.

Calvinism
Christian doctrine as interpreted by the Protestant reformer John Calvin (1509–64) and adopted in Scotland, parts of Switzerland, and the Netherlands; by the Puritans in England and New England, USA; and by the subsequent Congregational and Presbyterian churches in the USA. Its central doctrine is **predestination**, under which certain souls (the elect) are predestined by God through the sacrifice of Jesus to salvation, and the rest to damnation. Although Calvinism is rarely accepted today in its strictest interpretation, the 20th century witnessed a neo-Calvinist revival through the work of Karl **Barth**.

Cambridge Platonists
Group of 17th-century English philosophers and Puritan theologians, centred on Cambridge University. In opposing the **materialism** of their contemporary Thomas **Hobbes**, they drew on the ideas of **neo-Platonism** and **Plato** himself. They stressed in particular the individual's innate spiritual and moral nature. Leading members of the group included the theologian Benjamin Whichcote and the philosophers Ralph Cudworth and Henry More.

Camus, Albert (1913–1960)
Algerian-born French writer. His earlier works, such as the novel *The Outsider* (1942), owe much to **existentialism** in their emphasis on the absurdity and arbitrariness of life (see **absurd, the**). *The Myth of Sisyphus* (1943) is a philosophical treatment of the same concept. At this time, during World

Cover of the French edition of La Peste/The Plague *by Albert Camus.*

FOOTBALL AND PHILOSOPHY

As a young man, Camus played in goal for Racing Universitaire de'Alger, but his sporting career was cut short by an attack of tuberculosis. He later maintained that football had given him a complete education in ethics.

War II, Camus was active in the French Resistance. With his novel *The Plague* (1948) and the philosophical *The Rebel* (1951), Camus moved away from metaphysical alienation and began to explore the problem of suffering in its more historical manifestations, and the concept of revolt. Camus's criticism of communism in *The Rebel* led to a protracted quarrel with Jean-Paul Sartre. Camus was awarded the Nobel Prize for literature in 1957. He was killed in a car crash.

❝ What is a rebel? A man who says no. ❞

Albert Camus, *The Rebel*

Cantor, Georg (1845–1918)
German mathematician, notable for his work on the foundations of mathematics, and for establishing set theory and the mathematics of **infinity**. Cantor considered **metaphysics** to be a science into which mathematics, and especially set theory, could be integrated.

capitalism
Economic system in which the principal means of production, distribution, and exchange are in private (individual or corporate) hands and competitively operated for profit. A 'mixed economy' combines the private enterprise of capitalism and a degree of state monopoly, as in nationalized industries and welfare services. Most capitalist economies are actually mixed economies, but some (such as the US and Japanese) have a greater share of the economy devoted to free enterprise.

Karl **Marx** offered the first systematic critique of capitalism, and adherents of **communism** and **socialism** have continued to criticize the exploitative nature of capitalism, which reduces labour to a commodity and leads to the **alienation** of workers. Defenders of capitalism point out that it has been shown to be the most efficient economic system, and that it is only right that the risk-taking capitalist be highly rewarded. Critics in turn point out that workers are also at risk, in that they face unemployment if their employer goes out of business. **See also:** *conservatism; liberalism.*

> ❝ Capital as such is not evil; it is its wrong use that is evil. Capital in some form or other will always be needed. ❞
>
> **Mahatma Gandhi**, in Harijan, 28 July 1940

Carnap, Rudolf (1891–1970)

German philosopher, in the USA from 1935. He was a member of the **Vienna Circle** and a leading exponent of **logical positivism**. He tried to show that **metaphysics** arose from a confusion between talk about the world and talk about language.

Carroll, Lewis (1832–1898)

Pen name of Charles Lutwidge Dodgson, English mathematician and author of the children's classics *Alice's Adventures in Wonderland* (1865) and its sequel *Through the Looking-Glass* (1872). He was fascinated by the limits and paradoxes of language and thought, the exploration of which leads to the apparent nonsense of Alice's adventures. These have provided a rich source of inspiration to philosophers. Dodgson also published many popular mathematical games and problems requiring the use of logic, and several of these suggest an awareness of **set theory**, which was then only just being formulated by Georg **Cantor**.

Alice, having sampled the contents of the bottle labelled 'Drink me', and shrunk as a consequence, has to stand on tiptoe to talk with the caterpillar sitting on a toadstool and smoking a Hookah. John Tenniel illustration from Alice's Adventures in Wonderland.

NOT AMUSED

Queen Victoria enjoyed Alice in Wonderland so much that she asked its author, Lewis Carroll, to send her a copy of his next work. She was not amused to receive *Syllabus of Pure Algebraical Geometry*.

> ❝ What I tell you three times is true. ❞
>
> **Lewis Carroll**, *Hunting of the Snark*

Cartesianism

Term applied to the philosophy of René **Descartes** and his followers. By 1700 Cartesian rationalism dominated the physical sciences, but was gradually undermined by **empiricism**. Nevertheless, aspects of Cartesianism, particularly the dualism of mind and matter, continue to engage philosophers today (see **mind–body problem**).

casuistry

The application of an ethical theory to particular cases or types of case, especially in theology and dogmatics. Casuistry is contrasted with **situationism**, which considers each moral situation as it arises and without reference to ethical theory or moral principles. Most ethical theories can be shown to be inadequate, if sufficient effort is devoted to identifying increasingly subtle features in a particular moral situation. Hence, casuistry has fallen into disrepute.

categorical imperative

Technical term in **Kant's** moral philosophy designating the supreme principle of morality for rational beings. The imperative orders us to act only in such a way that we will the 'maxim', or subjective principle, underlying our action to be a universal law.

category

In philosophy, a fundamental concept applied to objects or concepts that cannot be reduced to anything more elementary. Various philosophers have attempted to come up with lists of irreducable categories. **Aristotle**, for example, listed ten categories: substance, quantity, quality, relation, place, time, position, state, action, and passion. **See also:** *category mistake.*

category mistake

An error involving the attribution of a feature of one **category** to something belonging to a different category. An example would be to attribute a smell to music (unless one was speaking metaphorically). Many apparent paradoxes are actually based on category mistakes. **Plato**, for example, mocked those who constructed paradoxes that relied on a confusion between the **predicate and subject** of a sentence. **See also:** *is/ought problem.*

causality or causation

The connection between cause and effect. We usually assume that this relationship is inevitable, for example a dry match will always light if we strike it.

If an event is assumed to have a cause, two important questions arise: what is the relationship between cause and effect, and must it follow that every event is caused? Hume considered these questions to be, in principle, unanswerable. He argued that our idea of an effect following necessarily from its cause arises by habit from the repeated observation of regularities, such as the striking of dry matches being followed by ignition. We can observe that this is a 'constant conjunction', but never know with absolute certainty that the one will always follow the other.

The concept of causality in science has been undermined by **quantum mechanics** and the **uncertainty principle**. **See also:** *chaos theory; determinism; reasons and causes.*

ARISTOTLE'S FOUR CAUSES

Aristotle held that there were four causes of things. The four causes of a man, for example, are:

- The 'efficient cause' (his father).
- The 'material cause' (flesh).
- The 'formal cause' (form of man).
- The 'final cause' (end or purpose of human life).

Only two of Aristotle's causes answer to English usage – the efficient and the final causes. The Greek word translated as 'cause' means something more like 'responsible factor' or 'necessary condition'.

---

cave, Plato's

An analogy in *The Republic*, in which **Plato** says we are like prisoners chained in a darkened cave, whose **knowledge** of reality is limited to the shadows cast by a fire on the wall in front of them. In the same way, humans have only an incomplete grasp of true reality. Plato held that this true reality consisted of **Forms** (abstract ideas independent of matter), which can only be known through reason, not the senses.

certainty

The condition of accepting something without doubting its truth. The degree to which we can be certain of something may vary, as can the ways in which something can be certain:

- **Logic** and **mathematics** offer the greatest degree of certainty, relying on **deduction**.
- The **laws of nature** (in science), based on empirical observation and **induction**, may appear for all *practical* purposes (such as prediction) to

be certain, although there is no *logical* necessity for this to be the case, as David Hume pointed out (see science, philosophy of; **scientific method**).

• Another sceptical philosopher, René **Descartes**, pointed out that there was no irrefutable reason why we should believe our senses, although again for practical purposes that is what we do.

People with religious **faith** talk about the certainty of their beliefs, and we have no reason to doubt their certainty, even if we doubt the truth of their beliefs. **See also:** *a priori; belief; doubt; scepticism; truth.*

> ❝ The only certainty is that nothing is certain. ❞
>
> **Pliny the Elder**, attributed remark

chain of being

In metaphysics, an ancient principle with many variations, originating in **neo-Platonism**. Essentially, the principle asserts the unity, continuity, and perfection of the universe. The principle assumes that the universe is a hierarchy of different grades of beings – the higher grades of beings possessing more reality or perfection than the lower ones. At the top of the hierarchy is the most perfect being of all – God or the One – or, sometimes, the most perfect creature – Man. **See also:** *Plotinus.*

chance

See *probability.*

change

The nature of change has concerned philosophers since the time of the ancient Greeks.

• Heraclitus believed that change is the ultimate reality of the universe, whereas **Parmenides** and **Zeno of Elea** asserted that change and motion are illusory.

• For **Plato**, although matter is prone to change, absolute reality exists in the **Forms**, which are timeless and unchanging.

• Christian theologians and philosophers have stressed the unchanging nature of God, however much his creation is mutable.

• In Eastern philosophical traditions, such Hinduism and Buddhism, reality consists in a continuous cycle of birth, death, and rebirth – change within an unchanging system.

• Similarly, some Western philosophers, such as Giambattista Vico in the 18th century, have proposed that **history** repeats itself in cycles.

Scientists have sometimes had to revise their ideas of what is unchanging. For example, 19th-century physicists were sure that the amount of matter in the universe never changed. However, Einstein's theory of **relativity** showed mass can change into energy, and vice versa. **See also:** *Darwinism; progress; teleology; time.*

> 6 Change alone is unchanging. 9
>
> **Heraclitus**, remark attributed in *Herakleitos and Diogenes*

chaos theory
Branch of mathematics that attempts to describe irregular or unpredictable systems – that is, deterministic systems whose behaviour is difficult to predict because there are so many variable or unknown or apparently random factors. Chaos theory, which attempts to predict the probable behaviour of such systems, based on a rapid calculation of the impact of as wide a range of factors as possible, emerged in the 1970s with the development of sophisticated computers. First developed for use in meteorology, it has also been used in such fields as economics. **See also:** *causality; determinism.*

THE BUTTERFLY EFFECT

An apparently chaotic system such as the weather is prone to tiny variations in initial conditions leading to radically different outcomes. Thus whether a hurricane occurs may depend on whether or not a particular butterfly flaps its wings.

> 6 In all chaos there is a cosmos, in all disorder a secret order. 9
>
> **Carl Jung**, *The Archetypes and the Collective Unconscious*

Chinese room
See *artificial intelligence.*

Chomsky, Noam (1928–)
US linguist and philosopher. He proposed a theory of 'transformational generative grammar', which attracted widespread interest because of the claims

it made about the relationship between language and the mind, and the universality of an underlying language structure.

Chomsky distinguished between knowledge and behaviour, and maintained that the focus of scientific enquiry should be on knowledge. In order to define and describe linguistic knowledge, he posited a set of abstract principles of grammar that appear to be universal and may have a biological basis (see **innate idea**). Chomsky has also been a leading critic of the imperialist tendencies of the US government.

> ❝ Colourless green ideas sleep furiously. ❞
>
> **Noam Chomsky**, example of a meaningless, but grammatically correct sentence, in *Syntactic Structures*

Cicero, Marcus Tullius
(106–43 BC)
Roman orator, writer, and politician. His speeches and philosophical and rhetorical works are models of Latin prose. Among his philosophical writings are works on ethics, religion, human rights, and **natural law**. Involved on one side or another during the Roman civil wars of the period, he was eventually executed by agents of Mark Antony.

> ❝ Salus populi suprema est lex. ❞
> ❝ The good of the people is the chief law. ❞
>
> **Cicero**, *De Legibus*

A Roman bust depicting Cicero.

circular argument
An argument in which one of the premises is dependent on, or even the same as, the conclusion, thereby making the argument futile. **See also:** *syllogism*.

civil liberties or civil rights
Rights of the individual citizen, derived from the concept of **natural rights**

proposed by John **Locke** in the 17th century. In a liberal **democracy** civil liberties usually include:

- Freedom of speech.
- Freedom of the press.
- Freedom of assembly.
- Freedom of religion.
- Freedom from discrimination (on grounds such as race, gender, and religion).
- The right to vote.
- The right to privacy.
- The right to private property.

In many countries they are incorporated into the **constitution**, to ensure equal treatment for all citizens. Civil liberties are sometimes regarded as a subset of **human rights**. **See also:** *freedom; individualism; liberalism; libertarianism; toleration.*

⟨ The liberty of the individual must be thus far limited; he must not make himself a nuisance to other people. ⟩

John Stuart Mill, *On Liberty*

---

civil society
Part of a society or culture outside the government and state-run institutions. For **Marx** and **Hegel**, civil society was that part of society where self-interest and materialism were rampant, although the economist Adam Smith (1723–1790) believed that enlightened self-interest would promote the general good. Classical writers and earlier political theorists such as John **Locke** used the term to describe the whole of a civilized society.

class
In mathematics, another name for a set (see **set theory**).

class
In sociology and political theory, any of several groupings used to describe the social stratification in industrial societies, based primarily on economic and occupational factors, but also referring to people's style of living or sense of group identity. Within the social sciences, class has been used both as a descriptive category and as the basis of theories about industrial society. Theories of class may see such social divisions either as a source of social stability (Emile **Durkheim**) or social conflict (Karl **Marx**).

Cogito, ergo sum
See *Descartes*.

cognition
In psychology, a general term covering the functions involved in synthesizing information – for example, **perception**, attention, **memory**, and reasoning (see **reason**). **See also:** *cognitive science; mind.*

cognitive science
Study of information-processing functions in humans and animals, covering their role in learning, memory, reasoning, and language development. Cognitive science involves several disciplines: **psychology, linguistics, artificial intelligence**, and, indeed, philosophy. Cognitive scientists use a number of experimental techniques, including laboratory-based research with normal and brain-damaged subjects, as well as computer and mathematical models to test and validate theories.

The study of cognition was largely neglected by psychologists for the early part of the 20th century after the demise of **introspection** as a method of investigation and the rise of **behaviourism**. However, several influential theorists continued to argue that in order to comprehend fully the determinants of behaviour, cognitive processes must be studied and understood, and in 1957 Noam **Chomsky's** critique of behaviourist approaches to language acquisition appeared. With the rise of computing, various theorists began to develop information-processing models of the brain. More recently, the limitations of these approaches, for example, in elaborating the role of **emotion** and motivation in cognitive processes, have become the focus of attention. **See also:** *mind.*

collectivism
In political theory, a position in which the collective (such as the state) has priority over its individual members. It is the opposite of **individualism**. Expressed in the works of **Rousseau, Hegel,** and **Marx**, collectivism appears in different guises in the ideologies of **socialism, communism**, and **fascism**. Collectivism, in a pure form impossible to attain, would transfer all social and economic activities to the state, which would assume total responsibility for them. In practice, it is possible to view collectivism as a matter of degree and argue that the political system of one state is more or less collectivist than that of another; for example, in the state provision of housing or education, or the extent of state intervention in the economy.

Collingwood, R(obin) G(eorge) (1889–1943)
English philosopher who believed that any philosophical theory or position could be properly understood only within its own historical context and not from the point of view of the present. His aesthetic theory, outlined in *Principles of Art* (1938), bases art on expression and imagination.

common sense

In philosophy, the doctrine that we perceive the external world directly, that what we perceive is what there is and how things are. It is thus opposed, for example, to the doctrines of **Plato** and other philosophers who either propose an ultimate reality beyond the reach of the senses, or doubt the reliability of sense data, or both. **Aristotle** was perhaps the first great common-sense philosopher. Other adherents of a common-sense approach include Thomas **Reid** and G E **Moore**. Although a useful antidote to complex metaphysical theories, common sense can mislead – for instance, common sense tells us that the world is flat.

> ❝ Common sense is the collection of prejudices acquired by age eighteen. ❞
>
> **Albert Einstein**, attr.

communism

Revolutionary **socialism** based on the theories of **Marx** and **Engels**, and the modifications of **Lenin**. It emphasizes common ownership of the means of production and a planned economy. The principle held is that each should work according to his or her capacity and receive according to his or her needs. Politically, it seeks the overthrow of **capitalism** through a proletarian revolution.

Marx and Engels in the *Communist Manifesto* (1848) put forward the theory that human society, having passed through successive stages of slavery, feudalism, and capitalism, must advance to communism. This combines with a belief in economic **determinism** to form the central communist concept of 'dialectical materialism'. Marx believed that capitalism had become a barrier to progress and needed to be replaced by a 'dictatorship of the proletariat' (working class), which would build a socialist society. In theory, communism posits the disappearance of classes and the withering away of the state as the oppressive institution of class domination, to achieve a situation akin to ideal **anarchism**.

Communism in practice has proved to be economically inefficient and politically oppressive, and between 1989 and 1991 the communist regimes of Eastern Europe and the Soviet Union all collapsed. **See also:** *collectivism; utopianism.*

> ❝ Communism I like, but communist intellectuals are savages. ❞
>
> **Jean-Paul Sartre**, quoted in the *Observer*, 1956

communitarianism

Political theory that emphasizes the primacy of the community, rather the individual or the state, in guiding policy. The duties or obligations of the citizen become as important as the citizen's rights. Communitarianism became fashionable during the 1990s as a 'third way' between **collectivism** and **individualism**.

computer science

Several aspects of computer science have proved of interest to philosophers, or have some overlap with philosophical concerns:

- In the broad area of logic, computers make use of such concepts as **algorithms** and **Boolean algebra**.

- In **cognitive science**, computers are used to model information-processing functions in humans.

- Some philosophers of **mind** draw on computational models in an attempt to clarify various issues, for example, by drawing an analogy between the software–hardware dichotomy and mind–body dualism (*see* **mind–body** problem).

- Finally, the field of **artificial intelligence** raises challenging questions regarding the nature of **consciousness**.

  See also: *Turing, Alan.*

Comte, Auguste (1798–1857)

French philosopher, famous as the father of **positivism**. He sought to establish sociology (a term he coined) as an intellectual discipline, using a scientific approach ('positivism').

Comte argued that human thought and social development evolve through three stages: the theological, the metaphysical, and the 'positive' or scientific. Although he originally sought to proclaim society's evolution to a new golden age of science, industry, and rational morality, his radical ideas were increasingly tempered by the political and social upheavals of his time. His influence continued in Europe and the USA until the early 20th century. **See also:** *altruism.*

> ❦ Men are not allowed to think freely about chemistry and biology; why should they be allowed to think freely about political philosophy? ❧
>
> **Auguste Comte**, *Positive Philosophy*

concept

In philosophy, the term 'concept' has superseded the more ambiguous **'idea'**. To have a concept of dog is to be able to distinguish dogs from other things, or to be able to think or reason about dogs in some way. Conceptual realists (see **realism**) hold that concepts are objectively existing **universals**, like real **essences**. Conceptualists hold that universals are mind-dependent concepts (this is the outlook of **nominalism**).

connotation and denotation

Two ways in which a word or phrase can have **meaning**.

The word 'animal' for example, denotes (indicates, designates) all living organisms belonging to the biological kingdom Animalia. This is the literal, most limited meaning of the word. If we were to be asked, in contrast, what the connotations (suggestions, associations) of the word 'animal' are, we might cite such things as 'wildness', 'primitiveness', 'irrationality', 'innocence', 'nature', and so on. Both connotation and denotation can depend on context, and connotation can often influence denotation. **See also:** *language, philosophy of.*

SIGNS AND SYMBOLS

Signs can be regarded as simply denotative (for example, the road sign for 'no entry'), while symbols usually carry some connotative **meaning** as well as their denotative meaning (for example, the cross stands for Christianity, but also conveys Christ's love, suffering, and sacrifice). **See also:** *signs and symbols.*

---

conscience

Inner sense of what is morally right and wrong. The English theologian Joseph Butler (1692–1752), the leading conscience theorist in ethics, saw the voice of conscience as 'the candle of the Lord'. He argued that conscience is the part of human nature that guides us towards the moral integration of the self. Critics of conscience theories argue that conscience is an unreliable guide. **Freud** described conscience in terms of the superego.

> 6 The one thing that doesn't abide by majority rule is a person's conscience. 9
>
> **Harper Lee**, *To Kill a Mockingbird*

consciousness

The state of being aware of oneself and one's surroundings. This awareness is not purely of external events or phenomena, but also of one's own feelings, beliefs, and mental events. Such introspective self-awareness, as opposed to merely responding to external stimuli, is generally taken to be a prerequisite for consciousness.

To what degree language or reasoning are intrinsic to consciousness is open to debate (see **reason** and **thinking and language**). This has a bearing on whether consciousness can be ascribed to animals as well as humans.

Psychologists and neurophysiologists have attempted to establish what processes are involved in consciousness, but with limited success. The question arises as to whether consciousness – which by its nature has a subjective component – can ever be entirely explained in materialist or mechanistic terms. **See also:** *artificial intelligence; mind; mind-body problem; self; unconscious.*

> ❧ A sub-clerk in the post-office is the equal of a conqueror if consciousness is common to them. ❧
>
> **Albert Camus**, *The Myth of Sisyphus*

consequentialism
A doctrine in ethics that holds that whether an act is right or wrong can only be judged by its consequences. This is the basis of **utilitarianism**. **See also:** *ends and means.*

conservatism
Political philosophy favouring the maintenance of traditional institutions, and identified with a number of Western political parties, such as the British Conservative, US Republican, and German Christian Democratic parties. Conservatism tends to be explicitly nondoctrinaire and pragmatic, but generally emphasizes free-enterprise **capitalism**, minimal government intervention in the economy, rigid law and order, and the importance of national traditions.

Conservative thinking derives from, among others, John **Locke**, Edmund **Burke**, the 18th-century economist Adam Smith, and the Austrian philosopher Friedrich **Hayek**. Conservatives generally oppose **collectivism** in favour of **individualism**, but while many adhere to traditional forms of authority, others, particularly on the 'New Right', are adherents of **libertarianism**. **See also:** *liberalism.*

constitution
Body of fundamental laws of a state, laying down the system of government and defining the relations of the legislature, executive, and judiciary to each other and to the citizens. Constitutions also often incorporate the **civil liberties** of the citizens.

Since the French Revolution (1789) almost all countries (the UK is an exception) have adopted written constitutions; that of the USA (1787) is the oldest.

Constitutions are intended to prevent government from becoming a tyranny, and to provide the framework and limitations within which political activity occurs. However, in most countries constitutions are open to change through political activity, so are not strictly separate from politics.

continental philosophy
Term applied to 20th-century developments in philosophy in mainland Europe. The term is often used by adherents of the British and US tradition of **analytic philosophy**, who largely disdain the interest of European philosophers in **metaphysics**, speculative systems, doctrines such as **Marxism, phenomenology**, and **existentialism**, and methods such as **structuralism, poststructuralism**, and **deconstruction**.

> 6 French philosophy aspires to the condition of literature or art. It's about picking up an idea and running with it, possibly over a cliff or into a brick wall. 9
>
> **Ted Honderich**, on BBC Radio, 1998

contingent and necessary
In the broad sense, 'contingent' means dependent on events, conditional, not necessary.

- In logic, a contingent proposition or statement is one that may be true under certain conditions, but false under others. This is contrasted with a necessary statement, which by the rules of logic must be true.
- In certain metaphysical systems, an object or being – such as those in the material universe – with a contingent existence does not necessarily need to exist. This is contrasted with entities with a necessary existence, which might include, for example, the human soul and God. **See also:** *a priori*.

conventionalism
The view that **a priori** truths, logical **axioms**, or scientific laws have no absolute validity but are disguised conventions representing one of a number of possible alternatives. The French philosopher and mathematician Jules-Henri Poincaré (1854–1912) introduced this position into the philosophy of science.

cosmogony
The study of the origin of the universe.

- Most mythologies offer some kind of explanation of creation, for example, the account in Genesis.

- Cosmogony was a particular concern in **pre-Socratic philosophy**, whose exponents offered speculative, proto-scientific explanations.

- Following **Aristotle**, Christian theologians such as Thomas **Aquinas** declared that there must be a **first cause** of the universe, namely God (see **cosmological argument**).

- Modern cosmology points to the big bang as the origin of the universe.

cosmological argument

Any line of reasoning for the existence of God that proceeds from the inexplicable existence of the universe to an allegedly self-explanatory being, God. It is one of the four traditional arguments for the existence of God, the others being the **argument from design**, the **moral argument**, and the **ontological argument**.

The cosmological argument originates in ancient Greece with **Aristotle** (who posited a 'prime mover'), and takes various forms. One version is that everything requires a cause, so God must exist as the first or sustaining cause of the universe (see **first cause**). **Aquinas** argued that the universe could have not existed, so there must be a being that could not but exist – that is, exists necessarily – on which it depends. Leibniz also used the cosmological argument.

Like the **ontological argument**, most versions of the cosmological argument rely on existence being a **property** or **predicate**, which **Kant** claimed was impossible. Another weakness is that the argument attempts a causal inference from the universe to God, when it only makes sense to speak of causal relations as holding between observable states of affairs.

cosmology

Branch of astronomy and physics that deals with the structure and evolution of the universe as an ordered whole. Modern cosmology began in the

---

GOD AND COSMOLOGY

Philosophers and scientists will continue to debate what bearing the big bang has on the existence or otherwise of a **first cause** (a variant of the cosmological argument for the existence of God). Some have suggested that the way that the universe has evolved in just the way it has (allowing, for example, human life to develop) supports the argument from design, although astrophysicists suggest the likelihood of parallel universes that are evolving in entirely different ways.

A reconstruction of the medieval conception of the universe, showing a flat earth surrounded by the crystalline spheres. The figure on the left has broken through the outermost of these to find the celestial mechanics by which they are moved.

1920s with the discovery that the universe is expanding, which suggested that it began in an explosion, the big bang. This theory is now generally accepted.

critical theory
See *Frankfurt School.*

Croce, Benedetto (1866–1952)
Italian philosopher, historian, and politician. He wrote extensively on aesthetics, and his *Philosophy of the Spirit* (1902–17) was a landmark in **idealism**. Like **Hegel**, he held that ideas do not represent reality but *are* reality; but unlike Hegel, he rejected every kind of transcendence.

CROCE THE ANTI-FASCIST

Croce was the personification of the intellectual opposition to fascism in his native Italy. A leading liberal, he served as minister of public instruction (1920–21) prior to Mussolini's coming to power, and in 1925 he published his 'Manifesto of Anti-Fascist Intellectuals'. Following Mussolini's fall, he again served as a minister (1943–44).

Cynic

Member of a school of Greek philosophy (Cynicism), founded in Athens about 400 BC by **Antisthenes** (a disciple of Socrates), who advocated a stern and simple morality and a complete disregard of pleasure and comfort. His followers, led by **Diogenes the Cynic**, not only showed a contemptuous disregard for pleasure, but despised all human affection as a source of weakness.

The Greek word cynic means 'dog-like', and was applied to the Cynic philosophers because of their 'snarling contempt' for ordinary people.

Cyrenaic

Member of a school of Greek hedonistic philosophy (see **hedonism**) founded about 400 BC by **Aristippus** of Cyrene. He regarded pleasure as the only absolutely worthwhile thing in life, but taught that self-control and intelligence were necessary to choose the best pleasures.

❝ It is not abstinence from pleasures that is best, but mastery over them without being worsted. ❞

Aristippus, quoted in *Diogenes Laertius, Lives and Opinions of Eminent Philosophers*

D

Dante Alighieri
(1265–1321)

Italian poet and philosopher. Renowned for the epic poem *The Divine Comedy* (1307–21), Dante is also known for his philosophical works. The treatise *The Banquet* (1306–08) includes a prose commentary to the glory of his mystical lady, Philosophy. *On World Government* (1310–13) is an attempt to reconcile the medieval debate over spiritual and temporal authority. It has been described as 'the most purely ideal of political works ever written'.

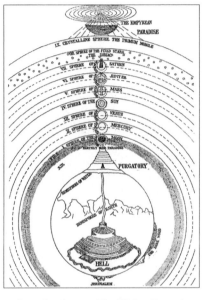

Dante's epic poem The Divine Comedy *describes a journey through Hell, Purgatory, and Paradise.*

Darwinism

The theory of evolution by natural selection, first proposed in a paper by the English naturalists Charles Darwin (1809–1882) and Alfred Russel Wallace (1823–1913) in 1858. The following year Darwin elaborated the theory in *On the Origin of Species by Means of Natural Selection*. Although earlier scientists had proposed various theories of evolution, natural selection – supported as it is by a mass of evidence – has come to be universally accepted in the scientific community.

The theory of natural selection proposes that individual organisms that are better adapted to their environment – owing to the possession of certain characteristics (some inherited) – are more likely to survive and produce offspring, passing on to their offspring their desirable characteristics. In this way species evolve. Darwin, in *The Descent of Man* (1871), showed that humans were no exception to this natural law, and that they shared common ancestors with the apes.

Darwin's theory of natural selection brought about an intellectual revolution:

- It showed that there was no fundamental biological difference between humans and other **animals**, and that humans had no special status, as they had been previously accorded in Christian doctrine and theories of the **chain of being**.

- It demonstrated that the account of the creation of life by God in Genesis could not be literally true, thus creating an unbridgeable rift between scientific and religious explanations.

- In showing that evolution operated by blind chance, with many evolutionary dead ends, it put an end to the idea that life might have evolved for some purpose (see **teleology**), or be subject to or caused by a divine will.

Adherents of **social Darwinism** attempted to use Darwin's scientific theory as the basis of social policy, so confusing explanation with prescription (see **is/ought problem**). **See also:** *religion, science,* and *philosophy.*

A cartoon of Charles Darwin from The London Sketch Book, *May 1874. This was a reaction to the views Darwin put forward in his Origin of Species.*

death

In biological terms, death is the cessation of all life functions, so that the molecules and structures associated with living things become disorganized and indistinguishable from similar molecules found in nonliving things. **See also:** *life.*

In medicine, a person is pronounced dead when the brain ceases to control the vital functions, even if breathing and heartbeat are maintained artificially. This position implies that human life is not to be defined by consciousness, as a person who is permanently unconscious would not necessarily be declared dead under the medical criterion. This is an issue of some debate in **medical ethics** and the law.

In religious belief, death may be seen as part of a continual cycle of birth, death, and rebirth (as in Hinduism and Buddhism). In Islam and Christianity, death marks the departure of the immortal **soul** from the body, prior to a day of judgement and consignment of the soul to heaven or hell. Judaism concentrates not on an afterlife but on survival through descendants who honour tradition.

WHY DIE?

Biologists have a problem in explaining the phenomenon of death. If proteins, other complex molecules, and whole cells can be repaired or replaced, why cannot a multicellular organism be immortal? The most favoured explanation is an evolutionary one. Organisms must die in order to make way for new ones, which, by virtue of sexual reproduction, may vary slightly in relation to the previous generation. Most environments change constantly, if slowly, and without this variation organisms would be unable to adapt to the changes.

---

deconstruction

In literary theory, a radical form of **structuralism** or **poststructuralism**, pioneered by **Derrida**, which views text as a 'decentred' play of structures, lacking any ultimately determinable meaning.

Through analysis of the internal structure of a text, particularly its contradictions, deconstructionists demonstrate the existence of subtext meanings – often not those that the author intended – and hence illustrate the impossibility of attributing fixed meaning to a work.

The French critic Roland **Barthes** originated deconstruction in his book Mythologies (1957), in which he studied the inherent instability between sign and referent in a range of cultural phenomena, such as toys, advertising, cookery, and wrestling. **See also:** *intertextuality*.

deduction

A form of argument in which the conclusion necessarily follows from the premises. It would be inconsistent logic to accept the premises but deny the conclusion (see **syllogism**). Compare **induction**. **See also:** *a priori; contingent and necessary*.

definition

A statement or explanation of the meaning of a word or phrase. This may take the form of an account of the essential properties of something by which it can be uniquely identified (see **essence**).

However, this is not always possible. Although we can define 'blue', for example, as any of a group of colours that have wavelengths in the range 490–445 nanometres, we cannot fully convey what 'blue' means without resorting to examples, such as 'the colour of a clear and cloudless sky'. Words as we use them may also carry connotations (associated meanings) beyond the simple definition that they denote (see **connotation** and **denotation**). **Wittgenstein** held that words do not have fixed meanings, but that meanings are dependent on contexts. **See also:** *language, philosophy of; meaning.*

> ❦ "When I use a word," Humpty Dumpty said in a rather scornful tone, "it means just what I choose it to mean, – neither more nor less." ❧
>
> **Lewis Carroll**, *Through the Looking Glass*

deism

Movement in the 17th and 18th centuries characterized by the belief in a rational 'religion of nature' as opposed to the orthodox beliefs of Christianity. Deists believed that God is the source of **natural law** but does not intervene directly in the affairs of the world, and that the only religious duty of humanity is to be virtuous.

The founder of English deism was Lord Herbert of Cherbury (1583–1648). Deism became prominent among European thinkers such as **Voltaire** during the **Enlightenment**. In the USA, many of the country's founders, including Benjamin Franklin and Thomas **Jefferson**, were essentially deists.

THE CULT OF THE SUPREME BEING

At the beginning of the French Revolution (1789) there was considerable hostility towards organized religion, in the form of Christianity, which was associated with the detested ancien régime. However, within a few years the Revolutionary leaders came to the conclusion that some kind of organized religion was necessary for social stability, and therefore introduced a 'Cult of the Supreme Being', which was based on deism.

> ❦ If God did not exist, it would be necessary to invent him. ❧
>
> **Voltaire**, *Epîtres*

demiurge

The supernatural maker of the world. In **Plato's** *Timaeus* the demiurge (Greek *demiourgos* 'artisan') is the creator of the universe, who copies the **Forms** on to the receptacle of space–time or womb of becoming. In later **cosmogonies**, such as that of **Gnosticism**, the demiurge is subordinate to the Supreme Being or God.

democracy

Government by the people (Greek demos, implying 'the populace at large'), usually through elected representatives, although sometimes by devices such as referendums. Modern 'liberal' democracy developed from the American and French revolutions, although earlier forms of democracy were practised in ancient Athens and elsewhere.

In practice the features of a liberal democracy include:

- Representative institutions based on majority rule, through free elections and a choice of political parties
- Accountability of the government to the electorate
- **Civil liberties** guaranteed by an independent judiciary
- Limitations on the power of government (see **constitution**).

There are few nation states today that do not claim to be democratic, but not all would qualify on the basis of these criteria.

The question of who 'the people' are is a matter of dispute; historically 'democracy' has by no means always designated universal adult suffrage. The question of what constitutes adequate exercise of the demos' power is also a matter for dispute, more particularly since modern social science has demonstrated the persistence of elite structures in electorally democratic societies.

> ❝ No man is good enough to govern another man without that other's consent. ❞
>
> **Abraham Lincoln**, speech, 1854

Democritus (c. 460–c. 370 BC)

Greek philosopher and speculative scientist. In his atomic theory of the universe all things originate from a vortex of tiny, indivisible particles, which he called atoms, and differ according to the shape and arrangement of their

> ❝ In reality we know nothing, for truth is in the depths. ❞
>
> **Democritus**, quoted in *Diogenes Laertius, Lives of the Philosophers*

atoms. Democritus' discussion of the constant motion of atoms to explain the origins of the universe was the most scientific theory proposed in his time.

De Morgan, Augustus (1806–1871)
British mathematician, who developed a theory of relations in **logic**. He devised a symbolism that could express such notions as the contradictory, the converse, and the transitivity of a relation, as well as the union of two relations. He also extended his syllogistic vocabulary using definitions, giving rise to new kinds of inferences, both direct (involving one premise) and indirect (involving two premises). He was thus able to work out purely structural rules for transforming a premise or pair of premises into a valid conclusion.

denotation
See *connotation and denotation*.

deontology
Ethical theory that the rightness of an action consists in its conformity to **duty** (in the sense of what must and must not be done), regardless of the consequences that may result from it. Deontological ethics is thus opposed to any form of **utilitarianism** or **pragmatism**.

Derrida, Jacques (1930–)
French philosopher who introduced the **deconstruction** theory into literary criticism. His approach involves looking at how a text is put together in order to reveal its hidden meanings and the assumptions of the author. His analysis of language draws on **Nietzsche, Husserl, Heidegger,** and **Saussure**. Although obscurely presented, his conclusions have some similarity to those of Anglo-American linguistic philosophers.

Descartes, René (1596–1650)
French philosopher and mathematician, the inventor or coordinate geometry and a leading exponent of **rationalism**.

Descartes believed that commonly accepted knowledge was doubtful because of the subjective nature of the senses. Rigorously applying this extreme scepticism, he held that the only rational certainty was *Cogito, ergo sum* ('I think, therefore I am'), and on the basis of this dictum he attempted to rebuild human knowledge.

Descartes believed that the entire material universe could be explained by means of thinking, in the form of rational **deduction**, using mathematical physics, rather than by observation and experiment. However, to avoid serious controversy with the church, he held that everything has a cause, and that the initial impulse for the motion of matter comes from God.

Descartes identified the 'thinking thing' (*res cogitans*), or mind, with the human soul or consciousness. The body, though somehow interacting with the soul, was a physical machine, secondary to, and in principle separable from, the soul. This distinction led him to postulate two quite different substances: spatial substance, or matter, and thinking substance, or mind. This 'Cartesian dualism' is an aspect

Descartes proposed the pineal gland as the site of the interaction between body and soul.

of the **mind–body** problem that still concerns philosophers and scientists. His philosophy and that of his followers is known as **Cartesianism**, and was the dominant intellectual doctrine in Europe into the 18th century.

> ❝ It is not enough to have a good mind. The main thing is to use it well. ❞
>
> **René Descartes**, *Discourse on Method*

design, argument from
See *argument from design*.

determinism
The view that every event has a cause that makes the occurrence of the event inevitable. This chain of cause and effect may be posited as resulting from the will of God, for example, or from some immutable scientific law of nature.

- In antiquity, determinism was a feature of **Stoicism**.
- In Christian theology, the doctrine of **predestination** is deterministic.
- In science, the physics of Isaac **Newton** appeared to establish a wholly mechanistic, and thus deterministic, universe.
- Deterministic theories of history include that of Karl **Marx**, who interpreted blind economic forces as the causes of human action.
- Human behaviour is now often seen as the outcome of a combination of genetic make-up and environmental influence.

Underlying determinism is the concept of **causality** – the inevitable following of cause by predictable effect – which may itself be just a habit of the mind, as David **Hume** suggested, without any logical validity. Certain developments in physics in the 20th century, namely quantum mechanics and the **uncertainty principle** – also fundamentally undermine our understanding of causality, and the concept of a deterministic universe.

> ❝ Fate, then, is a name for facts not yet passed under the fire of thought; for causes which are unpenetrated. ❞
>
> **Ralph Emerson**, *The Conduct of Life*, 'Fate'

FREE WILL AND DETERMINISM

Some philosophers have held that determinism denies the possibility of free will, and thus absolves humans of their moral responsibilities. Other philosophers, even while they might accept that we live in a deterministic universe, hold that we, as humans, think and act as if free will exists. Existentialists such as Jean-Paul Sartre regard it as bad faith to deny that we are free to choose. Conversely, Hegel held that freedom is the recognition of necessity.

Dewey, John (1859–1952)
US philosopher and educationist. Influenced by William **James,** Dewey became a leading proponent of **pragmatism**. He developed the theory of **instrumentalism**, that ideas are just tools or instruments for dealing with problems in the real world. He maintained that the only reality is that which we encounter through scientific and everyday experience, and made 'inquiry' the essence of logic. He extended these ideas to his educational theories, and founded a progressive school in Chicago.

dialectic
Greek term, originally associated with the philosopher Socrates' method of argument through dialogue and conversation (see **Socratic method**). For **Hegel** and **Marx**, dialectic is an interpretive method in which the contradiction between a thesis and its antithesis is resolved through synthesis.

In Hegel's **idealism**, the development of a concept is 'dialectical', involving three stages:

- The first stage is the thesis, or indeterminate concept (for example, a thing in space).
- Then the dialectic moves to the antithesis, or determinate concept (for example, an animal).
- Finally, the dialectic moves to the synthesis (for example, a cat), which is the resolution of what Hegel thinks is the contradiction between the indeterminate and determinate concepts.

As logic, Hegel's dialectic is worthless. As an account of how intellectual and social development occurs, it is shrewd. Marx's **dialectical materialism** put it on a materialistic basis.

dialectical materialism
Term applied (especially by communists) to **Marxism**. Marx and Engels borrowed the method of Hegel's **dialectic**, but rejected his **idealism** in favour of **materialism**.

Diderot, Denis (1713–1784)

French philosopher. He was a leading figure of the **Enlightenment**, and was editor of the *Encyclopédie* (1751–80), a work that exerted an enormous influence on contemporary social thinking with its **materialism** and anti-clericalism (see **Encyclopédistes**). Diderot saw the natural world as nothing more than matter and motion, and proposed a purely mechanical account of the origin and development of life.

> ❝ There is only one passion, the passion for happiness. ❞
>
> **Denis Diderot**, *Elements of Physiology*, 'Will, Freedom'

Dilthey, Wilhelm (1833-1911)

German philosopher, a major figure in the interpretive tradition of **hermeneutics**. He argued that the 'human sciences' could not employ the same methods as the natural sciences, but must use the procedure of 'understanding' to grasp the inner life of an alien culture or past historical period. Thus Dilthey extended the significance of hermeneutics far beyond the interpretation of texts to the whole of human history and culture.

Ding-an-sich

See *thing-in-itself*.

Diogenes the Cynic (c. 412–c. 323 BC)

Greek **Cynic** philosopher, who upheld the virtues of **asceticism**. He believed in freedom and self-sufficiency for the individual, and that the

DIOGENES THE DOG

When Alexander the Great asked him if he wanted anything, Diogenes replied, with typical cantankerousness, 'Stand out of my sun a little.' He was nicknamed 'the Dog', and his followers were known as Cynics ('doglike'). The story of his having lived in a barrel arose when Seneca said that was where a man so crabbed ought to have lived.

Diogenes, the Greek philosopher who founded the Cynic sect.

virtuous life was the simple life. He disregarded social mores, and any distinctions based on rank. No writings of Diogenes survive, but he was famous for teaching through action. He is said to have carried a lamp during the daytime, looking for one honest man.

Diogenes Laertius (3rd century AD)
Greek writer. He was the author of *Lives and Opinions of Eminent Philosophers*, an important compilation of anecdotes and quotations from the ancient Greek philosophers. It is the sole source of information we have about many of the philosophers it covers.

Dionysiac
See *Apollonian and Dionysiac.*

divine right of kings
Christian political doctrine that justified the system of absolute monarchy in Europe for many centuries. The doctrine holds that:

- Hereditary monarchy is the system approved by God.

- Monarchs are the direct representatives of God, and owe obedience to God alone.

- Monarchs are to receive the unquestioning obedience due to God's viceroy on earth, and so any rebellion is blasphemous.

The doctrine had its origins in the 8th century, and was at its peak in 16th- and 17th-century Europe as a weapon against the claims of the papacy. Louis XIV was a notable exponent. In 17th-century England it was maintained by the supporters of the Stuarts in opposition to the democratic theories of many in Parliament, and was a factor in the outbreak of the English Civil War. The most influential exposition of divine right in English is to be found in Sir Robert Filmer's *Patriarcha* (1680), which argues by analogy that the powers of God over the universe, of father over family, and sovereign over people, are all divinely ordained and absolute. The success of John **Locke**'s *Two Treatises on Government* (1690) signalled the decline of the theory in England, although it persisted for some time in other parts of Europe.

dogma
The authoritative truths accepted by members of a particular faith, regardless of reason, evidence, or experience. In the Roman Catholic Church the dogmas are transmitted through scripture or church traditions or papal authority, whereas the Reformed Churches insist on scripture alone as the source of authority. Much **Enlightenment** thinking was directed against the dogmas of organized religion.

doubt
A position in which judgement as to the truth or falsity of a proposition is suspended. To doubt a proposition is not to claim that it is false, but to be

uncertain as to whether it is true or not. Doubt regarding a particular proposition may be provisional, where there is insufficient evidence; this does not rule out the possibility that sufficient evidence may eventually be forthcoming. Doubt regarding another proposition may be absolute or permanent, in the sense that the proposition is judged by its very nature to be unverifiable. **See also:** *certainty; Descartes; scepticism; truth.*

dualism

The belief that reality is essentially dual in nature. **Descartes**, for example, held that thinking and material substance interact but are fundamentally separate and distinct. Dualism is contrasted with 'monism', the theory that reality is made up of only one substance. It is also contrasted with **materialism**, which would explain **mind** and **consciousness** and any other phenomena in strictly physical terms. **See also:** *Manichaeism; mind–body problem.*

Duns Scotus, John
(*c.* 1265–*c.* 1308)
Scottish philosopher, a member of the Franciscan order, and a leading figure of **scholasticism**. In the medieval controversy over universals he advocated **nominalism**, maintaining that classes of things have no independent reality. On many points he turned against the orthodoxy of Thomas **Aquinas**; for

> **THE FIRST DUNCE**
>
> Although he was known as Doctor Subtilis ('the subtle teacher'), the church rejected the ideas of Duns Scotus. The word 'dunce' is derived from Dunses, a term of ridicule applied to his followers.

example, he rejected the idea of a necessary world, favouring a concept of God as absolute freedom capable of spontaneous activity.

Durkheim, Emile (1858–1917)
French sociologist, one of the founders of modern sociology, who also influenced social anthropology. He worked to establish sociology as a respectable and scientific discipline, capable of diagnosing social ills and recommending possible cures. He examined the bases of social order and the effects of industrialization on traditional social and moral order (for example, developing the concept of **alienation**). He proclaimed **positivism** as the way forward for sociology as a science.

duty

Moral obligation experienced as required or demanded by the moral law. Moral conflicts may occur where a number of duties make apparently irreconcilable demands on us. In moral philosophy, the greatest emphasis on duty is found in **Stoicism** and in the thinking of Immanuel **Kant**. The ethical theory that the rightness of an action consists in its conformity to duty, regardless of the consequences that may result from it, is known as deontology. Compare **utilitarianism** and **pragmatism**.

Eco, Umberto (1932–)

Italian writer, semiologist, and literary theorist. His works include a *Theory of Semiotics* (1975), *The Role of the Reader* (1979). He is best known to a wider audience for his philosophical novels, *The Name of the Rose* (1983) and *Foucault's Pendulum* (1988), which incorporate various theories of signs.

A PHILOSOPHICAL DETECTIVE STORY

The Name of the Rose is set in a 14th-century monastery. The Sherlock-Holmes-like hero, William of Baskerville, solves seven murders by interpreting and deducting from a variety of signs. The novel involves the nature of truth, and alludes to some of the debates of medieval **scholasticism**.

---

efficient cause

In Aristotle's philosophy, one of the four causes of things. **See** *causality* (box).

egalitarianism

Belief that all citizens in a state should have equal rights and privileges. Interpretations of this can vary, from the notion of equality of opportunity to equality in material welfare and political decision-making. Some states reject egalitarianism; most accept the concept of equal opportunities but recognize that people's abilities vary widely. Even those states that claim to be socialist find it necessary to have hierarchical structures in the political, social, and economic spheres. Egalitarianism was one of the principles of the French Revolution. **See also:** *equality*.

egoism

In ethics, the doctrine that we seek only our enlightened self-interest and that all our desires are self-referential. Notable ethical theorists who have held versions of egoism are **Aristotle**, Thomas **Hobbes**, and Benedict **Spinoza**. Compare **altruism**.

Eleatic School

Collective term for the pre-Socratic philosopher **Parmenides** and his followers (notably **Zeno**), who lived in Elea (a Greek colony in southern Italy) in the early 5th century BC. They taught that reality is single and unchanging, and that sense experience is illusory.

Emerson, Ralph Waldo (1803–1882)

US philosopher, essayist, and poet. He settled in Concord, Massachusetts, where he worked alongside Henry **Thoreau** and others to develop **transcendentalism**, particularly its theological aspects, as a protest against dogmatic **rationalism** in religion. In *Nature* (1836) he states the movement's main principles, emphasizing the value of self-reliance and the godlike nature of human souls. His philosophical views also appear in two volumes of *Essays* (1841, 1844) and other works.

> ❦ Belief consists in accepting the affirmations of the soul;
> unbelief, in denying them. ❧
>
> **Ralph Emerson,** *The Conduct of Life,* 'Worship'

emotion

A mental state of feeling, rather than thinking or knowing. Today, most researchers regard emotions as having three components:

- Our conscious, subjective experience of the emotion.
- The objectively observed behaviour that is the external expression of the emotion.
- The physiological and neurophysiological changes that are associated with the emotion.

US philosopher William **James** argued in the 1890s that emotional feeling is our perception of the way our body is behaving, for example, a frightening sight makes our heart beat quicken, and it is our perception of quickened heart rate that constitutes the emotion of fear. In the 1960s it was suggested that emotions are 'motivational states', expressions of some imbalance in the organism that requires remedial action.

Neurophysiologists have found out more and more about what is happening in our brains and nervous systems when we experience emotions. For example, feelings of unhappiness are accompanied by low levels of the chemical serotonin. However, given the complex relations between the external circumstances prompting an emotion, our perception of these circumstances, our experience of feeling the emotion, and the associated physiological events in our bodies, it is not clear which is cause and which is effect. Purely mechanistic accounts of emotion exclude the element of cognition in emotion, for example, the role of perception and learning. **See also:** *consciousness; Langer, Susanne.*

EMOTION AND REASON

In Western culture, **Romanticism** encouraged the view that reason and emotion are engaged in a perpetual battle, whereas Classicism treats them as complementary aspects of being human and recommends rational reflection on which emotion is the most appropriate to feel in any particular circumstance. Scottish 18th-century philosopher David **Hume** argued that reason is 'the slave of the passions', or emotions.

---

emotivism

A philosophical position in the theory of **ethics**. Emotivists deny that moral judgements can be true or false, maintaining that they merely express an attitude or an emotional response. The concept came to prominence during the 1930s, largely under the influence of *Language, Truth and Logic* (1936) by the English philosopher A J **Ayer.**

Empedocles (c. 493–433 BC)

Greek philosopher and scientist who proposed that the universe is composed of four elements – fire, air, earth, and water – which through the action of love and discord are eternally constructed, destroyed, and constructed anew. He lived in Acragas (Agrigento), Sicily, and according to tradition, he committed suicide by throwing himself into the crater of Mount Etna.

Empedocles. His works describe the fall of Man, redemption, and the transmigration of souls.

❝ The nature of God is a circle of which the centre is everywhere and the circumference is nowhere. ❞

Empedocles, attributed, and quoted in *Le Roman de la Rose*

empiricism

The belief that all knowledge is ultimately derived from sense experience. It is suspicious of metaphysical schemes based on **a priori** propositions, which are claimed to be true irrespective of experience. It is often contrasted with **rationalism**.

Empiricism developed in the 17th and early 18th centuries through the work of John **Locke**, George **Berkeley,** and David **Hume**, sometimes known as the British empiricist school. At this time, the dominant intellectual view in Europe was the rationalism of **Descartes**, who believed that the universe could be explained solely by means of **deduction** – using mathematics alone, without observation or experiment. However, the discoveries of the three laws of motion and the law of gravity by Isaac **Newton**, using observation and experiment, gave great impetus to empiricism as the most successful approach to **scientific method.**

Encyclopédistes

Group of 18th-century French intellectuals who contributed to the Encyclopédie (1751–77). This monument to **Enlightenment** thinking was enormously influential in eroding respect for organized religion, and in promoting scientific **materialism**. Denis **Diderot** and Jean le Rond d'Alembert (1717–1783) were the co-editors of the *Encyclopédie* until d'Alembert withdrew in 1757. The contributors also included **Voltaire** and Jean-Jacques **Rousseau**.

ends and means

The question as to whether ends justify means is a central one in ethics. Some moral philosophers hold that the rightness of an action should be judged without reference to the result of the action. For example, **Kant** held that the rightness of an action consists in its conformity to **duty**, regardless of the consequences that may result from it (this is called 'deontological ethics').

In contrast, **utilitarianism** holds that the rightness of an action can only be judged by the 'utility' of its outcome – the greatest happiness of the greatest number, in **Bentham's** formulation. The most notorious proponent of ends justifying means was **Machiavelli**, although his theories merely reflect time-honoured political practice.

Other philosophers again have held that the rightness of an action should be judged by its intention, rather than for itself, or by its actual outcome. **See also:** *categorical imperative; ethics; good; right, the.*

Engels, Friedrich (1820–1895)

German social and political philosopher, regarded as the co-founder, with his life-long friend Karl **Marx,** of modern **communism**.

Engels spent much of his working life in England, managing his family's cotton factory in Manchester. He met Marx in 1844. The two worked out the materialist interpretation of history, and in 1847–48 they wrote the *Communist Manifesto*. They briefly returned to Germany during the revolutions of 1848–49, and thereafter, back in England, Engels gave continual financial support to the Marx family. After Marx's death Engels was largely responsible for the wider dissemination of his friend's ideas; he edited the second and third volumes of Marx's *Das Kapital* (1885 and 1894).

Engels's own later works, such as *Origins of the Family, Private Property, and the State* (1884) – which linked patriarchy with the development of private **property** – developed such concepts as historical materialism. His use of **positivism** and **Darwinism** gave Marxism a scientific and deterministic flavour, which was to influence later Soviet thinking. Although Engels himself regarded his ideas as identical with those of Marx, discrepancies between their works are the basis of many Marxist debates.

> ❦ English socialism arose with [Robert] Owen, a manufacturer, and proceeds therefore with great consideration towards the bourgeoisie and great injustice towards the proletariat. ❧
>
> **Friedrich Engels**, *The Condition of the Working Classes in England*

Enlightenment, the
European intellectual movement that reached its high point in the 18th century. Enlightenment thinkers were believers in social progress, toleration, and in the liberating possibilities of rational and scientific knowledge. They were often critical of existing society, and were hostile to the church and its dogmas, which they saw as keeping the human mind chained down by superstition. Leading representatives of the Enlightenment included **Voltaire**, Gotthold **Lessing**, Denis **Diderot**, and David **Hume**.

The primacy of reason
The Enlightenment had its roots in 17th-century England. The empiricism of John **Locke** and the scientific discoveries of **Newton** gave considerable impetus to the questioning of traditional teaching, particularly that of the church. The ideas of Newton and Locke were introduced to France by Voltaire in his *Philosophical Letters* (1734), and taken up by the group of French thinkers known as the **Philosophes**. Many of these contributed to Diderot's *Encyclopédie* (1751–77), which spread the new ideas to a wider audience (see **Encyclopédistes**). The concept of God was not entirely abandoned, however, as many Enlightenment thinkers were adherents of **deism**, the belief in a supreme being based on reason rather than revelation.

Political and economic ideas
In the area of political theory, Locke developed the idea of a **social contract** between government and governed, and the idea of people's **natural rights**. Such ideas were in complete opposition to the theory of the **divine right of kings** that underpinned the absolute monarchies ruling most of Europe at this time. In his *Spirit of the Laws* (1748), **Montesquieu** outlined the basis of democratic constitutional government, and argued that systems of law and morality are relative. Jean-Jacques **Rousseau** extended Locke's ideas in his *Social Contract* (1762). Meanwhile, the Scottish thinker Adam Smith (1723–90) advocated a free-market economic system based on enlightened self-interest.

The Enlightenment legacy
Enlightenment ideas, particularly regarding rights, influenced the American and French revolutions. Thomas **Jefferson** encouraged the incorporation of many Enlightenment principles into the US Constitution. However, by the later 18th century, some thinkers – notably Rousseau himself – began to react against the Enlightenment emphasis on reason. This marked the beginning of **Romanticism**.

Epictetus (*c.* AD 55–135)
Greek philosopher, an advocate of **Stoicism**. He encouraged people to refrain from self-interest and to promote the common good of humanity. He believed that people were in the hands of an all-wise providence and that they should endeavour to do their duty in the position to which they were called.

Epicureanism
System of moral philosophy named after the Greek philosopher **Epicurus**. He argued that pleasure is the basis of the ethical life, and that the most satisfying form of pleasure is achieved by avoiding pain, mental or physical. This is done by limiting desire as far as possible, and by choosing pleasures of the mind over those of the body.

Epicurus (341–270 BC)
Greek philosopher, founder of **Epicureanism**. His theory of knowledge stresses the role of sense perception, and in his ethics the most desired condition is a serene detachment based on the avoidance of anxiety and physical pain. He was influential on both Greek and Roman thinking. For example, his theory that all things are made up of atoms was adopted by the Roman Epicurean **Lucretius**.

epiphenominalism
Theory regarding the **mind–body problem** that mind has distinctive and irreducible qualities but no power over the body.

epistemology
Branch of philosophy that examines the nature of knowledge and attempts to determine the limits of human understanding. **See** *knowledge.*

equality
In political theory, the condition of being equal or the same in given respects, as advocated, for example, in **liberalism, socialism,** and **feminism**. The efforts of these and other ideologies and movements have secured a basis in law for equality on racial, sexual, and other grounds. Absolute equality is rarely advocated. Instead, debates about equality concern to what extent individuals or groups ought to have equality of opportunity, of respect, of rights, of treatment, equality before the law, and so on. Belief that all citizens in a state should have equal rights and privileges is called **egalitarianism**.

Erasmus, Desiderius (*c.* 1469–1536)
Dutch scholar and a leading figure in Renaissance **humanism**, who travelled widely in Europe. He was opposed to dogmatism and the abuse of church power, and his encouragement of reform contributed both to the Protestant Reformation and the Catholic Counter-Reformation, although he himself took an independent stance during **Luther's** conflict with the pope. *His Praise of Folly* (1511), a satire on church and society, quickly became an international bestseller. He made a pioneering translation of the Greek New Testament in 1516, published *Colloquia,* dialogues on contemporary subjects, in 1519, and also edited the writings of the early Christian leaders.

❝ Among the blind the one-eyed man is king. ❞

Desiderius Erasmus, *Adagia*

Erigena, Johannes Scotus (*c.* 815–*c.* 877)
Medieval philosopher, thought to have been Irish. He defied church orthodoxy in his writings on cosmology and **predestination**, and tried to combine Christianity with **neo-Platonism**.

Desiderius Erasmus.

THE WANDERING SCHOLAR

According to tradition, Erigena travelled in Greece and Italy. The French king Charles the Bald invited him to France, where he became head of the court school. He is said to have visited Oxford, to have taught at Malmesbury, and to have been stabbed to death by his pupils.

---

eschatology
Collective term for doctrines relating to the end of time. Christian eschatology concerns the end of this Earth and of time; the resurrection of the dead; the Antichrist; the return of Jesus Christ to overthrow the Antichrist; and the culmination of history with the destruction of this world. In more general terms, it refers to the moral significance of the belief that time and history are working towards an ultimate end. **See also:** *teleology*.

essence
All that makes a thing what it is and is indispensable to the thing. Philosophers have often distinguished 'nominal essences' from 'real essences':

- A nominal essence is a group of terms used to define a **concept**; thus, the nominal essence of the concept of a horse could be 'anything that neighs and has a mane and four legs'. **See also:** *definition*.

- A real essence is either a group of **universals** objectively given in nature (this is also called a **form**) or (as in the work of John **Locke**) the underlying structure of an object; for example, its atomic structure.

  See also: *existence; property*.

ethics or moral philosophy
Branch of philosophy concerned with the systematic study of human values. It involves the study of theories of conduct and goodness, and of the meanings of moral terms. It is usually distinguished from actual moral teaching, although in practice the distinction has not always been clear cut.

The Greeks
Ethics as a systematic study first appears with the Greek philosopher **Socrates** in the 5th century BC.

- **Plato** thought that objective standards (**Forms**) of justice and goodness existed beyond the everyday world.

- **Aristotle** argued that virtue is natural and so leads to happiness, and that moral virtues are acquired by practice, like skills.

- Both Plato and Aristotle combined the doctrine of **hedonism** (that pleasure is the greatest good) and **rationalism** (that reason is the best guide to behaviour).
- Other ancient schools and doctrines of ethics include the **Cynics**, the **Cyrenaics**, **Epicureanism**, and **Stoicism**.

Christian ethics
The 'Christian ethic' is mainly a combination of New Testament moral teaching with ideas drawn from Plato and Aristotle. Medieval **scholasticism** saw God's will as the ethical standard, but tempered it with Aristotelian ethics.

The Modern Period
From the time of the Renaissance philosophers have re-examined the basis of ethics.

- David **Hume** argued that moral judgements are based on feelings about pleasant and unpleasant consequences.
- For **Kant**, morality could not have a purpose outside itself, so the good person acts only in accordance with the **categorical imperative.**
- In contrast, in **utilitarianism** (devised by Jeremy **Bentham** and refined by J S **Mill** in the 19th century), actions are to be judged by their consequences.
- **Existentialism**, originating in the 19th century with **Kierkegaard**, has also been highly influential, with its emphasis on choice and responsibility.

See also: *consequentialism; deontology; determinism; duty; ends and means; evil; existentialism; free will; good; happiness; Hutcheson, Francis; is/ought problem; Moore, G E; naturalism; pragmatism; right, the; situationism.*

ETHICAL ISSUES

Ethics is closely linked to other disciplines, such as anthropology, law, political theory, psychology, and sociology. Increasingly, moral philosophers analyse such ethical problems as **war** and **violence, animal rights, suicide, punishment, abortion, euthanasia,** and embryo research. Various specialized branches have emerged, such as business ethics, **medical ethics**, and the ethics of science (**see science, philosophy of**).

---

euthanasia
In medicine, mercy killing of someone with a severe and incurable condition or illness. Euthanasia is an issue that creates much controversy on medical and ethical grounds. A patient's right to refuse life-prolonging treatment is recognized in several countries. **See also:** *violence.*

evil

'Evil' as an adjective or noun may be applied to that which is morally wrong, or wicked. It usually implies an extreme of wickedness or badness. Evil has been thought of in a number of ways by philosophers and theologians, for example:

- Evil as an abstract but real entity (personified, for example, by the devil) of which evil things, people, and actions partake.

- Evil as a quality of certain actions in themselves, regardless of their effects. In this interpretations ends never justify means (see **ends and means**).

- Similarly, although someone's actions might be judged evil, they themselves may not be (this might depend on their **intention**).

- Evil as only residing in the outcomes of actions, thus the term is restricted to anything that is bad for, or harmful to, human beings (this may be extended to anything that is harmful to animals, for example, or the environment).

Another distinction is the traditional division of evil into 'moral evil' and 'natural evil'. Moral evil originates in human action, whereas natural evil originates independently of human action – for instance, earthquakes or epidemics. The 'problem of evil' is the difficulty of explaining the existence of evil if the world was created by a perfect and omnipotent God (see **theodicy**). **See also:** *Arendt, Hannah.*

The devil carrying off a child promised to him by his parents under a pact.

> ❧ More people are killed out of righteous stupidity than out of wickedness. ❧
>
> **Karl Popper**, *Conjectures and Refutations*

existence

What is common to everything that there is. Like **being**, existence is a fundamental notion in metaphysics generally. Existence can be contrasted with being or **essence**, as in the work of Thomas Aquinas and in some types of **existentialism**. Existentialists such as **Heidegger** and **Sartre** held that 'existence precedes essence', implying that we make ourselves what we are by free choice.

In medieval and rationalist metaphysics, existence is perfection. The **ontological argument** – God is perfect; existence is a perfection; therefore God exists necessarily – turns on whether existence can be a **predicate** or **property**, which Immanuel **Kant** denied.

> ❝ All existence is a theft paid for by other existences; no life flowers except on a cemetery ❞
>
> **Rémy De Gourmont**, *The Dissociation of Ideas*

existence of God, arguments for
See *argument from design; cosmological argument; moral argument; ontological argument*.

existentialism
Modern philosophical movement based on the situation of the individual in an absurd or meaningless universe where humans have **free will**. Existentialists argue that people are responsible for and the sole judge of their actions as they affect others.

The origin of existentialism is usually traced back to **Kierkegaard** in the 19th century. Among its proponents were Karl **Jaspers** and Martin **Heidegger** in Germany and Jean-Paul **Sartre** in France.

All self-aware individuals can grasp or intuit their own existence and freedom, and individuals must not deny their freedom to choose, or to allow their choices to be constrained by anything – not even reason or morality. To do so is **bad faith**. Human existence consists of the freedom to choose; both are rooted in nothingness or nonbeing, and this can provoke **anguish**. Existentialism has many variants. Kierkegaard emphasized the importance of pure choice in ethics and Christian belief; Sartre tried to combine existentialism with Marxism.

experience
Direct personal involvement in the world, and the knowledge derived from such involvement. It is sometimes restricted to knowledge derived directly through the senses. The reliability of knowledge from **experience** is upheld by empiricism, and doubted by **rationalism** (see, for example, **Descartes**). **See also:** *idealism*.

experiment
In science, a practical test designed with the intention that its results will be relevant to a particular **theory** or **hypothesis**. **See** *empiricism; science, philosophy of; scientific method; thought experiment*.

F

faith

In religion, trust and belief in God's provision; the 'assurance of things hoped for, the conviction of things not seen' (St Paul). Faith includes moral or liturgical obedience, although in Christianity the Protestant reformers made a sharp distinction between faith (belief in Jesus Christ as the only way to salvation) and works (practical actions), which they taught did not bring salvation. **See also:** *bad faith; belief; doubt; fideism.*

> ❝ There lives more faith in honest doubt,
> Believe me, than in half the creeds. ❞
>
> **Alfred, Lord Tennyson,** *In Memoriam*

fallacy

In philosophy, a type of mistake in reasoning or inference (deduction or conclusion drawn from what has been implied). In Aristotelian logic (see **syllogism**) and in modern formal logic, there are rules for detecting and preventing fallacies, and ensuring that an inference is valid.

Fallacies in everyday reasoning can be less easy to detect. Begging the question is a fallacy that occurs when one of the premises of an argument could not be known to be true unless the conclusion were first assumed to be true. Other fallacies include fallacies of ambiguity; of arguing against a person (an *AD hominem* argument), rather than against what the person says; and of arguing that something is true simply because there is no evidence against it.

For the 'naturalistic fallacy' see **is/ought problem**. For the 'quantifier shift fallacy', see **quantification**.

fascism

Totalitarian political ideology that denies all rights to individuals in their relations with the state. It first emerged after World War I in Italy, where Mussolini's Fascist Party held power from 1922 to 1943, and was adopted by Hilter's Nazi Party in Germany, which held power from 1933 to 1945. There were also fascist parties in other European countries between the two world wars, and neo-fascist parties have re-emerged in postwar Europe, the USA, and elsewhere.

Fascism is a form of extreme, militaristic, racist **nationalism**:

- At the core of fascism is a heavily cultivated myth of the superiority of a state and its people over other states and peoples.

- Fascism is opposed to both **communism** and **capitalism**, although it tends to protect the existing social order by forcible suppression of the working-class movement and by providing scapegoats for popular anger such as Jews, foreigners, or blacks.

- Private property, labour, education, and all other aspects of people's lives are made subservient to the needs of the state.

Mussolini, Italian dictator and founder of the Fascist Movement in 1911.

- This is often part of an economic and psychological mobilization of all a state's resources for expansionist war.

It has been suggested that the appeal of fascism is to those people who, for whatever reason, feel that their sense of community is being threatened. For such people, it has been argued, fascism provides a total, highly structured, intellectually undemanding, yet psychologically satisfying, resort.

Fascism is not a discrete phenomenon but has different characteristics in different countries, and merges into other forms of right-wing authoritarianism. Its loose employment as a term of abuse for political opponents of whatever complexion to the right has tended to erode the analytical utility of the term.

fatalism
The view that the future is fixed, irrespective of our attempts to affect it. Seldom held as a philosophical doctrine, fatalism has been influential as an attitude towards life (as in **Stoicism**) and as a literary theme (for example, in the Oedipus legend). **See also:** *determinism.*

felicific calculus or hedonic calculus
A technique devised by Jeremy **Bentham** for establishing the rightness and wrongness of an action. Using the calculus, one can supposedly attempt to

work out the likely consequences of an action in terms of the pain or pleasure of those affected.

feminism

Active belief in equal rights and opportunities for women, or, more broadly, the belief that the relationship between the sexes is one that involves the subordination, oppression, **alienation**, and **reification** of women.

Early campaigners of the 17th–19th centuries fought for women's right to own property, to have access to higher education, and to vote. These campaigners included Mary **Wollstonecraft** and Emmeline Pankhurst in the UK, and Susan B Anthony and Elizabeth Cady Stanton in the USA. The women's movement was also supported by J S **Mill**.

Once women's suffrage was achieved in the 20th century, the emphasis of the movement shifted to the goals of equal social and economic opportunities for women, including employment. After World War II a new impetus was given to the women's movement by such theorists as Simone de **Beauvoir**, Betty Friedan, Kate Millett, Gloria Steinem, and Germaine Greer. From the late 1960s feminists argued that women were oppressed by the male-dominated social structure as a whole, which they saw as pervaded by sexism, despite legal concessions towards equality of the sexes. In this period the women's movement has been critical of the use of women as sex objects in advertising, and has also opposed their indoctrination into passive and accommodating roles within the family and society in general.

> ❝ Women's liberation is the liberation of the feminine in the man and the masculine in the woman. ❞
>
> **Corita Kent**, quoted in the *Los Angeles Times*, 11 July 1974

Feuerbach, Ludwig (1804–1872)

German philosopher who studied under **Hegel**, but abandoned Hegel's idealism for a form of **materialism**. Feuerbach argued that religion is the elevation of human qualities into an object of worship. He influenced Karl **Marx,** although Marx was critical of some aspects of Feuerbach's thinking. **See also:** *anthropology*.

Feurbach's main work, *The Essence of Christianity* (1841), was translated into English by the novelist George Eliot in 1854.

> ❝ Man is what he eats. ❞
>
> **Ludwig Feuerbach**, *Blätter für Literarische Unterhaltung*

Fichte, Johann Gottlieb (1762–1814)

German philosopher, who developed a comprehensive form of subjective **idealism**, expounded in *The Science of Knowledge* (1794). He was an admirer of **Kant**, and in 1792 published Critique of Religious Revelation, a critical study of **Kant's** doctrine of the **thing-in-itself**. For Fichte, the absolute ego posits both the external world (the non-ego) and the finite **self**. Morality consists in the striving of this finite self to rejoin the **absolute**. He was an important influence on **Romanticism**, and his *Addresses to the German People* (1807–08) had an impact on contemporary liberal **nationalism**.

Ficino, Marsilio (1433–1499)

Italian philosopher, who created an influential synthesis of **Platonism** and medieval theology, and who established the **Platonic Academy** in Florence.
He assigned to the human soul the central place in the hierarchy of the universe (see **chain of being**), and he believed that the soul ascended towards God through contemplation. He translated both **Plato** and **Plotinus**, the

Among those influenced by Ficino's philosophy of beauty was the painter Sandro Botticelli.

founder of **neo-Platonism**, into Latin, thus becoming one of the principal channels of their diffusion through Renaissance Europe.

fideism

A theological position that religious truth and belief is a matter of **faith**, and cannot be established by reason. It is thus opposed to **natural theology**. Modern fideism, based on the Christian existentialism of **Kierkegaard**, can take the form of a conscious choice or 'will' to believe, given the apparent purposelessness and absurdity of the universe.

> ❝ Certum est quia impossibile est.'
> 'It is certain because it is impossible ❞
>
> **Tertullian**, *De Carne Christi*

first cause

An argument for the existence of God as creator or cause of the world. The first cause argument – a version of the **cosmological argument** – turns on the idea that everything requires a cause or reason. God must exist to be the first cause, because it is assumed either that an infinite regress of causes is impossible or that the existence of the universe itself needs explanation.

For **Aristotle,** matter has always existed, so the first cause, or 'prime mover' as he calls God, is not the first cause in time but the cause of the universe's continuing existence – a sustaining cause, or reason for its existence. For Thomas **Aquinas**, the first cause is both a sustaining cause of the world and the first cause in all the causal series that make up the world.

> ❝ I have too much respect for the idea of God to make it responsible for such an absurd world. ❞
>
> **Georges Duhamel**, *Chronique des Pasquier*

flux
See *Heraclitus*.

form
In Greek and medieval European philosophy (**scholasticism**), that which makes a thing what it is.

For **Plato**, a Form was an immaterial, independent object, which could not be perceived by the senses and was known only by reason; thus, a horse was a thing participating in the Form of horseness. (In Platonic philosophy Form is generally capitalized and is synonymous with his use of idea.)

For **Aristotle**, forms existed only in combination with matter: a horse was a lump of matter having the form of a horse – that is, the essential properties (see **essence**) and powers of a horse. However, Aristotle, like the medieval philosophers after him, does not make it clear whether there is a different form for each individual, or only for each type or species.

form
In logic, the form of a proposition is the kind or species to which it belongs; see **syllogism**.

Foucault, Michel (1926–1984)
French philosopher who argued that human knowledge and subjectivity are dependent upon specific institutions and practices, and that they change through history. In particular, he was concerned to subvert conventional assumptions about 'social deviants' – the mentally ill, the sick, and the criminal – who, he believed, are oppressed by the approved knowledge of the period in which they live.

Foucault rejected **phenomenology** and **existentialism**, and his historicization of the self challenges the ideas of **Marx**. He was deeply influenced by **Nietzsche**, and developed an analysis of the operation of power in society using Nietzschean concepts.

> ❝ Man is neither the oldest nor the most constant problem that has been posed for human knowledge. ❞
>
> **Michel Foucault**, *The Order of Things*

Frankfurt School

The members of the Institute of Social Research, set up at Frankfurt University, Germany, in 1923 as the first Marxist research centre. With the rise of Hitler, many of its members went to the USA and set up the institute at Columbia University, New York.

In the 1930s, under its second director Max Horkheimer (1895–1973), a group that included Erich Fromm (1900–80), Herbert **Marcuse**, and T W **Adorno** attempted to update Marxism and create a coherent and viable social theory. Drawing on a variety of disciplines as well as the writings of **Marx** and **Freud**, they produced works such as *Authority and the Family* (1936) and developed a Marxist perspective known as 'critical theory'.

After World War II the institute returned to Frankfurt, although Marcuse and some others remained in the USA. The German and US branches diverged in the 1950s, and the institute was dissolved in 1969 after Adorno's death, although Jürgen **Habermas** and others have since attempted to revive its theory and research programme.

freedom

A concept most usually applied to personal liberty to act according to the individual will and without any physical or other form of restraint.

Negative and positive freedom
The absence of restraint is known as 'negative freedom', while a state of self-mastery or self-realization is sometimes referred to as 'positive freedom'. Those holding the negative view of freedom include **Locke, Mill,** and **Hobbes**. Those holding the positive view include **Rousseau** and **Hegel.**

Liberalism and Marxism
Negative freedom is at the heart of **liberalism**, with its belief in **civil liberties.** In 19th-century liberalism, there is also the belief in unrestrained capitalist free enterprise, a position shared by modern **conservatism. See also:** *libertarianism.*

> ❦ Better starve free than be a fat slave. ❧
>
> **Aesop,** *Fables*, 'The Dog and the Wolf'

A different perspective on the concept of freedom is found among Marxist thinkers, who hold that freedom from poverty and hunger, freedom from inequality, and freedom from exploitation are more fundamental than civil liberties, and are certainly more important than the free play of the market, which is interpreted as the freedom of the few to exploit the many. This perspective was reflected in communist states in the 20th century. **See also:** *human rights.*

> ❝ Absolute freedom mocks at justice. Absolute justice denies freedom. ❞
>
> **Albert Camus**, *The Rebel*, 'Historical Murder'

The freedom to choose
Yet another perspective on freedom is found in **existentialism**, in which the freedom to choose (**free will**) is the fundamental condition of human beings. In **determinism**, in contrast, free will is denied.

> ❝ The misfortune that befalls man from his once having been a child is that his liberty was at first concealed from him, and all his life he will retain the nostalgia for a time when he was ignorant of its exigencies. ❞
>
> **Simone de Beauvoir**, *Pour une morale de l'ambiguité*

free will
The doctrine that human beings are free to control their own actions, and that these actions are not fixed in advance by God or fate or any mechanism of cause and effect. Some Jewish and Christian theologians assert that God gave humanity free will to choose between good and evil; others that God has decided in advance the outcome of all human choices (**predestination**), as in Calvinism. Modern philosophers tend to discuss the existence or otherwise of free will in relation to socio-historical and/or scientific **determinism** – are we really free to choose if we are conditioned by a mixture of genetic makeup and environmental circumstances? In **existentialism**, to deny one's freedom to choose is **bad faith**.

> ❝ Freedom is not something that anybody can be given; freedom is something people take and people are as free as they want to be. ❞
>
> **James Baldwin**, *Nobody Knows My Name*, 'Notes for a Hypothetical Novel'

Frege, Gottlob (1848–1925)
German philosopher, the founder of modern mathematical logic. He also made important contributions to the philosophy of **language**. Frege created

symbols for concepts like 'or' and 'if ... then', which are now in standard use in mathematics.

Frege's work on the foundations of arithmetic influenced Bertrand **Russell** and Ludwig Wittgenstein, but in 1902 Frege was devastated when Russell inquired how his logical system coped with a particular logical paradox in set theory (see **Russell's paradox**). Frege's system was not able to resolve it, and he was forced to acknowledge his system to be useless.

Freud, Sigmund
(1856–1939)

Austrian physician who pioneered the study of the **unconscious** mind. He developed the methods of free association and interpretation of dreams that are basic techniques of **psychoanalysis**. Freud held that unconscious forces influence people's thoughts and actions, and that the repression of infantile sexuality is the root of neuroses in the adult. Following the Nazi annexation of Austria in 1938, Freud sought refuge in London and died there the following year.

Sigmund Freud, the founder of psychoanalysis.

❝ I am actually not at all a man of science ... I am by temperament nothing but a conquistador – an adventurer ... – with all the curiosity, daring and tenacity characteristic of a man of this sort. ❞

Sigmund Freud, letter, 1900

FREUD: INFLUENCE AND CRITICISM

Freud's influence has permeated the world to such an extent that it may be discerned today in almost every branch of thought. His theories have changed the way people think about human nature, brought about a more open approach to sexual matters, and have led to wider expression of the human condition in art and literature.

Nevertheless, Freud's theories have caused disagreement among psychologists and psychiatrists, and his methods of psychoanalysis cannot be applied in every case. In addition, many scientists and philosophers have questioned whether Freud's theories have anything to do with science, on the grounds that they can neither be proved nor disproved.

friendship
Mutual benevolence that is independent of sexual or family love. **Aristotle** distinguished three levels of friendship:

- The useful (friendship as a common enterprise).
- The pleasant (friendship as entertaining companionship).
- The good or virtuous (friendship as mutual esteem).

See also: *love.*

Galileo Galilei (1564–1642)

Italian mathematician, astronomer, and physicist, whose influence on both scientific and philosophical thought was enormous. His work founded the **scientific method** of inferring laws to explain the results of observation and experiment.

Galileo's observations, and his pioneering application of mathematics to physics, were unwelcome refutations of the **Aristotelianism** dominant in the universities, largely because they made plausible for the first time the Sun-centred theory of Polish astronomer Nicolaus Copernicus (1473–1543). Galileo's persuasive *Dialogues on the Two Chief Systems of the World* (1632) was banned by the church authorities in Rome, and he was made to recant by the Inquisition.

Galileo observing the chandelier in Pisa cathedral. This led to his work on the isochronism of the pendulum and eventually, through Huyghens, to the development of the pendulum clock.

> ❛In questions of science the authority of a thousand is not worth the humble reasoning of a single individual.❜
>
> **Galileo**, attributed remark

Gandhi, Mahatma (1869–1948)

Indian nationalist leader and social reformer. A pacifist, he led the struggle for Indian independence from the UK by advocating nonviolent noncooperation (satyagraha, defence of and by truth) from 1915.

Gandhi's belief of the inseparability of **ends and means**, and his philosophy of peaceful civil disobedience as the way to right injustice, have been widely influential, for example in the struggle for black civil rights in the USA in the 1950s and 1960s. He was assassinated by a Hindu nationalist in the violence that followed the partition of British India into India and Pakistan.

> 6 Freedom and slavery are mental states. 9
>
> **Mahatma Gandhi**, *Non-Violence in Peace and War*

Gentile, Giovanni (1875–1944)

Italian philosopher and politician. His doctrine of 'actualism' (a form of highly subjective **idealism**) was seized on by the Fascist Party to justify their authoritarian policies. As Mussolini's minister of education from 1924, Gentile reformed both the school and university systems. He was assassinated by partisans.

Gestalt

A term (from the German for 'form') applied to a concept of a unified whole that is greater than, or different from, the sum of its parts; that is, a complete structure whose nature is not explained simply by analysing its constituent elements. A chair, for example, will generally be recognized as a chair despite great variations between individual chairs in such attributes as size, shape, and colour. **See also:** *holism.*

GESTALT PSYCHOLOGY

Gestalt psychology was founded in Germany in the early 20th century by Wolfgang Köhler and Kurt Koffka. It regards all mental phenomena as being arranged in organized, structured wholes, as opposed to being composed of simple sensations. For example, learning is seen as a reorganizing of a whole situation (often involving insight), as opposed to the behaviourists' view that it consists of associations between stimuli and responses (see **behaviourism**).

Gestalt psychologists' experiments show that the brain is not a passive receiver of information, but that it structures all its input in order to make sense of it, a belief that is now generally accepted (see **cognitive science**) However, other principles of Gestalt psychology have received considerable criticism.

Geulincx, Arnold (*c.* 1625–1669)

Flemish philosopher, who formed the theory of 'occasionalism', according to which God synchronizes body and mind, like two clocks that act together but have no influence on each other. Occasionalism was his solution to the **mind–body problem**.

ghost in the machine

See *Ryle, Gilbert.*

Gnosticism

Esoteric cult of divine knowledge, which flourished during the 2nd and 3rd centuries ad. It was a synthesis of Christianity, Greek philosophy, Hinduism, Buddhism, and the mystery cults of the Mediterranean, and was a rival to, and influence on, early Christianity. It also influenced **Manichaeism**, the medieval French Cathar heresy, and the modern Mandean sect in southern Iraq.

Gnosticism envisaged the world as a series of emanations from the highest of several gods. The lowest emanation was an evil god (the demiurge) who created the material world as a prison for the divine sparks that dwell in human bodies. The Gnostics identified this evil creator with the God of the Old Testament, and saw the Adam and Eve story and the ministry of Jesus as attempts to liberate humanity from his dominion, by imparting divine secret wisdom.

God

The concept of a supreme being, a unique creative entity, basic to several monotheistic religions (for example Judaism, Christianity, Islam). In these religions God is usually ascribed a variety of features, such as transcendence (being beyond or apart from the natural universe), immanence (operating within the natural universe), omnipotence, omniscience, omnipresence, and timelessness.

In many polytheistic cultures (for example Norse, Roman, Greek), the term 'god' refers to a supernatural being who personifies the force behind an aspect of life (for example Neptune, Roman god of the sea).

Traditionally, Christian philosophers have offered four arguments for the existence of God:

- the **argument from design**
- the **cosmological argument**
- the **moral argument**
- the **ontological argument**.

Since the 17th century, advances in science and the belief that the only valid statements were those verifiable by the senses have had a complex influence on the belief in God (see, for example, **religion, science, and philosophy).**

See also: *agnosticism; atheism; belief; deism; ethics; faith; fideism; first cause; natural theology; pantheism; religion, philosophy of; theism; theodicy; theology.*

> ❝ You cannot plumb the depths of the human heart, nor find out what a man is thinking; how do you expect to search out God, who made all these things, and find out his mind or comprehend his thoughts? ❞
>
> **Apocrypha**, Judith 8:14

Gödel, Kurt (1906–1978)
Austrian mathematician and philosopher, who emigrated to the USA following the Nazi annexation of Austria in 1938. Examining the logical basis of mathematics devised by Russell and **Whitehead** in *Principia Mathematica*, Gödel proved in 1931 that a mathematical system always contains statements that can be neither proved nor disproved within the system. In other words, mathematics can never be totally consistent and totally complete.

Godwin, William (1756–1836)
English philosopher and novelist. His *Enquiry Concerning Political Justice* (1793) put forward a theory of **anarchism** based on a faith in people's essential rationality. His philosophical outlook was deterministic, yet he believed that people should increase their awareness of moral choices. Morality was defined by reference to the greatest general good (see **utilitarianism**), and he argued that selfish actions bring less pleasure than benevolent ones. His novel *The Adventures of Caleb Williams* (1794) promoted his views.

Godwin was the husband of the pioneering feminist Mary **Wollstonecraft**, and the father by her of Mary Shelley, the author of Frankenstein, and wife of the poet Percy Bysshe Shelley.

Goethe, Johann Wolfgang von (1749–1832)
German poet, novelist, dramatist, scientist, and thinker. He is generally considered the founder of modern German literature, and was the leader of the *Sturm und Drang* movement, a forerunner of **Romanticism**, although he later worked towards the classical Greek ideal of calm and harmony.

In his thinking Goethe was influenced by philosophers such as **Plato, Spinoza,** and **Kant**. His belief in the unity of nature and the inseparability of mind and matter amounts to a kind of **pantheism**. These views pervaded not only his literary work, but also his scientific research, in which he combined keen observation and poetic intuition.

GOETHE'S FAUST

Goethe's masterpiece is the poetic play Faust (1808 and 1832), a work of unique biographical interest. Faust, like Goethe, struggles for perfection, often yields to evil, but never comes to love it or to lose his belief in the right and good. His failure in the quest for absolute knowledge leads him to despair, from which he is rescued only by a life of useful labour.

golden rule

A guideline, found in the ethical systems of many cultures, that one should act towards others in such a way that one would wish others to act towards oneself:

- 'What you do not want done to yourself, do not do to others.' (Confucius, *Analects*, 6th–5th century BC)

- 'Therefore all things whatsoever ye would that men should do to you, do ye even so unto them.' (Matthew 7:12)

J S **Mill** claimed that the golden rule lay at the heart of **utilitarianism**. **See also:** *categorical imperative.*

> ❝ Do not do unto others as you would they should do unto you. Their tastes may not be the same ❞
>
> **George Bernard Shaw**, *Man and Superman*, 'Maxims for Revolutionists'

good

That property or characteristic of a thing giving rise to commendation. Philosophers have distinguished different types of 'goods':

- 'Intrinsic goods' are those things that we value in themselves, for their own sakes or as ends.

- 'Extrinsic goods' are those that owe their goodness to things outside themselves – for example, surgery is good in so far as it promotes health.

- 'Non-moral good' can originate in human action (for example, taking exercise), or it can originate independently of human action (for example, good weather).

- 'Moral good' or 'goodness' (see **morality**) originates in human action.

Ethics is, in part, the systematic study of theories about morality and goodness. **See also:** *evil; happiness; right, the.*

A HIGHEST GOOD?

Many philosophers have identified a highest good:

- Plato held that our highest good was experience of the Form of the Good – which is goodness itself and the transcendent source of goodness.
- Aristotle held that it was an integrated life of virtuous behaviour and intellectual contemplation.
- St Augustine of Hippo and St Thomas Aquinas, both Christian philosophers, held that the highest good is beatitude or a state of blessedness.

Others, such as Thomas Hobbes, have denied that there is any such thing as a highest good.

Goodman's paradox

Riddle of **induction** (reasoning from the particular to the general) formulated by US philosopher Nelson Goodman (1906–). He invents a property 'grue', which applies to any green thing examined before a given time and also to any blue thing at any time, and uses it to show that in inductive reasoning some events do, and some do not, establish regularities from which we can make predictions, and that what determines our habits of classification is how deeply a property is entrenched in our thinking.

- A prediction that all emeralds examined before the given time will be green, and a prediction that they will be 'grue', are both equally likely to be true.
- However, if, after the given time, we examine an emerald and it is 'grue', it must be blue and not green.
- Moreover, if the confirmation of predictions is defined in terms of past success, anything can be made to confirm anything else by inventing strange properties like 'grue'.

Some philosophers have criticized the device of a time-linked property as artificial.

Gramsci, Antonio (1891–1937)

Italian Marxist who attempted to unify social theory and political practice. He helped to found the Italian Communist Party in 1921 and was elected to parliament in 1924, but was imprisoned by the Fascist leader Mussolini from 1926. His *Prison Notebooks* were published posthumously in 1947.

Gramsci believed that politics and ideology are independent of the economic base. His concept of 'hegemony' argued that real class control in capitalist societies is ideological and cultural rather than physical, and that only the working class 'educated' by radical intellectuals could see through and overthrow such bourgeois propaganda. His humane and gradualist approach, specifically his emphasis on the need to overthrow bourgeois ideology, influenced European Marxists in their attempt to distance themselves from the orthodox economic determinism of Soviet communism.

greatest happiness
See *utilitarianism*.

Grosseteste, Robert (c. 1169–1253)
English scholar, who became bishop of Lincoln and chancellor of Oxford University. His prolific writings include scientific works as well as translations of **Aristotle** and commentaries on the Bible. He was a forerunner of the empirical school, being one of the earliest to suggest testing ancient Greek theories by practical experiment.

Grotius, Hugo (1583–1645)
Dutch jurist and politician. His book *De jure belli et pacis* ('on the law of war and peace', 1625) is the foundation of international law. Grotius held that the rules governing human and international relations are founded on human nature, which is rational and social. These rules constitute a **natural law** binding on citizens, rulers, and God.

❝ Not to know something is a great part of wisdom. ❞

Hugo Grotius, *Docta Ignorantia*

Habermas, Jürgen (1929–)

German social theorist, a member of the **Frankfurt School**. His central concern is how a meaningful engagement in politics and society is possible in a society dominated by science and the technology and bureaucracy based on it.

In *Theory and Practice* (1963) and *Knowledge and Human Interest* (1968), he argued that reason, which had long been a weapon of intellectual and political freedom, has been appropriated by science. Far from being a disinterested pursuit of knowledge, it is an instrument for achieving a range of unquestioned social and political ends. In *Theory of Communicative Action* (1981) he describes how a 'communicative rationality' can be developed, reclaiming lost ground and allowing rational political commitment.

haecceity

Literally 'thisness', a term used in philosophy for an individual **essence**, the property that uniquely identifies an individual object or person.

Halevi, Judah (c. 1080–1140)

Spanish poet, philosopher, and physician. His religious verses are still used as prayers by Jewish congregations. His philosophical dialogue *The Book of the Khazar* is a defence of Judaism and an examination of the nature of religious truth.

Hamilton, William (1788–1856)

Scottish philosopher, a follower of the 'common sense' philosophy of Thomas **Reid,** whose views he combined with those of **Kant**. His theory of knowledge was criticized by J S **Mill**.

Hampshire, Stuart (1914–)

English philosopher. In *Thought and Action* (1959), he argued, against **Descartes**, that awareness of selfhood requires that a person possess a physical body acting in a physical world (see **mind–body problem**). Hampshire sees human action as involving freedom, in that humans have some power to decide. His ethical views are influenced by those of **Spinoza**.

happiness

Happiness is sometimes seen as residing in pleasure, and sometimes in such things as self-fulfilment. It is often (although by no means universally) identified with the **good**.

The ethical theory known as **hedonism** holds that happiness lies in pleasure, the main goal in life. In the ancient world this doctrine was put forward by the **Cyrenaics** and the Epicureans (see **Epicureanism**). Hedonism is also at the core of **utilitarianism**, which holds that the best action is that which results in the 'greatest happiness of the greatest number of people'.

In contrast, other philosophers have looked for happiness beyond pleasure, a psychological state or sensation, to the nature of a person's whole life. For example, **Aristotle** held that happiness lies in the use of reason, both in thought and as a guide to virtuous living.

> ❝ If merely 'feeling good' could decide, drunkenness would be the supremely valid human experience. ❞
>
> **William James**, *The Varieties of Religious Experience*,
> 'Religion and Neurology'

Hayek, Friedrich (1899–1992)
Austrian-born British economist and political theorist, who shared the 1974 Nobel Prize for economics. In *The Road to Serfdom* (1944) he set out to combat the wartime vogue for **collectivism** in Britain, and argued that economic **freedom** was the necessary precondition for political freedom and democracy. His ideas were enthusiastically devoured by the leaders of the resurgent free-market **conservatism** in the late-1970s and 1980s, although these disciples did not always share Hayek's commitment to liberal values.

heap, paradox of the
A traditional paradox that asks 'How many grains of sand make a heap?' One or two or three grains of sand obviously do not constitute a heap, while a thousand grains obviously do. The question is at what point, if we add a grain at a time, do we have a heap? And if we take one grain away, do we cease to have a heap?

The paradox is partly due to an inappropriate application of logic, and party due to our use of language, specifically the vagueness of collective nouns. One might equally well ask, for example, 'How many birds make a flock?' An analogous, but more morally pressing, question, is, 'At what point does a developing embryo change from being a collection of cells into a human being?' (see **abortion**).

hedonic calculus
See *felicific calculus*.

hedonism
Ethical theory that pleasure or **happiness** is, or should be, the main goal in life. In ancient Greece the **Cyrenaics** held that the pleasure of the moment

is the only human good, while **Epicureanism** advocated the pursuit of pleasure under the direction of reason. Modern hedonistic philosophies, such as **utilitarianism**, regard the happiness of society as the aim. **See also:** *deontology; ethics.*

> ❝ Twere too absurd to slight
> For the hereafter the today's delight! ❞
>
> **Robert Browning**, *Sordello*

Hegel, G(eorg) W(ilhelm) F(riedrich) (1770–1831)

German philosopher, in whose 'absolute **idealism**' the distinction between reality and our knowledge of it breaks down. Of all the great philosophers, Hegel is the most difficult to understand. Even so, the impact of his systematized philosophy has been immense, particularly as an interpretation of social and historical processes. Those influenced by him include **Marx**, **Feuerbach**, **Bradley**, **Croce**, and **Sartre**.

Spirit and the dialectic
Influenced by **Spinoza**, Hegel conceived of mind and nature as two abstractions of one indivisible whole, 'Spirit'. His system traces the emergence of Spirit in the logical study of concepts and the process of world history. To Hegel, Spirit has purposes and ends of its own, which finite spirits serve. It lives only through human beings, but is not identical with the human spirit. For Hegel, concepts unfold, and in unfolding they generate the reality that is described by them. To understand reality is to understand our ideas, and vice versa. The development of a concept is 'dialectical', involving three stages: thesis, antithesis, and synthesis (see **dialectic**).

Freedom, ethics, and the state
Hegel believed that freedom lies in the rational understanding of the dialectical process of history, and that 'The history of the world is none other than the progress of the consciousness of freedom.' In a society based on reason, it is possible to realize fully a freedom that does not constrain the freedom of others; in such a society **duty** and self-interest coincide.

Hegel himself regarded the Prussian state and Lutheran Christianity of his day as the supreme social synthesis. In contrast, Hegel's leftist followers,

> ❝ Only one man ever understood me … And he didn't
> understand me. ❞
>
> **G W F Hegel**, last words (attributed)

including Marx, tried to use his dialectic to show the inevitability of radical change and to attack both the religion and social order of their times. **See also:** *history, philosophy of; organicism.*

> 6 Hegel filled the universe with copulating contradictions. 9
>
> **Bertrand Russell,** *History of Western Philosophy*

hegemony
See *Gramsci, Antonio.*

Heidegger, Martin (1889–1976)
German philosopher, regarded as a leading exponent of **existentialism**. He was influenced by, among others, **Kierkegaard, Nietzsche**, and the **phenomenology** of **Husserl**. His major work is *Being and Time* (1927).

Heidegger believed that Western philosophy had 'forgotten' the fundamental question of the 'meaning of Being', and his work concerns the investigation of what he thought were the different types of being appropriate to people and to things in general. Among his key concepts were those of **authenticity** and *Angst* (**anguish**). His sympathy with the Nazis damaged his reputation, although he influenced younger philosophers such as **Sartre.**

Heisenberg's uncertainty principle
See *uncertainty principle.*

Heraclitus (*c.* 544–*c.* 483 BC)
Greek philosopher. Rejecting the doctrine of **Parmenides** that motion and change are illusory, and that reality is unitary and static, Heraclitus held that reality consists of constant change (flux) and motion, and that objects comprise a harmony of opposing tensions. He held that behind this process was a **logos**, an organizing principle analogous to human reason. His influence has been discerned in such divergent philosophers as **Hegel, Heidegger**, and **Wittgenstein**.

> 6 You could not step twice into the same river; for other waters are ever flowing on to you. 9
>
> **Heraclitus,** quoted in Hippocrates, *On the Universe*

Herbert of Cherbury, Lord
See *deism.*

hermeneutics
Philosophical tradition concerned with the nature of understanding and interpretation of human behaviour and social traditions. From its origins in

problems of biblical interpretation, hermeneutics has expanded to cover many fields of enquiry, including aesthetics, literary theory, and science. Wilhelm **Dilthey** and Martin **Heidegger** were among the influential contributors to this tradition.

hermeticism

The belief that there is a secret, ancient body of wisdom, surviving in written texts of the 1st–3rd centuries AD, that accurately describes the workings of the natural and supernatural worlds, and that mastery of these texts provides an enhanced understanding and control of nature. The belief was common in Renaissance times and persisted into the 17th century.

The secret body of wisdom was identified with various combinations of:

- The writings of Hermes Trismegistus (supposedly the Egyptian god Thoth, but the writings actually date from the 1st–3rd centuries AD),

- Christian Rosenkreuz, the probably mythical founder of Rosicrucianism, who supposedly lived in the 14th–15th centuries,

- The **kabbala**, an ancient Jewish mystical tradition,

- The neo-Platonists of the 3rd to 6th centuries AD (see **neo-Platonism**),

- Texts of ritual magic,

- Egyptian hieroglyphics (which were not deciphered until the discovery of the Rosetta Stone in 1799).

Devotees included Giordano **Bruno**, and, in England, John Dee (1527–1608), and Robert Fludd (1574–1637).

The Jewish elements led to people believing that the texts had foretold the coming of Jesus, and this enabled much of the mysticism and magic within the texts to be used by Christian writers. This strongly influenced the growth of Christian mysticism and fuelled a fascination with Egypt as a land of esoteric knowledge.

Hilbert, David (1862–1943)

German mathematician, philosopher, and physicist whose work was fundamental to 20th-century mathematics. Hilbert attempted to put mathematics on a logical foundation through defining it in terms of a number of basic principles, which Kurt **Gödel** later showed to be impossible.

In 1900 Hilbert proposed a set of 23 problems for future mathematicians to solve, many of which are still outstanding.

historicism

Term referring to two contrasting views on the nature of historical and social research;

- The first claims that historians must interpret each age in terms of its values, assumptions, and concerns, and that a modern perspective uncritically distorts historical phenomena.
- The second argues for the need to understand historical change in terms of broad, all-embracing laws of historical growth and development.

Karl **Popper** used the term in this second sense in the *Poverty of Historicism* (1957) to attack the theories of **Hegel** and **Marx**, both of whom saw the course of history as working towards a goal.

history, philosophy of

One of the fundamental questions in the philosophy of history is whether history can be objective. Historical facts can in most cases be shown to be true or false. But facts in isolation are not very useful to our understanding of the past; what we look for are reasons, causes, and explanations.

To do this, historians must select what they think are pertinent facts, and marshal them together into a structure. These processes are interpretative, and will inevitably be coloured to a degree by the historian's own time and culture, however objective or empathetic he or she may attempt to be.

The uses of history

The writing of history has often, through the ages, had some ulterior purpose, usually religious or political. In many cases it has been written to maintain the hegemony of the ruling elite, concentrating on the lives of 'great men'.

Many modern historians have been concerned to reverse this trend, and to rescue from obscurity the lives and significance of the ordinary people of the past, of ignored minorities such as women or blacks. But even here the investigation of the past is informed by a current ideological concern.

It is of course not necessarily a problem, as long as one is aware of it, that historical writing should have some purpose or utility. Many have argued that history helps us to understand the present, or to avoid the mistakes of the past.

history as system

Some philosophers, such as **Vico**, have seen history as a series of repeating cycles. Others, such as **Hegel** and **Marx**, detected in history the deterministic operation of non-human forces acting on the actions of humanity according to certain laws and towards some goal.

Although Marx's emphasis on economic and social history has been highly influential, many historians and philosophers have rejected his account as an entire explanation of history, emphasizing the role of chance, the plurality of histories, and questioning the inevitability of cause and effect in history. **See also:** *historicism.*

> ❦ [History repeats itself] the first time as tragedy,
> the second as farce. ❧
>
> **Karl Marx**, *The Eighteenth Brumaire of Louis Napoleon*

Hobbes, Thomas (1588–1679)

English philosopher, best known for his political work *Leviathan* (1651), which justified absolute monarchy as the best means of preserving peace. Hobbes was also the first thinker since **Aristotle** to attempt to develop a comprehensive theory of nature, including human behaviour. A **materialist**, he analysed everything in terms of matter and motion. His moral philosophy was largely secular: he held that moral rules had to be obeyed to ensure 'peaceable, social, and comfortable living'. This, like his political thinking, anticipates **utilitarianism**.

Thomas Hobbes.

Hobbes's political theory was prompted by the breakdown of social and political order during the English Civil War of the 1640s. In *Leviathan* he advocated absolutist monarchy as the only means of preventing life from being 'nasty, brutish, and short', as he alleged it was in a state of nature. He argued that government resulted from a **social contract** among individuals, who willingly surrendered their power to an absolute monarch for the sake of ensuring order, and security. If the monarch failed to provide this, then the people had a right to change their allegiance to a stronger ruler.

> ❦ They that approve a private opinion, call it opinion; but
> they that mislike it, heresy: and yet heresy signifies no more
> than private opinion. ❧
>
> **Thomas Hobbes**, *Leviathan*

holism

The concept that 'the whole is more than the sum of the parts', a phrase coined by Aristotle in his *Metaphysics*. Holism implies that in certain systems the relationships between the parts are an important part of the whole. Holism is opposed to **reductionism**, although both are relative terms, and it is possible for one thinker to propose a holistic interpretation of one topic and not of another. Holistic approaches are found in subjects such as biology, medicine, the social sciences, and in the study of mind (see, for example, **Gestalt**) and language.

human being

The question as to what it is to be human – as opposed to anything else – has been addressed in a number of ways:

- **Plato** and many philosophers after him regarded **reason** as a uniquely human property. However, David **Hume's** scepticism on this matter in the 18th century has been justified by research that indicates that other apes are capable of degrees of reasoning.

- **Consciousness** has also been held up as something that distinguishes us from the other animals, but here again the distinction may be a matter of degree.

Some philosophers have been less concerned with what makes us uniquely different and more with what we are, with the metaphysical notion of **being**. In **existentialism**, for example, being human means being free to choose.

See also: *human nature; innate idea; life; life, meaning of.*

humanism

Belief in the importance of human beings. The term implies a greater interest in humans, their actions and their potential than in God or religious or transcendental values.

Classical humanism

In ancient Greece, **pre-Socratic philosophy** was largely concerned with cosmology, but with **Socrates, Plato, Aristotle** and others the emphasis turned to human-centred areas of interest such as ethics and politics. At the same time, classical Greek art focused on representations of the idealized human form. With the advent of Christianity, art, literature, and philosophy were largely concerned with God, humans being regarded as fallen and imperfect.

Renaissance humanism

Renaissance humanism originated in the studies of ancient Greek and Roman texts, a process that began in the 14th century with Petrarch and continued with scholars such as Erasmus. Renaissance humanism culminated as a cultural force in the 16th century, when man as opposed to God began to take centre stage in literature, art, and scholarship. Although God was rarely denied the role of creator and supreme authority, he was regarded as distant from human affairs.

Humanism and reason

Renaissance humanism provided the background to the Scientific Revolution that began in the 16th century. The potential for human reason to fathom the workings of the universe was demonstrated in the discoveries of Copernicus, **Galileo**, **Newton**, and many other scientists, and was celebrated by the thinkers of the 18th-century **Enlightenment**.

Since the 19th century 'humanism' has been associated with **atheism** and **agnosticism**; the term has also implied opposition to totalitarianism, and a concern for the welfare of human beings. However, modern humanists do not necessarily hold that reason can provide the answer to all questions, such as those of morality.

> ❝ In all humanism there is an element of weakness, which in some circumstances may be its ruin, connected with its contempt of fanaticism, its patience, its love of scepticism; in short its natural goodness. ❞
>
> **Thomas Mann**, *Europe Beware*

human nature

The concept of human nature implies that humans will always behave in certain ways. But does human nature actually exist? And if it does, what is it?

The Christian tradition holds that humans are in a state of 'original sin'. Similar views on the intrinsically flawed nature of humanity have been used by political theorists such as Thomas Hobbes to justify authoritarian government, and still provides a basis for the social and economic policies of modern **conservatism**.

In contrast is the view that humans are innately good. This was the position taken by

Adam and Eve were expelled from the Garden of Eden (left) because they ate the fruit from the Tree of Knowledge (right).

Rousseau, for example, who believed that people's natural goodness was corrupted by society.

The view that there is no such thing as human nature, that humans are 'blank slates' at birth (as proposed for example by John **Locke**), is a third strand that has influenced political thinking. In such accounts, the way that humans behave is entirely due to environmental factors.

This being the case, given the right social conditions, education, and so on, human beings can be perfected. Beliefs in the innate goodness or in the perfectability of humans are fundamental to the political theories of **anarchism, communism, and socialism**.

See also: *human being; innate idea.*

NATURE AND NURTURE

Modern social, psychological, and genetic research indicates that the way that humans behave is the result of a complex mixture of genetic and environmental factors. Genetic factors (partially determined by human evolution) may give certain people, or all of us, predispositions to behave in certain ways; environmental factors may similarly provide such predispositions. But to say that we inevitably will behave in certain ways is a very extreme form of determinism.

---

human rights

A term sometimes used interchangeably with **civil liberties** (or civil rights), but sometimes implying something more fundamental. Whereas the concept of civil liberties usually implies constraints on the state's power to circumscribe individual freedom, human rights may also imply additional duties of the state to act positively to ensure the well-being of its citizens.

This distinction is reflected in the two United Nations covenants on human rights drawn up in 1966 (building on the UN's 1948 Universal Declaration of Human Rights):

- The first covenant deals with civil and political rights.

- The second deals with economic, social and cultural rights, such as the right to work, the right to an adequate standard of living, the right to health care, and the right to education.

The idea of human rights is rooted in the concept of *natural rights*, and is tied up with ideas of **natural law, justice,** and **freedom**. Political thinkers such as John **Locke** in the 17th century and Jean-Jacques **Rousseau** and Thomas **Paine** in the 18th century incorporated ideas of individual rights into their theories of government, and these had a great influence on both the French and American revolutions, and on the subsequent evolution of liberal **democracy**.

In general, liberal, capitalist democracies have placed greater emphasis on civil and political rights, while communist states have emphasized the importance of social and economic rights.

See also: *constitution.*

Hume, David (1711–1776)

Scottish philosopher renowned for his **scepticism**. His *Treatise of Human Nature* (1739–40) is a central text of British **empiricism**, the theory that experience is the only source of knowledge.

Kant claimed that Hume's scepticism woke him from his 'dogmatic slumbers', and he continues to be highly influential. Hume himself was influenced by **Newton's** scientific method and by the theories of knowledge of **Locke** and **Berkeley**. Hume held that impressions are primary to ideas, and that ideas are derived from impressions by such mental activities as imagination and memory.

Meticulously examining our modes of thinking, Hume concluded that they are more habitual than rational. Consequently, he not only rejected the possibility of knowledge that goes beyond the bounds of experience (speculative metaphysics), but also arrived at generally sceptical positions about reason (especially **induction**), **causality**, necessity, identity, and the self.

In moral philosophy, 'Hume's law' states that it is never possible to deduce evaluative conclusions from factual premises; this has come to be known as the **is/ought problem**. He held that moral judgements are based on sentiment rather than reason.

> ❝ Hume's philosophy, whether true or false, represents the bankruptcy of eighteenth-century reasonableness ... he arrives at the disastrous conclusion that from experience and observation nothing is to be learnt. ❞
>
> **Bertrand Russell**, *A History of Western Philosophy*

Husserl, Edmund (1859–1938)

German philosopher, regarded as the founder of **phenomenology**, the study of mental states as consciously experienced. His early phenomenology resembles linguistic philosophy because he examined the meaning, and our understanding, of words. He hoped phenomenology would become the science of all sciences. He influenced Martin **Heidegger** and other existentialists, and affected sociology through the work of Alfred Schütz (1899–1959). **See also:** *intentionality.*

Hutcheson, Francis (1694–1746)

Scottish philosopher who held that humans are born with an innate 'moral sense'. Hutcheson believed that humans instinctively know right from wrong, and thus moral judgements are based on feeling rather than reason. This influenced his contemporary David **Hume**, and was echoed in 20th-century emotivism. Hutcheson also anticipated **utilitarianism** when he coined the phrase 'the greatest happiness for the greatest number' as the criterion for judging any action.

Hypatia (*c.* 370–*c.* 415)

Greek philosopher and mathematician, born in Alexandria. She studied **neo-Platonism** in Athens, and succeeded her father Theon as professor of philosophy at Alexandria. She was murdered, it is thought, by Christian fanatics, who at this time associated science and learning with paganism.

It is thought that Hypatia was murdered by fanatical Christians.

hypothesis

In the **scientific method**, an idea concerning an event and its possible explanation. The term is one favoured by the followers of the philosopher Karl **Popper**, who argue that the merit of a scientific hypothesis lies in its ability to make testable predictions. **See also:** *science, philosophy of.*

> ❝ The great tragedy of Science – the slaying of a beautiful hypothesis by an ugly fact ❞
>
> **T H Huxley**, 'Biogenesis and Abiogenesis'

Ibn Gabirol, Solomon ben Judah (*c.* 1020–*c.* 1057)

Poet and philosopher, born in Moorish Spain, also known as Avicebron. Some of his hymns have been incorporated into the Jewish liturgy. His main philosophical work is Fons vitae. This is neo-Platonic in thought (see **neo-Platonism**), yet also contains elements of **Aristotle** and **Philo Judaeus.** It influenced **Duns Scotus**, **Spinoza**, **Schopenhauer**, and the **kabbala**.

Ibn Rushd

See *Averroës.*

Ibn Sina

See *Avicenna.*

idea

A word derived from the Greek *eidos* ('form', 'that which is seen'), which in philosophy has had a variety of technical usages. Modern philosophers prefer more specific terms such as 'sense datum', 'image', and '**concept**'. An **innate idea** is a concept not derived from experience.

- **Plato's** Ideas (also called **Forms**) were immaterial universals or essences existing objectively in nature.

- In **neo-Platonism** and in medieval **scholasticism**, ideas tended to be in the mind of the One or God.

- Since the 17th century, 'idea' has nearly always been used for something in or having reference to the **mind**.

- **Locke** believed that ideas are formed in the mind by abstraction from experience.

- For **Kant**, an idea was a representation of something that cannot be experienced.

- For **Hegel**, the term meant something like the overall pattern or purpose in the universe.

See also: *idealism; thinking and language.*

    ❝ Old ideas give way slowly; for they are more than abstract logical forms and categories. They are habits, predispositions, deeply ingrained attitudes of aversion and preference. ❞

John Dewey, *The Influence of Darwinism on Philosophy*

idealism

In its technical philosophical sense, any of various theories that the external world does not exist independently of the human mind, or is not knowable apart from our conceptions of it. Compare **materialism** and **naturalism**.

Although Plato held that the ultimate reality resides in Ideas (or **Forms**), these have a reality outside the mind, so he is not strictly an idealist, but rather a realist (see **realism**).

- The first idealist philosopher was George **Berkeley**, according to whose 'subjective idealism' everyday objects are collections of ideas or sensations; something exists only if it is perceived by the mind.

- In **Kant's** 'transcendental idealism' (or 'critical idealism') knowledge of things is dependent on the conceptual apparatus of the mind; we cannot know 'things-in-themselves'.

- In **Hegel's** 'absolute idealism', the distinction between reality and our knowledge of it breaks down; to understand reality is to understand our concepts, and vice versa.

- The philosophical approach known as **phenomenology** concentrates on phenomena as objects of perception, rather than as facts or occurrences that exist independently.

Other idealist philosophers include **Fichte, Schelling, Bosanquet,** and **Bradley. See also:** *absolute; concept; idea; mind–body problem.*

ideology

Set of ideas, beliefs, and opinions about the nature of people and society, providing a framework for a theory about how people should live, as well as how society is or should be organized. Ideologies in this sense are often all-embracing systems of supposedly universal applicability, and at the same time programmes for action. **See also:** *political theory.*

A second sense of the term 'ideology' is found in Marxist social analysis. Here the term is applied to the set of beliefs and values of a particular society. The dominant ideology of a society is determined by economic factors, and serves to keep the ruling class in power. The concept of ideology in this sense was refined by Antonio **Gramsci**.

illusion

Generally, a delusion, deception, or false perception. Illusion is, like **appearance**, usually contrasted with reality. The concept is often used in the philosophy of **perception** and in epistemology (the philosophy of **knowledge**). It is only by trusting some experiences that we can identify others as illusory, so the occurrence of illusions does not mean that everything is illusory. **See also:** *cave, Plato's; Descartes; empiricism; rationalism.*

imagination

The ability of the mind to conjure up things that are not the objects of current **perception** (present to the senses) or **cognition** (known to be real).

Proponents of **idealism** believe that only our minds and their contents exist, so the concept of imagination has provided them with little difficulty. However, for other philosophers, the nature of imagination, and the relationship between imagination and 'reality', poses a variety of questions:

- Is our imagination restricted by data from **sensation** and **memory**?
- How does imagination differ from dreaming, and does the **unconscious** play a role in it?
- Is it what separates human intelligence from **artificial intelligence**?
- Can imagination be incorporated into a mechanistic explanation of **mind**)?
- Is imagination always distinct from **reason**?

Imagination is often thought of as the prerogative of the artist, but the dualism of science and imagination, like that of **emotion** and reason, probably originates in **Romanticism**. Philosophers of science have increasingly realized the role that the creative imagination plays in the **scientific method** in terms of devising hypotheses.

See also: *intentionality; phenomenology.*

⟨ It's no use trying,' she [Alice] said: 'one can't believe impossible things.'
'I dare say you haven't had much practice,' said the Queen.
'When I was your age, I always did it for half an hour a day. Why, sometimes I've believed as many as six impossible things before breakfast. ⟩

Lewis Carroll, *Alice Through the Looking Glass*

---

immortality

State of perpetual or eternal life attributed in most religions to **God**, the gods, or other divine beings, and in some traditions to the human **soul**. Many of the ancient Greeks (including the philosophers **Socrates** and **Plato**) believed in the immortality of the soul, although not in terms of a resurrected body. Christianity teaches both the immortality of the soul and the resurrection of the body – although the resurrected body is not carnal but spiritual. **See also:** *reincarnation.*

> ❝ I don't want to achieve immortality through my work. I want to achieve it through not dying. ❞
>
> **Woody Allen**, attributed remark

imperative, categorical
See *categorical imperative.*

indeterminacy
See *uncertainty principle; determinism.*

individualism
In political theory, a view in which the individual takes precedence over the collective: the opposite of **collectivism**.

Individualism emphasizes the civil, political and economic **freedom** of the individual, and individual rights are enshrined in the concept of **civil liberties**. Individualism is a key belief of **liberalism** and of the non-authoritarian aspects of **conservatism**, and is found in its most radical form in **libertarianism**.

The roots of individualism can perhaps be traced to the **humanism** of the Renaissance, and its central tenets were expressed in the 17th century by John **Locke**. The term 'possessive individualism' has been applied to the ideas of Locke and Jeremy **Bentham**, who described society as comprising individuals interacting through market relations.

> ❝ There is no such thing as society. There are individual men and women, and there are families. ❞
>
> **Margaret Thatcher**, attributed remark

induction
The process of observing particular instances of things in order to derive general statements and **laws of nature**. It is the opposite of **deduction**, which moves from general statements and principles to the particular. Induction is the basis of **empiricism**, and is crucial to the **scientific method**.

Induction was criticized by **Hume** because it relies upon belief rather than logical reasoning. In the philosophy of science, the 'problem of induction' is a crucial area of debate: however much evidence there is for a proposition, there is the possibility of a future counter-instance that will invalidate the explanation. Therefore, it is argued, no scientific statement can be said to be true in the absolute sense.

See also: *abduction; a posteriori; a priori; Goodman's paradox; Popper, Karl; science, philosophy of.*

inference

In philosophy, the process of concluding something by reasoning. Philosophers identify three types of inference: **deduction**, **induction**, and **abduction** (sometimes regarded as a type of induction).

infinity

Mathematical quantity that is larger (or smaller) than any fixed assignable quantity. The paradoxes of **Zeno of Elea,** such as the **Achilles paradox**, introduced the problem of infinity. The infinitely small (yet greater than zero) was a concept required by the mathematical calculus devised by **Newton** and **Leibniz**. The **set theory** developed by **Cantor** introduced the possibility of different infinities, for example the set of all the natural (counting) numbers would appear to be larger than the set of just the even natural numbers. Mathematicians do not seem to be unduly disturbed by this. Outside of mathematics, infinity remains difficult for the mind to grasp. **Kant** among others believed it was beyond the scope of human reason. **See also:** *intuitionism; space and space-time.*

> ❦ If the doors of perception were cleansed everything would appear as it is, infinite. ❧
>
> **William Blake**, 'A Memorable Fancy'

innate idea

A **concept** prior to, and not derived from, experience. Innate ideas are therefore related to **a priori** knowledge. In the history of philosophy the existence of innate ideas (such as the idea of God, or beauty, or the good) has been upheld by the adherents of **rationalism**, and opposed by the adherents of **empiricism**, who, following John **Locke**, have argued that the mind is a 'blank slate' at birth.

The debate continues today, although in rather different terms, namely over whether evolution, via genetic mechanisms, has resulted in certain conceptual frameworks being 'hard-wired' in our brains. For example, **Chomsky** holds that we have an innate tendency to learn and to use certain grammatical structures.

instrumentalism

Doctrine, derived from **pragmatism** by John **Dewey**, that ideas such as scientific theories are not necessarily true accounts of reality, but rather instruments or tools for dealing with problems in the real world. The value of any theory thus lies not in its truth but in its success, for example in enabling us to order and predict for practical ends. **See also:** *science, philosophy of.*

intention
In the philosophy of mind, intention is related to **volition**. In ethics, some moral philosophers hold that acts should be judged by the intentions of their authors, rather than in themselves or for their outcomes.

> 6 All acts are in themselves indifferent and only become good or evil according to the intention of their author. 9
>
> **Peter Abelard**, quoted in J P Migne (ed), *Patrologia Latina*

intentionality
The property of **consciousness** whereby it is directed towards an object, even when this object does not exist in reality (such as 'the golden mountain'). Intentionality is a key concept in the *phenomenology* of Edmund **Husserl**.

intertextuality
Theory in **deconstruction** that draws attention to the interdependence of literary texts. The principles of intertextuality are as thoroughly demonstrated in the critical writings of its advocates as in the literary works they discuss. Behind assertions of intertextuality lies the more general theory that authors cannot achieve a 'closure' of their writings as self-contained artefacts in the manner assumed by much traditional literary criticism. **See also:** *postmodernism*.

introspection
Observing or examining the contents of one's own mind or consciousness: for example, 'looking at' and describing a 'picture' or image in the 'mind's eye', or trying to examine what is happening when one performs mental arithmetic.

The use of introspection as an approach to the study of the mind has a history dating back, at least, to **Socrates**. It was first proposed as an experimental method by Wilhelm Wundt (1832–1920), the founder of modern psychology, in the late 19th century, in accord with his view that **psychology** is 'the science of inward and immediate experience'.

Wundt himself eventually became dissatisfied with the method and, following severe criticism as to the reliability of introspective data, the method fell into disuse. Following the advent of **behaviourism**, the systematic study of mental processes was largely eschewed by psychologists for half a century, only returning as a course of serious study in the 1960s.

intuition
In philosophy, knowledge of a concept that does not derive directly from the senses. Thus, we may be said to have an intuitive idea (or **innate idea** or **a priori** knowledge) of God, beauty, or justice. Bertrand Russell proposed a similar concept in his theory of 'knowledge by acquaintance'. In both cases, it is contrasted with empirical knowledge. **See also:** *transcendentalism*.

intuitionism

In mathematics, the theory founded by L E J **Brouwer** that propositions can be built up only from intuitive concepts that we all recognize easily, such as unity or plurality. The concept of **infinity**, of which we have no intuitive experience, is thus not allowed.

irony, Socratic

Simulation of ignorance in order to lead on and eventually confute an opponent. The technique was used by **Plato** in his dialogues, in which **Socrates** elicits truth through a pretence of naïvety.

irrationalism

A philosophical approach rather than a movement, involving a denial that the world can be comprehended by **reason** or conceptual thought.

Irrationalism is a feature of **Romanticism**, which emphasized **emotion** and **imagination** in contrast to the optimistic **Enlightenment** belief in the power of reason. Some thinkers, such as **Schopenhauer** and **Freud**, have viewed the human mind as being at least partially determined by **unconscious** (and therefore irrational) forces. In **existentialism**, neither reason nor morality nor any other consideration provides a constraint on the absolute freedom to choose.

In religious thinking, the belief that reason and **faith** are compatible was upheld by medieval **scholasticism** (notably by St Thomas **Aquinas**), while Enlightenment **deism** held that human reason rather than divine revelation is the correct means of ascertaining truth and regulating behaviour. These positions of theological rationalism have been opposed by, among others, **Luther, Kierkegaard**, and **Barth**.

Confusingly, the opposing doctrine to *philosophical* rationalism (the view that only knowledge derived by deduction from **a priori** propositions is valid) is usually taken to be empiricism, which is by no means irrationalist in the senses mentioned above.

is/ought problem

The problem as to whether prescriptions or value judgements can be derived from descriptive statements. David **Hume** held that is never possible to deduce evaluative conclusions from factual premises, a process that G E **Moore** described as the 'naturalistic fallacy'. Hume believed that moral judgements are based on sentiment rather than reason.

Other moral philosophers have argued that we cannot (and indeed should not) make moral decisions in a factual vacuum. Nevertheless, it is important to be aware of the difference. For example, if we accept that 'the survival of the fittest' *is* the way that evolution operates (according to **Darwinism**), should we necessarily agree (with **social Darwinism**) that this is the way that human society *ought* to operate?

James, William (1842–1910)

US psychologist and philosopher. He was among the first to take an approach emphasizing the ends or purposes of behaviour and to advocate a scientific, experimental psychology. He was the brother of the novelist Henry James.

In his classic *Principles of Psychology* (1890), James introduced the notion of the 'stream of consciousness' (thought, consciousness, or subjective life regarded as a flow rather than as separate bits), and propounded the theory of **emotion** now known as the James–Lange theory. His *Varieties of Religious Experience* (1902) is one of the most important works on the psychology of religion.

In *Pragmatism, a New Name for Some Old Ways of Thinking* (1907) James attempted to give an account of truth in terms of its satisfactory outcomes, an account that owes much to **Peirce's** ideas on **pragmatism**. In Essays in Radical Empiricism (1912) he proposed that ultimate reality consists of 'pure experience', defining this as 'the immediate flux of life which furnishes the material to our later reflection'.

> ❝ The art of being wise is the art of knowing what to overlook. ❞
>
> **William James**, *Principles of Psychology*

Jansenism

Christian teaching of the theologian Cornelius Jansen (1585–1638), which divided the Roman Catholic Church in France in the mid-17th century.

Emphasizing the element of **predestination** in **St Augustine's** teaching, Jansenists held that people are saved by God's grace, not by their own willpower, because all spiritual initiatives are God's. The Jesuits disagreed with this because they believed their spiritual exercises trained the will to turn towards God.

Jansenism was supported by the philosopher **Pascal** and Antoine Arnauld (a theologian linked with the abbey of Port Royal). Jansenists were first declared heretics in 1653, and were excommunicated in 1719.

See also: *Calvinism.*

Jaspers, Karl (1883–1969)

German philosopher, regarded as one of the founders of **existentialism**. His voluminous writings are filled with highly subjective paraphrases of the great philosophers, followed by appeals to the readers to be concerned with their own existence. He was a particular admirer of **Nietzsche** and **Kierkegaard**. For Jaspers the self is existence, not just 'being-in-the-world', but the potential to realize one's freedom of being.

JASPERS AND THE NAZIS

Jaspers broke with his friend Martin **Heidegger** when the latter joined the Nazi Party. Jaspers refused to compromise with the Nazis, and, because his wife was Jewish, he was dismissed from his university post, and forbidden to publish. He was given permission to emigrate to Switzerland in 1942, but his wife was not, so he stayed in Germany, where his wife went into hiding.

In 1946 he published *The Question of German Guilt*, and when this was largely ignored he accepted the offer of a post in Basel. The experience of Nazism and World War II led Jaspers to believe in the necessity of unity and toleration among nations, and to develop a 'world philosophy' to allow for the free communication of ideas. Following the hostile reception of *The Future of Germany* (1967), he surrendered his German citizenship.

Jefferson, Thomas (1743–1826)

US political philosopher, statesman, and president of the USA (1801–09). He was perhaps the first politician in a position to apply **Enlightenment** ideas. His political thinking was rooted in the idea of the **social contract**, and he rejected inherited privilege in favour of a meritocracy.

Jefferson was the chief author of the Declaration of Independence (1776), and he was influential in the drafting of the US Constitution in the 1780s, both of which documents have had a major influence on the modern concept of **democracy**. He was also responsible for the Virginia Statute for Religious Freedom (1786), which initiated the separation of church and state (he himself was an adherent of **deism**).

Jefferson's vision of America as an 'agrarian democracy' placed responsibility for upholding a virtuous republic mainly upon a citizenry of independent yeoman farmers – although he himself was a slaveholder with a large plantation. Ironically, his two terms as president saw the adoption of some of the ideas of his political opponents, the Federalists.

❝ The tree of liberty must be refreshed from time to time with the blood of patriots and tyrants. It is its natural manure. ❞

Thomas Jefferson, *Letter to W S Smith*, 13 November 1787

Judah ha-Levi
See *Halevi, Judah*.

Jung, Carl Gustav (1875–1961)
Swiss psychiatrist and pioneer of **psychoanalysis**. He studied myth, religion, and dream symbolism, and saw the **unconscious** as a source of spiritual insight. He collaborated with **Freud** from 1907 until their disagreement in 1912 over the importance of sexuality in causing psychological problems.

In P*sychology of the Unconscious* (1912) – which provoked the rift with Freud – Jung proposed that the unconscious contains both personal experiences and an inherited 'collective unconscious' made up of instincts, memories and experiences common to other members of the same people, or to all humanity. These components may resolve themselves into archetypes (mental images or symbols), and manifest in dreams, behaviour, and so on.

Dr Carol Jung founded the school of psychotherapy at Zurich. Once a disciple of Freud, he came to disagree with him on important issues and developed his own theories.

JUNG AND PERSONALITY

In Psychological Types (1921) Jung introduced the concept of introverts and extroverts, and proposed that the mind has four basic functions: thinking, feeling, sensations, and intuition. He held that any particular person's personality can be ascribed to the predominance of one of these functions.

> ❝ The images of the unconscious place a great responsibility upon a man. Failure to understand them, or a shirking of ethical responsibility, deprives him of his wholeness and imposes a painful fragmentariness on his life. ❞
>
> **Carl Jung**, *Memories, Dreams, Reflections*

justice

A goal of political activity and a subject of political enquiry since **Plato**. The term has been variously defined as fairness, equity, rightness, the equal distribution of resources, and positive discrimination in favour of underprivileged groups. It is most directly applied to the legal systems of states, and to decisions made by the recognized authorities within them – although it has often been observed that justice and **law** do not necessarily coincide. Consideration of justice is a component of the philosophy of **law**. **See also:** *egalitarianism; equality; human rights; natural law; natural rights; punishment; violence.*

> ❝ It is not merely of some importance, but is of fundamental importance that justice should not only be done, but should manifestly and undoubtedly be seen to be done. ❞
>
> **Gordon Hewart**, in Rex v. Sussex Justices, 9 November 1923

kabbala or cabbala

Ancient esoteric Jewish mystical tradition of philosophy containing strong elements of **pantheism**, yet akin to **neo-Platonism**. The word is Hebrew for 'tradition'. Kabbalistic writing reached its peak between the 13th and 16th centuries, and influenced **hermeticism**. It is largely rejected by current Judaic thought as medieval superstition, but is basic to the Hasid sect.

Kant, Immanuel
(1724–1804)

German philosopher who inaugurated a revolution in philosophy by turning attention to the mind's role in constructing our knowledge of the objective world. His position is known as 'transcendental **idealism**', although he preferred the term 'critical idealism'.

Born in Königsberg (in what was then East Prussia), Kant was professor of logic and metaphysics at the university there from 1770 to 1797. His main works are *Critique of Pure Reason* (1781), *Critique of Practical Reason* (1788), and *Critique of Judgement* (1790).

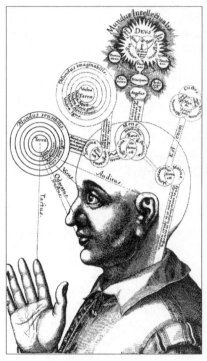

Robert Fludd's Kabbalistic analysis of the mind and the send, attributing different functions to different regions of the brain. Fludd (1574–1637) derived his ideas from many diverse sources, including the Jewish Kabbala.

Kant claimed that it was David **Hume** who woke him from his 'dogmatic slumbers'. Kant believed that knowledge is not merely an aggregate of sense impressions but is dependent on the conceptual apparatus of the human understanding, which is itself not derived from experience (see **a priori** knowledge). We cannot know 'things-in-themselves', the unknowable sources of the sensory component of our experience. We acquire knowledge from experience by the process of **apperception**, and our ideas or concepts are representations of those things that cannot be experienced directly. **See also:** *phenomena and noumena; analytic; synthetic.*

In ethics, Kant argued that **right** action cannot be based on feelings or inclinations but conforms to a law given by reason, the **categorical imperative**. Actions are right in themselves in so far as they conform to **duty**, regardless of any **good** that may come out of them. Freedom consists in acting in accordance with reason. Kant also originated the **moral argument** for the existence of God, while refuting the **cosmological argument** and the **ontological argument**.

> ❝ Two things fill the mind with ever-increasing wonder and awe ... the starry heavens above me and the moral law within me. ❞
>
> **Immanuel Kant**, *Critique of Practical Reason*, conclusion

Kierkegaard, Søren (1813–1855)

Danish philosopher, often considered to be the originator of **existentialism**. He held that God cannot be known through reason, but only by a 'leap of faith', made through free choice (see **fideism**). He maintained the subjective nature of truth and existence, and attacked all rational systems of thought (especially that of **Hegel**), which he argued were incapable of explaining the unique experience of the individual.

Kierkegaard's philosophical works are of great literary value. His thinking is often dressed up in the guise of fictions, in which the reader is obliged to choose between the alternative possibilities.

- In *Either/Or* (1843) the choice is between two ways of life, the hedonist (or aesthetic) and the ethical/religious.

- In *Fear and Trembling* (1843) the choice is between the ethical and a higher duty, to God, leading to a sense of the absurdity of faith.

- In *The Concept of Dread* (1844) Kierkegaard argues that **anguish** is the necessary psychological state for the realization of freedom, and the acceptance of the challenge of Christian faith.

- A third way of life, the religious, is explicitly added to the aesthetic and the ethical in *Stages on Life's Way* (1845). In the religious mode, there is an acceptance of suffering and a detachment from everyday concerns, including ethical considerations.

In his last works, such as *Sickness unto Death* (1849), Kierkegaard attacked social institutions, especially the church, for denying the individual self or spirit. The answer to anguish or despair is faith, a freely made choice to believe in God.

killing
See *abortion; death; euthanasia; punishment; suicide; violence; war.*

Kindi, al-
See *al-Kindi.*

knowledge
Awareness of or familiarity with something or someone, or confidence in the accuracy of a fact or other information. Knowledge is often defined as justified true **belief**, although philosophers dispute what would count as justification here, and some philosophers have argued that knowledge does not involve but replaces belief.

The philosophy of knowledge is called epistemology, which attempts to determine the limits of human understanding. Central issues include how knowledge is derived and how it is to be validated and tested.

- For **Plato**, knowledge is of the **Forms**, or universals, whereas belief is of changing, material things.
- For **Locke,** knowledge is 'the perception of the agreement or disagreement of two ideas'.
- *Descartes* held that his *'cogito ergo sum'* ('I think, therefore I am') was the only certainty, and from this basis attempted to rebuild human knowledge by inductive reasoning.
- In contrast, **Hume** rejected the possibility of knowledge that goes beyond the bounds of experience.
- **Kant** emphasized the role of the mind in constructing our knowledge of the objective world.
- For **Hegel**, the distinction between reality and our knowledge of it breaks down.

- In **logical positivism**, the only meaningful propositions are those that can be verified empirically.
- Gilbert **Ryle** contrasts knowing *how* and knowing *that*: moral knowledge is knowing how to behave, whereas factual knowledge is knowing that something is the case (See also: **is/ought problem**).

See also: *a posteriori; a priori; belief; certainty; deduction; doubt; empiricism; idealism; induction; instrumentalism; materialism; phenomenology; pragmatism; rationalism; science, philosophy of; scientific method; scepticism; solipsism;* and articles on many individual philosophers.

Kropotkin, Peter (1842–1921)

Russian prince, revolutionary, geographer and zoologist, who attempted to provide a scientific basis for **anarchism**. In *Mutual Aid* (1902) he applied his political beliefs to an interpretation of **Darwinism**. Drawing on numerous examples from the animal kingdom, he argued that cooperation rather competition is the driving force of evolution. Among his other works are *Memoirs of a Revolutionist* (1899), and *Modern Science and Anarchism* (1903).

A REVOLUTIONARY LIFE

Imprisoned for revolutionary activities in 1874, Kropotkin escaped to the UK in 1876 and later moved to Switzerland. Expelled from Switzerland in 1881, he went to France, where he was imprisoned 1883–86. He lived in Britain until 1917, when he returned to Moscow. Unsympathetic to the Bolsheviks, he retired from politics after the Russian Revolution.

Kuhn, Thomas (1922–1996)

US historian and philosopher of science, who showed that social and cultural conditions affect the directions of science. *The Structure of Scientific Revolutions* (1962) argued that even scientific knowledge is relative, dependent on the 'paradigm' (theoretical framework, both scientific and sociological) that dominates a scientific field at the time. Such paradigms (for example, **Darwinism** or the theories of **Newton**) are so dominant that they are uncritically accepted as true, until a 'scientific revolution' creates a new orthodoxy. Kuhn's ideas have also influenced ideas in the social sciences. **See also:** *science, philosophy of.*

Lacan, Jacques (1901–1981)

French psychoanalyst and theorist. His attempt to reinterpret **Freud** in terms of the structural linguistics of **Saussure** has influenced studies in literature, social ideology, aesthetics, and philosophy, but has had little effect on the practice of **psychoanalysis**. His main work is *Ecrits/Writings* (1966).

Lacan rejects the notion of a stable, coherent, autonomous self, and argues that the self is formed in a complex network (the 'symbolic order') of language and social customs. It follows that the self is inherently unstable and 'neurotic'. In Lacan's theories, Freud's Oedipal stage is replaced by the child's entry into language and society, the secure sense of narcissistic self-sufficiency giving way to a realization of difference, alienation, and loss.

Langer, Susanne (1895–1985)

US philosopher. Her seminal work *Philosophy in a New Key* (1942) portrayed symbolism as the key in uniting such fields as logic, psychology, and art. She argued that art, especially music, symbolizes or represents **emotion** better than scientific language can. Langer traced the development of the mind in *Mind: An Essay in Human Feeling* (1967–82).

language, philosophy of

The analysis of such notions as truth, facts, meaning, concepts, and sentences. It is different from 'linguistic philosophy', which is not a subject but an approach to philosophy involving ordinary language.

Meaning, reference, and sense

Both **Plato** and **Locke** believed that general terms (words such as 'horse' or 'beauty') named **ideas**, so for them the meaning of a word was its 'reference' – what it stands for.

However, as Gottlob **Frege** pointed out, two different words (or phrases) can stand for the same thing, and yet carry different meanings or 'senses'; for example, 'Lizzie' and 'Her Majesty the Queen' (See also: **connotation and denotation**). Similarly, the same word, such as 'you' or 'here', carry different meanings in different contexts.

Meaning and verifiability

Bertrand **Russell** developed the approach to discourse analysis known as **logical atomism**, in which propositions are true if they correspond to facts.

Supporters of **logical positivism** made **verifiability** the criterion of meaning in a proposition.

Peter **Strawson** subsequently distinguished between 'meaning' and 'reference': a word such as 'you' has a fixed meaning (its **definition**), but its reference will change, depending on the person being spoken to. Thus a sentence can have meaning but lack either verifiability or truth. **See also:** *liar paradox.*

Language and use

Perhaps the most influential modern theory of meaning – and language in general – is that of Ludwig **Wittgenstein**, for whom the meaning of a word or expression is to be found in its use. Thus the meaning of a word or sentence is not subjective and private but public, because it requires social conventions for its use.

More generally, Wittgenstein talks about different 'language games' being played by different rules in different human activities (for example, science and religion), and suggests that many philosophical difficulties arise from confusing different language games.

Another influential theory is that of J L **Austin**, who regarded sentences not as reporting facts but as performing 'speech acts'. This initiated various theories of language as behaviour (pragmatics).

See also: *definition; linguistics and philosophy; predicate and subject; proposition; semantics; semiology; signs and symbols; structuralism.*

law, philosophy of

Philosophical issues arising out of the law overlap with other areas, such as **ethics, political theory,** and even **epistemology** (the philosophy of **knowledge**). Law is intended by society as the instrument of **justice**, but that assumes that the laws themselves are just. Law is also often used by a particular society to implement its **morality**.

Natural law

Philosophers such as **Plato, Aristotle, Aquinas,** and **Grotius** believed in **natural law**, which is universal, 'natural' to humanity, identical with morality, and the standard against which all secular laws should be judged.

In the 18th century **Montesquieu** introduced a new relativism. In his *Spirit of the Laws* (1748) he showed how different circumstances in different societies produced different versions of morality and different laws. Nevertheless, the existence of international law and of international agreements on **human rights** indicates a continuing wide acceptance of something like natural law.

Law, government, and people

The existence of laws within a country (particularly those that make up the **constitution**) can be regarded as a restraint on tyranny, placing limits on the power of government. In a **democracy** laws are seen as expressions of the will of the people, and may be seen collectively as comprising the **social contract**.

The laws enshrine **civil liberties**, provide protection of **property** and of the person against **violence**, enforce civil contracts, and generally make clear the duties and rights of the citizen. They are intended to be administered impartially, whatever one's position in society.

The administration of justice
An important issue in the just administration of the law is the question of responsibility, and here the debate between **free will** and **determinism** is often raised, in one form or another. Other questions include what constitutes sufficient evidence, and indeed what is **truth**, and here issues such as **belief, certainty**, and **doubt** may come into play. Finally, there is the question of appropriate **punishment**.

> ❮ To say that authority, whether secular or religious, supplies no ground for morality is not to deny the obvious fact that it supplies a sanction. ❯
>
> **A J Ayer**, *The Meaning of Life and Other Essays*, title essay

law of nature
Scientific generalization that both explains and predicts physical phenomena; laws of nature are generally assumed to be descriptive of, and applicable to, the world. The three laws of thermodynamics are examples.

However, the first of **Newton's** laws of motion discusses the behaviour of a moving body not acted on by a net force, and this neither applies to the world nor describes it, because there are no such bodies. Hence, some philosophers of science have argued that the laws of nature are rules governing scientists' expectations and so are prescriptive rather than descriptive. Others have argued that laws are idealized descriptions to which the world approximates, as triangles on a blackboard approximate to Euclidean triangles.

See also: *instrumentalism; Kuhn, Thomas; science, philosophy of; scientific method.*

Leibniz, Gottfried Wilhelm (1646–1716)
German mathematician, philosopher, and diplomat. In philosophy he is best known for his theory of 'monads'. In mathematics he developed calculus independently of, but concurrently with, Isaac **Newton**. He was one of the founders of symbolic logic; free from all concepts of space and number, his logic was the prototype of future abstract mathematics. He was also

the first to make the distinction in logic between **contingent and necessary truths**.

In his metaphysical works, such as *The Monadology* (1714), Leibniz argued that everything consists of innumerable soul-like units, monads, the individual properties of which determine each thing's past, present, and future. The monads are independent of each other but coordinated by a 'pre-established harmony'. This means that Christian faith and scientific reason need not be in conflict and that 'this is the best of all **possible worlds**'. Leibniz's optimism is satirized in **Voltaire's** novel Candide.

Lenin, Vladimir Ilyich (1870–1924)

Russian revolutionary, first leader of the USSR, and theorist of **communism**. His modification of traditional **Marxism** to fit conditions prevailing in Russia became known as Marxism-Leninism, the basis of subsequent communist ideology.

In *What is to be Done?* (1902) Lenin advocated that a core of professional revolutionaries should spearhead the revolution in Russia. This was at odds with conventional Marxist theory, which held that communist revolution would first come about in the most industrialized countries in which there was a large urban proletariat. Lenin's leadership of the successful October Revolution in 1917 proved his point.

(from left to right) Karl Marx, Friedrich Engels, and Vladimir Lenin.

> 〈 Authority poisons everybody who takes authority on himself. 〉
>
> **V I Lenin**, letter to Kropotkin, May 1919

Lessing, Gotthold (1729–1781)

German philosopher, dramatist, and critic, who anticipated **Romanticism**. Although a believer in the **Enlightenment** ideals of reason and tolerance, his aesthetic point-of-view was anti-classical. In *Laocoon* (1766) he analysed the functions of poetry and the plastic arts, and espoused expressivity over formal constraint. In *Hamburg Dramaturgy* (1767–68) he reinterpreted the *Poetics* of **Aristotle** and attacked the restrictive form of French classical drama in favour of the freer approach of Shakespeare.

> ❝ A man who does not lose his reason over certain things has none to lose. ❞
>
> **Gotthold Lessing**, *Emilia Galotti*

Leucippus (lived 5th century BC)
Greek philosopher. He was the originator of the atomistic theory afterwards more fully developed by his pupil **Democritus**. The only words of his that survive form an early statement of **determinism**: 'Nothing happens at random. Everything happens according to a rational system, and of necessity.'

Lévi-Strauss, Claude (1908–)
French anthropologist. He helped to formulate the principles of **structuralism** by stressing the interdependence of cultural systems and the way they relate to each other. He maintained that social and cultural life can be explained by a postulated unconscious reality concealed behind the reality by which people believe their lives to be ordered. His thinking was influenced by the linguistics of **Ferdinand Saussure, psychoanalysis,** and **Marxism**.

In his analyses of kinship, myth, and symbolism, Lévi-Strauss sought to produce a scientific basis for anthropology and argued that, though the superficial appearance of these factors might vary between societies, their underlying structures were universal and could best be understood in terms of binary oppositions: left and right, male and female, nature and culture, the raw and the cooked, and so on, which represented the universal structure of the mind.

Lévi-Strauss has been extensively criticized by British and US anthropologists who adhere to a more empiricist approach. Nevertheless, his ideas have influenced many academic disciplines, ranging from philosophy, politics, and history, to art and literary criticism.

liar paradox
A paradox, originating in ancient Greece, that takes the form of statements such as, 'This sentence is not true.' If the statement is true, then it is false, and if it is false it is true. The paradox has continued to be of profound interest to philosophers of **language**, logicians, and those working on the foundations of mathematics. The paradox is an example of sentences that can be grammatically correct but that make no logical sense, indicating that truth cannot be defined in terms of the formal rules of language.

liberalism
Political and social theory that favours **democracy** in the form of representative government, **civil liberties**, the abolition of class privileges, and free

trade. It is historically associated with the Liberal Party in the UK, the Democratic Party in the USA, and similar parties elsewhere.

Origins of liberalism
Liberalism developed during the 17th–19th centuries as the distinctive theory of the industrial and commercial classes in their struggle against the power of the monarchy, the church, and the feudal landowners. It can be traced to John **Locke** in the 17th century, whose ideas influenced both the American and the French revolutions in the later 18th century. The classical statement of liberal principles is found in *On Liberty* (1859) and other works by J S **Mill**. Economically it was associated with *laissez faire* (nonintervention of the state in the free market), as well as free trade, drawing on the theories of the Scottish economist Adam Smith (1723–90).

Modern liberalism
In the late 19th and early 20th centuries liberal ideas were modified by the acceptance of universal suffrage and a certain amount of state intervention in economic affairs, in order to ensure a minimum standard of living and to remove extremes of poverty and wealth. Thus its original **individualism** has been modified by a degree of egalitarianism and collectivism (as in the writing of John **Rawls**). However, certain 'classical liberal' theorists, such as Friedrich **Hayek** and Robert **Nozick**, adhere to the principal of absolute economic **freedom**. **See also:** *libertarianism*.

> ❝ The worth of a State, in the long run, is the worth of the individuals composing it. ❞
>
> **John Stuart Mill**, *On Liberty*

libertarianism
Political theory that upholds the rights and **freedom** of the individual above all other considerations. It seeks to restrict the power of the state to the safeguarding of those rights. It is thus a strong form of **individualism**. At its most extreme it sees the state as having no legitimate power to interfere with people's lives, since permission for such interference has not been granted by the individual concerned. Individuals should be free to do whatever they like so long as it does not affect the rights of others.

Within libertarianism there are different strands: left-leaning libertarians have much in common with aspects of **anarchism**, while right-leaning libertarians (drawing on 'classical' 19th-century **liberalism**) are strong supporters of completely free markets, and represent a non-authoritarian component of modern **conservatism**. Recent advocates have included the philosopher Robert **Nozick**.

liberty
See *civil liberties; freedom; human rights; liberalism; libertarianism.*

life
The first attempt to define life was made by **Aristotle**, who held that the characteristics of living things are their abilities to feed themselves, grow, and decay. Biologists have subsequently elaborated on this definition, pointing out that almost all living organisms share certain basic character-istics, which include reproduction, growth, metabolism, self-repair, movement, responsiveness, adaptation, and death.

But not every organism displays all these features, and even inorganic substances may exhibit some of them. For example, crystals can grow in a solution, and they can also dissolve ('die') back into the solution. Machines equipped with computers can respond to stimuli, and it is in theory possi-ble to design a machine that could repair itself and create replicas of itself by drawing on outside materials. Biologists tend to fall back on the way that living organisms work, based on the cell, but even here there are difficul-ties. For example, a virus is non-cellular, and is lifeless until it becomes active inside a living cell.

See also: *artificial intelligence; consciousness; existence; mind; mind–brain problem.*

LIFE AND THE PHILOSOPHERS

The question as to what is the meaning of life, or whether it is meaningful to ask such a question, has long occupied philosophers (see **life, meaning of**). The right or otherwise of humans to deprive other humans or animals of their lives is a central ethical issue (see **animals; punishment; violence; war**). Determining at what point human life begins and ends is an important problem in **medical ethics**, for example in questions such as **abortion** and the definition of **death**.

---

life, meaning of
The big question, 'What is the meaning of life?', is not one that philosophers can definitively answer, although they can at least help to clarify it.
The big question can perhaps be divided into three questions:

- 'What is the meaning of my own (or any individual) life?'
- 'What is the meaning of human life?'
- 'What is the meaning of existence (the world, the universe, and every-thing)?'

And then there is the question as to what we mean by 'meaning'. The original question actually encompasses two questions:

- 'What is the purpose of life?'
- 'What is the value of life?'

Does life have purpose?
Christian theologians have generally answered the first question in terms of the fulfilment of a divine plan (see, for example, **eschatology**). In neo-Platonist **chain of being** theories, the purpose is usually the perfection of the universe.

On a more secular level, some have suggested that the evolution of life is both progressive and purposive, but this is to misrepresent entirely the findings of **Darwinism**. Some theories of history, such as those of **Hegel** and **Marx**, see human society evolving towards some form of perfection. Such beliefs are regarded by many philosophers and scientists as baseless. **See also:** *cosmology; teleology.*

Does life have value?
Virtually all societies and ethical systems value life to the extent of generally proscribing killing others (see **violence**). Most political philosophies aim in their own ways at improving people's lives, measuring improvement in terms of both material things (standard of living) and in qualitative ways (good education, pleasant environment, and so on). Many (but by no means all) moral philosophers have argued that the greatest **good** is **happiness**.

Life without meaning
A bleaker message is found in **existentialism**, which argues not only that the universe is absurd, but that, in the words of Jean-Paul **Sartre**, 'All human activities are equivalent, all are destined by principle to defeat.' Existing as a human entails only complete freedom: 'Man is nothing else but what he makes of himself.'

❢42.❡

Douglas Adams, *The Hitchhiker's Guide to the Galaxy*, providing the answer to 'life, the universe, and everything'

---

linguistics and philosophy
Linguistics is the scientific study of language. Linguistics has many branches, some of which are of particular interest to the philosophy of **language: semantics** (the study of meaning), grammar (the arrangement and modifications of words to convey a message), and pragmatics (language as behaviour).

More generally the elucidation of the way that language works can clarify the nature of various philosophical problems – this is the approach of **'linguistic philosophy'**, sometimes regarded as a part of analytic philosophy. For **Wittgenstein**, philosophy is conceived of as 'assembling reminders' about our use of language. Other exponents of this approach include G E **Moore**, Gilbert **Ryle**, and J L **Austin**.

Other areas of particular interest include **Chomsky's** theory of inbuilt language structures in the brain (reviving the notion of **innate ideas**), and the **structuralism of Saussure**, which has had a great influence on continental philosophy, notably the works of **Barthes, Derrida, Lacan, and Lévi-Strauss**. **See also:** *semiology*.

Locke, John (1632–1704)

English philosopher. His *Essay Concerning Human Understanding* (1690) maintained that experience is the only source of knowledge. This work is the foundation of **empiricism**, and was directly opposed to **Descartes**, who held that no knowledge derived from experience was reliable. Locke was equally influential in the area of political philosophy. His *Two Treatises on Government* (1690) helped to form contemporary ideas of liberal **democracy**.

Theory of knowledge

Locke rejected the traditional concept of **innate ideas**, believing that at birth the mind is a blank, and that all ideas come by a process of abstraction from sense impressions. He held that 'we can have knowledge no farther than we have ideas' derived in this way. However, knowledge is 'the perception of the agreement or disagreement of two ideas', and this involves the use of reason: 'Reason must be our last judge and guide in everything.'

Theory of government

Locke's Two Treatises on Government supplied the classical statement of Whig and later liberal theory (see **liberalism**), and provided a justification for the Glorious Revolution that had taken place just two years before, in 1688. The work enjoyed great influence in America and France, where it provided much of the ideological underpinning of the American and French revolutions.

Locke rejected the traditional doctrine of the **divine right of kings**, and proposed that governments derive their authority from popular consent. This popular consent is granted in a **social contract**, by which individuals exchange their **natural rights** (to life, liberty, and property) for civil rights, which it is the duty of the government to protect (see **civil liberties**). If a government infringes such fundamental rights of the people as religious freedom, then it may be rightly overthrown.

> ❝ It is one thing to show a man that he is in error, and another to put him in possession of the truth. ❞
>
> **John Locke**, Essay Concerning Human Understanding

logic

Branch of philosophy that studies valid reasoning and argument. It is also the way in which one thing may be said to follow from, or be a consequence of, another (deductive logic; see **deduction**). Logic is generally divided into the traditional formal logic of **Aristotle** and the symbolic logic derived from Friedrich **Frege** and Bertrand **Russell**, which is close to mathematics.

Aristotle's *Organon* is the founding work on logic. Aristotelian methods (such as the syllogism) were revived by Peter **Abelard** in the 12th century, and were used in the synthesis of ideas aimed at in medieval **scholasticism**.

As befitted the spirit of the Renaissance, Francis **Bacon** considered many of the general principles used as premises by the scholastics to be groundless. He envisaged that in science principles worthy of investigation would emerge by 'inductive' logic, which works backwards from the accumulated facts to the principle that accounts for them. However, the reliability of **induction** has been questioned, notably by David **Hume**, and is a central problem in the philosophy of science.

FUZZY LOGIC
The concept of 'fuzzy logic' was proposed 1965 to enable computer-controlled devices to deal with vague concepts.

See also: *a posteriori; a priori; empiricism; rationalism; logical atomism; logical positivism; predicate and subject; proposition; language, philosophy of; scientific method; validity; verifiability.*

> ❝ "Contrariwise," continued Tweedledee, "if it was so, it might be; and if it were so, it would be: but as it isn't, it ain't. That's logic." ❞
>
> **Lewis Carroll**, *Through the Looking Glass*

logical atomism

Philosophical theory associated with Bertrand **Russell** and the early **Wittgenstein**. It seeks to analyse thought and discourse in terms of indivisible components, or atomic propositions, for example, 'Jane is clever', 'Tom loves Jane'. Atomic propositions are true if they correspond directly to atomic facts.

An atomic fact, such as 'This table is red', is the simplest kind of fact, expressible in a sentence in which there are no logical connectives (stated or implied) such as 'and', 'or', 'not', and so on. Thus an atomic fact involves the possession of a quality by a particular, individual thing. One of many difficulties with the theory is how negative propositions, such as 'Jane does not love Tom', can correspond to atomic facts so defined.

logical positivism

Doctrine that philosophy should be scientific, and that the only meaningful propositions are those that can be verified empirically. Metaphysics, religion, and aesthetics are therefore meaningless. However, the doctrine itself cannot be verified empirically and so is self-refuting.

Logical positivism was characteristic of the **Vienna Circle** in the 1920s and 1930s, and was also espoused by A J **Ayer**. It was influenced by Friedrich **Frege**, Ernst **Mach**, Bertrand **Russell**, and Ludwig **Wittgenstein** (See also: **logical atomism**) Logical positivists have expended much effort in trying to resolve its inherent contradiction.

logos

A Greek word (literally 'word') that has a variety of meanings in Greek, Judaic, and Christian philosophy and theology:

- In Greek philosophy, especially in **Heraclitus** and **Anaxagoras** and in **Stoicism**, logos is the divine reason immanent in the cosmic process. Their systems are forms of pantheism, involving no transcendent god and teaching that this truth or reality (half hidden, half revealed in the visible world) can be found in the self.

- In the Septuagint (the Greek translation of the Old Testament) logos signifies the uttered word or wisdom of God expressed in creation, providence, and revelation.

- **Philo Judaeus** (1st century AD) and the Alexandrian–Jewish school combined these two originally separate meanings. Philo's logos may be said to correspond to **Plato's** idea of the Good endowed with the creative activity or universal causality proposed by the Stoics.

- Several of the New Testament writers took over Philo's conception of the logos, which they identified with Christ, the second person of the Trinity.

love

Affectionate or passionate devotion to another being. The Greeks often distinguished three types of love:

- Fondness or **friendship** (*philis*)
- Erotic love (*eros*)
- Selfless love (*agape*).

Plato and **Aristotle** both held that love is ultimately the desire of the imperfect for the perfect. 'Platonic love' transcends the physical, and culminates in the 'love of wisdom' (the literal meaning of 'philosophy').

Cupids. In Roman mythology, Cupid is the god of love.

The Christian concept
Christian thinking holds that love arises from the concern of the perfect (God) for the imperfect (human beings). St **Augustine** defines virtue as *ordo amoris* ('the order of love'), which occurs when the love of God replaces the love of self. For **Aquinas**, natural love concerns the passions and will, whereas supernatural love is natural love to which has been added habitual unselfishness.

Romantic love and its critics
The notion of romantic love is often interpreted as a social and cultural construct, originating in the courtly poetry of 12th-century France. In reaction to this notion, certain philosophers have reduced love to sex (**Schopenhauer**), or a power struggle (**Nietzsche**). In modern **feminism**, romantic love has been depicted as a male ideological construct for the oppression of women.

A sociobiological interpretation (arising out of **Darwinism**) would suggest that love as physical attraction to a particular person has evolved for purposes of reproduction, and as emotional attraction as a form of pair-bonding for the successful raising of children to reproductive age.

> ❦ We must love one another, yes, yes, that's all true enough, but nothing says we have to like each other. ❧
>
> **Peter De Vries**, *Glory of the Hummingbird*

Lucretius (*c.* 99–55 BC)
Roman poet and **Epicurean** philosopher. His long didactic poem *De rerum natura* ('on the nature of things') envisaged the whole universe as a combination of atoms, and includes a concept of evolutionary theory. According to Lucretius, animals are complex but initially quite fortuitous clusters of atoms, only certain combinations surviving to reproduce. The chief aim of

the poem is to free men from superstition, to accustom them to the idea of complete annihilation at death, and to rid them of the idea of divine interference in human affairs.

> 〆 Nothing can be created out of nothing. 〇
>
> **Lucretius**, *De rerum natura*

Lukács, Georg (1885–1971)

Hungarian philosopher and literary critic, who developed a version of Marxism opposed to that of the official communist movement.

In *History and Class Consciousness* (1923) Lukács discussed the process of **reification**, reintroducing **alienation** as a central concept, and argued that bourgeois thought was 'false consciousness'. He argued for realism in literature and opposed modernism. He also wrote on aesthetics and the sociology of literature.

LUKÁCS THE STATESMAN

Lukács was deputy minister of education during the short-lived Hungarian Soviet Republic of 1919. He joined the anti-Soviet government during the Hungarian Uprising of 1956, and was briefly imprisoned following the crushing of the revolt by Soviet tanks.

Luther, Martin (1483–1546)

German church reformer, regarded as the instigator of the Protestant Reformation. Lutheranism is now the predominant religion of many north European countries.

In theological matters, Luther dismissed reason as 'the Devil's Whore', so rejecting the belief of St Thomas **Aquinas** that reason and faith are compatible. He believed that reason was corrupted by original sin, and that human will was incapable of following the good

Luther's criticisms of the Roman Catholic Church initiated the Protestant Reformation. He was excommunicated in 1520, but publicly burned the papal bull of excommunication, and continued his work.

(the reason for his rift with **Erasmus**). He rejected good works as a means to salvation, which he held only came through revelation and divine grace.

lying

The question of whether it is ever right to tell a lie has frequently been discussed by moral philosophers, especially with reference to difficult situations. For example, should a doctor withhold the truth from a patient with a fatal disease? Should one protect a friend or client with a lie when telling the truth would be a betrayal of confidence, or would do unnecessary harm? The question is an aspect of the **ends and means** debate. **See also:** *liar paradox.*

> ❝ A lie is an abomination unto the Lord, and a very present help in trouble. ❞
>
> **Adlai Stevenson**, speech, 1951

Lyotard, Jean François (1924–1998)

French philosopher, one of the leading theorists of **post-modernism**. His central concern is the role of knowledge in contemporary society. A member of Marxist groups in the 1950s and 1960s, he became disillusioned with the ideology of revolution, and developed a radical scepticism towards all attempts to make sense of history and society.

Mach, Ernst (1838–1916)
Austrian physicist and philosopher of science who influenced the development of **logical positivism**. He was an empiricist, believing that science is a record of facts perceived by the senses, and that acceptance of a scientific law depends solely on its standing the practical test of use. He proposed that every statement in physics has to state relations between observable quantities.

Machiavelli, Niccolò (1469–1527)
Italian politician and author. His name is synonymous with cunning and cynical statecraft, in which the ends justify the means. In his chief political writings, *The Prince* (1513) and *Discourses* (1531), he discussed ways in which rulers can advance the interests of their states (and themselves) through an often immoral and opportunistic manipulation of other people.

> ❢ One of the most powerful safeguards a prince can have against conspiracies is to avoid being hated by the populace. ❟
>
> **Niccolò Machiavelli**, *The Prince*

Maimonides, Moses (1135–1204)
Spanish-born Jewish rabbi and philosopher. He attempted to reconcile faith and reason, and his philosophical classic *The Guide to the Perplexed* (1176–91) helped to introduce Aristotelian thought into medieval philosophy. His codification of Jewish law is known as the Mishneh *Torah/Torah Reviewed* (1180); he also formulated the Thirteen Principles, which summarize the basic beliefs of Judaism.

Malebranche, Nicolas (1638–1715)
French philosopher. Inspired by **Descartes**, he maintained that exact ideas of external objects are obtainable only through God; and that mind and body interact only through the direct agency of God, a doctrine known as occasionalism (see **mind–body problem**).

Manichaeism
Religion founded in Persia by the prophet Mani (c. AD 216–276), influenced by both Christianity and **Gnosticism**. Despite persecution, Manichaeism spread and flourished until about the 10th century.

Based on the concept of **dualism**, Manichaeism held that the material world is evil, an invasion of the spiritual realm of light by the powers of darkness; particles of divine light imprisoned in evil matter were to be rescued by messengers such as Jesus, and finally by Mani himself (who was put to death at the instigation of the Zoroastrian priesthood).

Marcel, Gabriel (1889–1973)
French philosopher and dramatist. His Christian version of **existentialism** owes much to **Bergson, Nietzsche,** and the Russian novelist **Dostoevski**. Marcel differs from **Sartre** and other atheist existentialists in that despair or **anguish** at the absurdity of life are no part of his attitude. Despair is no more than a transient temptation, while hope is the essential condition of life.

Marcus Aurelius (AD 121–180)
Roman emperor (from 161) and philosopher. He expressed his **Stoicism** in the *Meditations*, comprising 12 books of aphorisms, among which are the following:

- 'Adapt thyself to the things amidst which thy lot has been cast and love in sincerity the fellow-creatures with whom destiny has ordained thou shalt live.'
- 'Let thy every action, word and thought be that of one who is prepared at any moment to quit this life.'
- 'Men exist for the sake of one another. Either teach them or bear with them.'
- 'Waste no more time arguing what a good man should be. Be one.'

He was also an active emperor, who died during a military campaign in Pannonia.

Marcuse, Herbert (1898–1979)
German-born political philosopher, who settled in the USA in 1934 as a refugee from the Nazis. His anti-authoritarian theories, combining an unorthodox Marxism and the thinking of Freud, were influenced by the **Frankfurt School**, and in turn influenced radical thought in the 1960s. His books include *One-Dimensional Man* (1964). Marcuse preached the overthrow of the existing social order by using the system's very tolerance to ensure its defeat; he was not an advocate of violent revolution.

Maritain, Jacques (1882–1973)
French philosopher. Originally a disciple of **Bergson**, he later became the best-known of the **neo-Thomists**, applying the methods of Thomas **Aquinas** to contemporary problems. Maritain distinguished three types of knowledge: scientific, metaphysical, and mystical.

Marx, Karl (1818–1883)
German philosopher, economist, and social theorist whose account of change through class conflict is known as historical, or dialectical, materi-

alism. His *Das Kapital/Capital* (1867–95) is the fundamental text of Marxist economics, and his systematic theses on class struggle, history, and the importance of economic factors in politics have exercised an enormous influence on later thinkers and political activists. **See** *Marxism*.

In 1844 Marx began his lifelong collaboration with Friedrich **Engels**. Together they prepared *The Communist Manifesto* (1848), the foundation of modern **communism**. In 1849, in the wake of the 1848 revolution, Marx was expelled from Prussia, and settled in London. Here he wrote many works, including the monumental *Das Kapital*. In 1864 the

Karl Marx, the founder of modern Communism.

International Working Men's Association ('First International') was formed, whose policy Marx largely controlled. It collapsed in 1872 owing to Marx's disputes with the anarchists, notably **Bakunin**.

> ❛ The philosophers have only interpreted the world in various ways; the point, however, is to change it. ❜
>
> **Karl Marx**, *Theses on Feuerbach*

Marxism

The philosophical and political system, and mode of social, economic and historical analysis, originated by Karl **Marx** and Friedrich **Engels**, and subsequently adapted by, among others, **Lenin, Gramsci, Lukács,** and **Marcuse**.
The Marxist dialectic

Marx's philosophical work owes much to the writings of **Hegel**, though he rejected Hegel's **idealism** in favour of **materialism**: 'Life is not determined by consciousness, but consciousness by life.'

In Marx's deterministic theory of history, events unfold according to a Hegelian dialectic, in which one system gives way to the next because of its internal contradictions, but in which the determining factors are blind economic forces and class struggle (rather than Hegelian 'Spirit').

The road to socialism
So, in simple terms:

- Feudalism gives way to bourgeois **capitalism**.
- Capitalism in its turn can only operate by exploiting the majority of the population, the industrial proletariat, who suffer **alienation** and **reification**.
- According to Marx, the workers will inevitably overthrow capitalism, and establish the 'dictatorship of the proletariat', under which **socialism** can develop.
- As true socialism develops, the state will 'wither away', and a classless society will appear, which will allow individuals to achieve their full potential through cooperation (a vision identical to that of **anarchism**): 'From each according to his abilities, to each according to his needs.'

See also: *historicism; history, philosophy of.*

materialism

In philosophy, the theory that there is nothing in existence over and above **matter** and matter in motion. Such a theory excludes the possibility of deities. In the **mind–body problem**, materialists hold that mind is an attribute of the physical. Materialism is opposed to **idealism**.

In ancient Greece, the atomism of **Democritus** reduces the universe to an assemblage of tiny particles of matter. **Stoicism** and **Epicureanism** were also materialist doctrines. In contrast, **Plato's** Forms, the ultimate reality, are immaterial, and although **Aristotle** had a largely materialistic approach, he believed that the soul transcends matter.

Among the many later materialist philosophers are Thomas Hobbes, Denis Diderot, Friedrich **Engels**, and Karl **Marx**. Other philosophers who have shown materialist tendencies include John **Locke**, David **Hume,** J S **Mill**, and Herbert **Spencer**.

See also: *empiricism; logical positivism; positivism.*

mathematics

The study of relationships between numbers, between spatial configurations, and abstract structures. Because it appears to rely entirely on logical **deduction** to achieve **certainty**, mathematics has traditionally been regarded as the closest thing to absolute **knowledge**.

Logical reasoning
In ancient Greece **Pythagoras** held that mathematical statements must be proved using a logical chain of reasoning starting from acceptable assumptions. The use of logical reasoning, the methods of which were summarized by **Aristotle**, enabled Greek mathematicians to make general statements instead of merely solving individual problems.

Mathematics and science
There were many advances in mathematics in the medieval period. However, it was not until the Renaissance that scientists such as **Galileo** began to apply mathematical models to physics. **Descartes** believed that the universe could only be understood by deduction from general principles (**rationalism**), using mathematics, whereas Newton's discoveries, although explained in mathematical terms, were derived from observation (**empiricism**).

The foundations of mathematics
From the mid-19th century mathematicians began to investigate the logical foundations of mathematics. George **Boole** showed how logical arguments could be expressed in algebraic symbolism, bringing **logic** (traditionally a branch of philosophy) closer to mathematics. Friedrich **Frege** and Giuseppe **Peano** considerably developed this symbolic logic.

Meanwhile, Georg **Cantor** had developed **set theory**, and it was in relation to set theory that Bertrand **Russell** pointed out a flaw in Frege's attempt to found mathematics on a logical basis. Nevertheless, in *Principia Mathematica* (1910–13) Russell, with A N **Whitehead**, attempted to show that mathematics could be reduced to a branch of logic.

In 1931 Kurt **Gödel**, examining the work of Russell and Whitehead, proved that a mathematical system based on a finite number of **axioms** always contains statements that can be neither proved nor disproved within the system. Therefore mathematics can never be totally consistent and totally complete.

See also: *infinity; intuitionism.*

❝ Mathematics may be defined as the subject in which we never know what we are talking about, nor whether what we are saying is true. ❞

Bertrand Russell, *Mysticism and Logic*

---

matter
In physics, anything that has mass. Theories of matter have been put forward throughout the history of science and philosophy. **Materialism**, a major school of thought in metaphysics since the time of the ancient Greeks, holds that there is nothing in existence apart from matter, so denying the possibility of non-material entities such as spirit, the soul, or God. The question arises, however, as to what matter is.

The earliest theory of matter of any importance is that of **Democritus** and **Lucretius**, who supposed that matter consisted of hard, indivisible atoms that could neither be created, destroyed, nor altered in any way. The atomic theory of matter was revived and substantiated in the 19th century, although from the end of the century the existence of subatomic particles began to be established.

Quantum mechanics showed that some of these particles sometimes behaved like particles, and sometimes like waves, undermining the concept of matter as being made up of solid 'stuff'. Furthermore, the earlier belief that matter could neither be created nor destroyed had to be abandoned when Einstein showed that mass can be converted into energy, and vice versa.

An illustration of the four Greek elements, earth, air, water, and fire, surrounded by the dome of the fixed stars. The Greek philosopher Empedocles believed that these made up the fundamental components of all matter. The central figure represents Archimedes.

mauvaise foi
See *bad faith.*

meaning
What is meant by words or things. In the philosophy of language, there are various theories about the meaning of words and sentences. When things have meaning, it is because we understand them ('Clouds mean rain') or they have significance ('This ring means a lot to me'). **See** *language, philosophy of; life, meaning of.*

mechanism
In philosophy, a system of adapted parts working together, as in a machine. Mechanists hold that all natural phenomena admit of mechanical explanation, and that no reference to **teleology** (purpose or design) is necessary.

In political philosophy, mechanists (like Thomas **Hobbes**, John **Locke**, Jeremy **Bentham**, and J S **Mill**) see the state as more or less the sum of the individuals composing it, and not as an entity in its own right (which is **organicism**).

mediation
Technical term in the philosophy of **Hegel**, and in Marxist philosophy influenced by Hegel, describing the way in which an entity is defined through its relations to other entities.

medical ethics
Moral guidelines for doctors governing good professional conduct. The basic aims are considered to be doing good, avoiding harm, preserving the

patient's autonomy, telling the truth, and pursuing justice. Ethical issues provoke the most discussion in medicine where these five aims cannot be simultaneously achieved – for example, what is 'good' for a child may clash with his or her autonomy or that of the parents.

Traditionally these principles have been set out in the Hippocratic Oath, introduced by Greek physician Hippocrates (5th–4th century BC) and including such injunctions as the command to preserve confidentiality, to help the sick to the best of one's ability, and to refuse fatal draughts. However, in recent decades rapidly advancing technology has raised the question of how far medicine should intervene in natural processes. Lack of resources may also confront doctors with the question of which patients to select for treatment, or how far to continue treatment. The issues of **euthanasia** and **abortion**, and the definition of **death**, are other problems of medical ethics.

memory
Ability to store and recall experiences such as observations and sensations. Memory does not seem to be based in any particular part of the brain; it may depend on changes to the pathways followed by nerve impulses as they move through the brain. Memory can be improved by regular use as the connections between nerve cells (neurons) become 'well-worn paths' in the brain. Research is just beginning to uncover the biochemical and electrical bases of the human memory.

However, the way we actually experience memories is an aspect of **consciousness**, and therefore may not be wholly susceptible to a mechanistic explanation. Our possession of unique individual memories is an important part of personal identity, and also poses some interesting questions regarding the relationship of past and present (see **time**). **See also:** *imagination; mind; self.*

> ❦ A memory is what is left when something happens and does not completely unhappen. ❦
>
> **Edward de Bono**, *The Mechanism of Mind*

Mendelssohn, Moses (1729–1786)
German philosopher and scholar, the grandfather of the composer Felix Mendelssohn. He promoted Jewish emancipation and is recognized as an important Jewish and **rationalist** thinker. His works include:

- *Jerusalem* (1783), a plea for freedom of conscience and a demand for the total separation of church and state.
- *Phädon* (1767), in support of immortality of the soul.
- *Morgenstunden* (1785–86), in refutation of **pantheism** and **Spinoza** and in defence of his friend Gotthold **Lessing**.

Merleau-Ponty, Maurice (1908–1961)

French philosopher, one of the most significant contributors to **phenomenology** after Edmund Husserl. He attempted to move beyond the notion of a pure experiencing **consciousness**, arguing in *The Phenomenology of Perception* (1945) that perception is intertwined with bodily awareness and with language. In his posthumously published work *The Visible and the Invisible* (1964), he argued that our experience is inherently ambiguous and elusive, and that the traditional concepts of philosophy are therefore inadequate to grasp it.

metaphysics

Branch of philosophy that deals with first principles, in particular '**being**' (ontology) and 'knowing' (epistemology; see **knowledge**), and that is concerned with the ultimate nature of reality. It has been maintained that no certain knowledge of metaphysical questions is possible.

Epistemology, or the study of how we know, lies at the threshold of the subject. Metaphysics is concerned with the nature and origin of **existence** and of **mind**, the interaction between them, the meaning of **time** and **space**, **causation**, **determinism** and **free will**, personality and the **self**, arguments for belief in **God**, and human **immortality**.

The foundations of metaphysics were laid by **Plato** and **Aristotle**. St Thomas **Aquinas**, basing himself on Aristotle, produced a metaphysical structure that is accepted by the Catholic church. The subject has been advanced in one way or another by, among others, **Descartes**, **Spinoza, Leibniz, Locke, Berkeley, Hume, Kant, Hegel, Schopenhauer**, and **Marx**.

In the 20th century the US and British tradition of **analytic philosophy** – in contrast to continental philosophy – tended to ignore metaphysical questions, or regard them as unanswerable.

Mill, John Stuart (1806–1873)

British philosopher and economist who wrote *On Liberty* (1859), the classic philosophical defence of **liberalism**, and *Utilitarianism* (1863), a version of the 'greatest happiness for the greatest number' principle in ethics. His progressive views inspired *On the Subjection of Women* (1869).

Mill was born in London, the son of the Scottish philosopher James Mill (1773–1836), who was a disciple of Jeremy **Bentham**, the founder of utilitarianism. Mill found his father's bleakly intellectual **utilitarianism** emotionally unsatisfying and abandoned it for a more human philosophy influenced by the poet S T Coleridge. Mill sat in Parliament as a Radical (1865–68) and introduced a motion for women's suffrage.

On Liberty moved away from the utilitarian notion that individual liberty was necessary for economic and governmental efficiency, and advanced the classical defence of individual **freedom** as a value in itself and the mark of a mature society; this change can be traced in the later editions of Mill's *Principles of Political Economy* (first published 1848).

> ❝ The true virtue of human beings is fitness to live together as equals; claiming nothing for themselves but what they as freely concede to everyone else; regarding command of any kind as an exceptional necessity, and in all cases a temporary one ❞
>
> **John Stuart Mill**, *The Subjection of Women*

mind

The presumed mental or physical being or faculty that enables a person to think, will, and feel; the seat of the intelligence and of memory; sometimes only the cognitive or intellectual powers (see **cognition**), as distinguished from the will and the emotions. The relation of mind to matter – the **mind–body problem – is a long-standing philosophical problem.**

See also: *artificial intelligence; behaviourism; cognitive science; consciousness; emotion; Gestalt; introspection; imagination; knowledge; memory; psychoanalysis; psychology; reason; thinking and language; unconscious; volition.*

> ❝ [Poets] are masters of us ordinary men, in knowledge of the mind, because they drink at streams which we have not yet made accessible to science. ❞
>
> **Sigmund Freud**, attributed remark

SCIENCE AND THE MIND

Attempts to understand the mind in material terms is an important part of current scientific endeavour. The computer model of the brain was at one time fashionable, but has been found to be of little use in explaining many mental processes, such as understanding. The way that a computer plays chess (and can beat humans) – involving massive amounts of number crunching – is not the way that a human plays chess.

Neurophysiologists point to the fact that the brain contains something like 100 billion neurons (nerve cells), and that there are something like 100 trillion connections between them, as an indication of the complexity involved. Some scientists have also suggested that there may be quantum effects in operation (see quantum mechanics), so that conventional models of cause and effect (see causation) may not always apply.

mind–body problem

A central problem in philosophy, concerning what mind is and how it relates to the body. Various schools of thought have emerged. **Idealism** holds that only the mind is real, whereas materialism holds that the body alone is real or that mental phenomena are identical with certain physical ones. In the materialist account, mind is seen as synonymous with the electrochemical processes within the brain, or as a function of the brain as a whole (see **mind**).

The idealist and the materialist views are both types of 'monism' – that is, that body and mind are one substance. There are various other forms of monism:

- The theory of **Aristotle**, that the mind is to the body as **form** is to matter.

- Neutral monism, **Russell's** theory that physical and mental phenomena can be analysed in terms of a common underlying reality.

- The double-aspect theory, that mind and matter as a whole are two aspects of a single substance. The double-aspect theory can refer either to individual minds and their corresponding bodies or to mind and matter as a whole; the latter view was advanced by **Spinoza**, who saw the one substance as God or Nature.

In contrast to monism, dualism asserts the distinctness of mind and body. Again, there are a variety of types of dualism:

- Cartesian **dualism** (proposed by René **Descartes**) is a type of interactionism – proposing that mind and body are different substances but still interact.

- Epiphenomenalism is the theory that mind has distinctive and irreducible qualities but no power over the body.

- Psychophysical parallelism is the theory that every mental event has a physical counterpart, and vice versa, but that mind and body do not interact.

- A version of psychophysical parallelism is occasionalism, the theory put forward by Arnold **Geulincx** and Nicolas **Malebranche** that body and mind do not interact but are synchronized by God.

Mirandola

See *Pico della Mirandola*.

monad

See *Leibniz*.

monism

See *mind–body problem*.

Montaigne, Michel de (1533–1592)

French writer. The ironical *Apologie de Raymond Sebond* (*c.* 1576), in which he refuses to trust the reasoning and rationality of other philosophies, reveals the full extent of his scepticism. His famous *Essais* (1580–88) have as their focus the search for self-knowledge and for general rules of conduct, leading to a fully humane and natural way of life. In England, Shakespeare and Francis **Bacon** were among those who were challenged and stimulated by his work.

> 〉 How many things served us but yesterday as articles of faith, which today we deem but fables? 〉
>
> **Michel de Montaigne** *Essays*, I

Montesquieu, Baron de (1689–1755)

French political philosopher, whose ideas influenced the **Enlightenment**. His best-known work is *De l'Esprit des lois/The Spirit of the Laws* (1748), a philosophical disquisition on politics and sociology as well as legal matters. In it he demonstrated the relative nature of both **morality** and **law**, showing how both evolved according to the particular circumstances of different cultures. He also advocated the separation of powers within government – that is, of the legislative, executive, and judicial functions. This doctrine became fundamental to liberal **democracy**, and formed the basis of many **constitutions**.

Moore, G(eorge) E(dward) (1873–1958)

English philosopher who generally defended common-sense views of the world and what is said about it in ordinary language. In *Principia Ethica* (1903) he attempted to analyse the moral question 'What is **good**?', and concluded that the concept of goodness is simple and indefinable, and that we intuitively know what goodness is. He held that any attempt to identify goodness with another concept, such as **happiness**, or to derive moral conclusions from factual premises, was a fallacy – the 'naturalistic fallacy' (see **is/ought problem**).

> 〉 I ... use the word 'beautiful' to denote that of which the admiring contemplation is good in itself. 〉
>
> **G E Moore**, *Principia Ethica*

moral argument

One of four traditional lines of reasoning for the existence of God. It has several subtle forms. One is that without a just God to ensure that virtue is rewarded by happiness, morality would be impossible; and since morality is possible, God must exist. The moral argument was originated by **Kant**, who claimed to have demolished the **cosmological argument** and the **ontological argument**. The remaining traditional argument is the **argument from design**.

morality

A system of beliefs about what is right and wrong. Morality is different from **ethics**, which is the study of theories of conduct and goodness, and of the meanings of moral terms. A morality can be defined as having three essential components:

- A community of responsible agents, for morality concerns our behaviour towards others and their behaviour towards us.

- A shared set of nonmaterial values, such as fairness, truth, and compassion, the pursuit of which constitutes one aim of community life (this distinguishes a morality from an economic system).

- A way of life involving a code of behaviour (this distinguishes a morality from, say, a set of aesthetic values).

Although he accepted that morality requires a community of responsible agents, **Kant** argued that the distinguishing feature of morality is that it involves judgements that conform to a law of reason (the **categorical imperative**).

moral philosophy

See *ethics*.

motives and reasons

See *reasons and causes*.

nationalism

In politics, any movement that consciously aims to unify a nation, create a state, or liberate it from foreign or imperialist rule. Nationalism was the sequel to the emergence of the modern nation-state out of medieval feudalism, and also arose from the concept of sovereignty as developed by **Machiavelli**, **Hobbes**, **Locke**, and **Rousseau**.

Nationalist movements became a potent factor in European politics during the 19th century, when they were often associated with **Romanticism** and **liberalism**. In the 20th century national liberation movements brought about the end of European empires in Asia and Africa. Following the dismemberment of the Soviet bloc in the late 1980s, nationalism revived strongly in Eastern Europe.

Perhaps the most prevalent influence on the concept of a particular 'nationality' is community of history, tradition, language, and culture. In political terms, nationalism can be pursued as an ideology that stresses the superiority of a nation and its inhabitants compared with other nations and peoples. Carried to an extreme, this can lead to racism and **fascism**.

> ❦ Patriotism is the last refuge of a scoundrel ❧
>
> **Samuel Johnson**, quoted in Boswell, *Life of Johnson*

naturalism

Term with two specific meanings in philosophy. Ethical naturalism claims that ethical terms such as goodness can be identified with 'natural' terms such as **happiness**. This was attacked as the 'naturalistic fallacy' by G E **Moore**. It also claims that there are empirically verifiable criteria for right action, a position attacked by David **Hume** among others (**see** *is/ought problem*).

The second type of naturalism is a form of **materialism**, in that it regards mind as part of nature, and is thus opposed to **idealism**. Naturalistic philosophers have included George **Santayana**.

naturalistic fallacy

See *is/ought problem; Moore, G E.*

natural law

Supposedly 'natural' and therefore universal moral standards that are seen as the basis of and sanction for **morality, political theory,** and **law.** Natural law is contrasted with 'positive law', the rules set out by a particular society. Versions of natural law were proposed by, among others, **Plato, Aristotle,** and **Aquinas**. In these versions, reason is the arbiter of what is natural in moral terms. Aquinas and other theologians associated natural law with divine law. **See also:** *is/ought problem*.

natural philosophy

Former name for physics, used in the days before physics was separated from philosophy and became a discipline in its own right. The term began to fall out of use in the late 18th century.

natural theology

In Christianity, learning about God from creation, using reason alone. In Greek and Roman philosophy, it refers to discourse on the 'divine' nature of things, rather than their accidental or transient nature. Thomas **Aquinas** was the first great proponent of Christian natural theology. It became a part of Roman Catholic dogma in 1870.

The aim of natural theology is to prove that God exists and to evolve a notion of God by reasoning. This it strives to do in six main arguments:

- The argument of general consent: the generality of religious belief bears witness to a law impressed in our nature.
- The **cosmological argument**
- The **argument from design**
- The **ontological argument**
- The **moral argument**
- The argument from design in history.

Aquinas elaborated the second and third into his five proofs of the existence of God.

In more recent times, there has been considerable debate on the validity of natural theology, particularly between Emil Brunner (1889–1966), who argued that some knowledge of God could be gained from creation, and that this is a necessary part of Christian thought, and Karl **Barth**, who said that human capacities, especially human reason, are so perverted by sin that they cannot teach anything about God, who can only be known through Jesus Christ and the Word of God.

natural rights

Doctrine, deriving from medieval philosophy but articulated by John **Locke**, that human beings as individuals have certain absolute moral claims or entitlements. Locke identified three natural rights: to life, liberty, and property. The first two are also included in the Universal Declaration of **Human Rights**, and most states pay at least lip service to the concept of civil liberties and human rights. The doctrine of natural rights has been criticized on the grounds that no rights are absolute and that natural rights are a myth.

NATURE – GOOD OR BAD?

Whether nature is superior or inferior to human uses and transformations of it has long been debated. Many have believed that there was a time when people and nature were part of one harmonious whole. Christians identify this period with Adam and Eve's life before the Fall. For Rousseau, a pure state of nature could still be found in the behaviour of animals, children, and 'noble savages', an idea that influenced Romanticism. Similar ideas can be found in the modern ecological movement. An opposing viewpoint may be represented by the dictum of Thomas Hobbes that in the natural state, the life of humans is 'nasty, brutish, and short'.

---

nature
Historically the word 'nature' has had a multiplicity of meanings, which can conveniently be reduced to three:

- Firstly, it refers to the **essence** or innate quality of a thing – that which makes it what it is. An example of this would be **human nature** – the characteristics that are supposedly common to all people.

- Secondly, it refers to the entire physical universe, including all living and non-living things (sometimes just restricted to living things). This material realm has often been contrasted by philosophers (such as **Plato**) and theologians with the ideal and the spiritual. *See also:* **pantheism**.

- Thirdly, it refers to those material phenomena that function independently of humans. This definition of nature is often contrasted with the artificial and the conventional; that is, with human modifications of the 'natural order of things'.

neo-Hegelianism
Term applied to the **idealism** of philosophers such as F H **Bradley**, Bernard **Bosanquet**, and John McTaggart Ellis McTaggart (1866–1925).

neo-Kantianism

Philosophical movement started about 1865 in Germany by Otto Liebmann (1840–1912), which lasted until the 1920s. Neo-Kantianism abandoned the wild speculations of the followers of **Hegel** and advocated a return to the theories of Immanuel **Kant**. The physicist Albert Einstein's philosophy of science is neo-Kantian. Other leading figures were Hermann Cohen (1842–1918) and Ernst Cassirer (1874–1945).

neo-Platonism

School of philosophy, largely founded by **Plotinus**, that flourished during the declining centuries of the Roman Empire (3rd–6th centuries AD). Neo-Platonists were influenced by those aspects of Plato's thought relating to the ideal **Forms**, the good, love, the soul, and immortality. They imagined a hierarchy of levels of being, known as the **chain of being**, at the bottom of which is the physical universe available to our senses. They argued that the highest stage of philosophy is attained not through reason and experience, but through a mystical ecstasy.

Neo-Platonism influenced many later thinkers, including medieval Islamic, Jewish and Christian philosophers such as **al-Farabi, Ibn Gabirol,** and **Aquinas,** the adherents of the **kabbala** and **hermeticism, Nicholas of Cusa,** members of the Renaissance **Platonic Academy** such as Marsilio Ficino, and the 17th-century **Cambridge Platonists**.

neo-Thomism

The revival of the medieval philosophy of St Thomas **Aquinas**, following Pope Leo XIII's declaration in 1879 that the works of Aquinas were the basis of Catholic theology. The most important figures in the movement have been the French Catholic philosophers, Jacques **Maritain** and Etienne Gilson (1884–1978).

Newton, Isaac (1642–1727)

English physicist and mathematician who laid the foundations of physics as a modern discipline. His discoveries include:

- The binomial theorem.
- Differential and integral calculus.
- That white light is composed of many colours.
- The three standard laws of motion.
- The universal law of gravitation.

Newton's greatest achievement was to demonstrate that scientific principles derived from observation and experiment are of universal application – the basis of the modern **scientific method**. In philosophical terms this

> ❝ Truth is ever to be found in simplicity, and not in the multiplicity and confusion of things ... He is the God of order and not of confusion. ❞
>
> **Isaac Newton**, quoted in R L Weber, *More Random Walks in Science*

achievement helped to validate **empiricism** and weaken the case for Cartesian **rationalism**, and paved the way for the 18th-century **Enlightenment**. His mechanistic account of the universe held sway until the advent of **relativity** and **quantum mechanics** in the early 20th century.

An artist's impression of Newton sitting in the garden of Woolsthorpe when an apple fell and set him thinking about gravity.

NEWTON'S PETS

'O Diamond! Diamond! Thou little knowest the mischief done!' So cried Newton when his dog knocked over a candle that burnt 'the almost finished labours of some years'. Newton also kept a cat, for whom he invented the first cat-flap.

Nicholas of Cusa (1401–1464)
German philosopher. Influenced by **neo-Platonism**, he was involved in the transition from **scholasticism** to the philosophy of modern times. He argued that knowledge is 'learned ignorance' since God, the ultimate object of knowledge, is above the opposites by which human reason grasps the objects of nature. He also asserted that the universe is boundless and has no circumference, thus breaking with medieval cosmology.

Nietzsche, Friedrich (1844–1900)
German philosopher whose questioning of the moral and intellectual foundations of Western civilization has been highly influential on both

philosophy and literature. His use of a multiplicity of perspectives in his critiques has led to his thinking being appropriated for a variety of purposes. Most notoriously, he was adopted by the Nazis as a precursor, although many of his views are incompatible with totalitarian ideology.

The crisis of civilization
Early influences on Nietzsche included **Schopenhauer** and the music of Richard Wagner, although he came to reject both of these. Nietzsche announced that 'God is dead', and that religion, metaphysics, reason and science have failed to establish either absolute knowledge or absolute values. He saw Western culture and society facing an impending crisis, and that there

Nietsche.

would follow a period of **nihilism** unless some more positive solution were found. To this end he attempted to create a 'philosophy of the future'.

Towards the superman
Rejecting the 'slave morality' of Christianity, which saps human vitality, he argued for the creation of new values, 'beyond good and evil'. Humans are to be seen as part of nature, like other animals, and the world as an interplay of forces without structure or purpose. Life is associated with the 'will to power'. 'Man is something to be surpassed', and certain exceptional humans can rise above the 'herd' and achieve the 'enhancement of life'. This is the ideal of the *übermensch*, or 'superman'; such creatures would have their own 'master' morality. The idea of the 'enhancement of life' is associated with creativity, and Nietzsche saw in art a glimmer of how we may transform both the world and ourselves.

Principal works
Nietzsche's works include *The Birth of Tragedy* (1872), which introduced the **Apollonian and Dionysiac** principles, *Human, all too Human* (1878), *The Gay Science* (1881–82), *Also sprach Zarathustra/Thus Spoke Zarathustra* (1883–85), *Beyond Good and Evil* (1885–86), *On the Genealogy of Morals* (1887), *Ecce Homo* (1888), *Die Götzen-Dämmerung/Twilight of the Idols* (1889). Nietzsche suffered a permanent breakdown in 1889. His edited notebooks were published posthumously as *The Will to Power*.

nihilism

The rejection of all traditional values, authority, and institutions. The term was coined 1862 by Ivan Turgenev in his novel *Fathers and Sons*, and was adopted by the nihilists, a group of Russian radicals of the period. Despairing of reform, they saw change as possible only through the destruction of morality, justice, marriage, property, and the idea of God. Since then nihilism has come to mean a generally negative and destructive outlook. Compare **anarchism**.

nominalism

The theory that objects of general terms (such as 'red' and 'dog') have nothing in common except the general term. Nominalists deny that the meaning of a general term is an independently accessible thing, concept, or **universal**. Nominalists also deny that any particular thing has an independently real **essence**. Consequently, nominalism makes our classifications arbitrary.

The opposite of nominalism is **realism**, and the dispute between these two theories has continued since at least the 11th century. Leading nominalists include William of **Occam**, Thomas **Hobbes**, Nelson Goodman (1906–), and W V O **Quine**.

normative

Relating to values or incorporating a value judgement against some norm as the criterion.

nothingness

Nonbeing. The concept is much used in **existentialism**, as that in which existence and the freedom to choose are grounded. Some philosophers think that the problem of why something, rather than nothing, exists is the deepest metaphysical conundrum, whereas others consider it irrelevant.

NOTHINGNESS AND LOGIC

In logic, it is an error to assume that every subject of a grammatical sentence is the name of a thing. So when 'nothingness' is used as the subject of a grammatical sentence, it must not be assumed that 'nothingness' is itself a thing, or the name of anything.

---

noumena

See *phenomena and noumena*.

nous

Greek term for mind or reason, especially that capable of comprehending the essential unchanging nature of things. It may also be regarded as the organizing principle of the universe. For **Aristotle** it was the prime mover of the universe (see **first cause**), while for the neo-Platonist Plotinus it was the realm of Platonic Ideas or **Forms**.

Nozick, Robert (1938–)

US political philosopher, an advocate of **libertarianism**. He argues that the state's existence can be justified only when it is limited to the narrow function of protection against force, theft, and fraud, and to the enforcement of contracts. Any more extensive activities by the state will inevitably violate individual **natural rights**. His main work is *Anarchy, State and Utopia* (1974).

objective and subjective
Objective statements, such as 'This table is made of oak', concern external phenomena ('objects') and can be shown to be true or false without reference to anybody's opinion. Subjective statements, such as 'I like this table', embody the feelings, perceptions and so on of individual people ('subjects'), and cannot be shown to be either true or false. In **ethics** the question as to whether moral judgements can be objective is a long-standing debate.

Occam, William of (*c.* 1300–1349)
English philosopher and logician. He was a leading figure in **scholasticism**, and revived the fundamentals of **nominalism**. The principle of reducing assumptions to the absolute minimum when attempting to explain something is known as 'Occam's razor'.

occasionalism
See *Geulincx; Malebranche; mind–body problem.*

ontological argument
One of four traditional lines of reasoning to support the existence of God. Crudely, the argument is that God has all perfections; existence is a perfection; so God exists necessarily. The argument dates back to St **Anselm**.

In various forms, the ontological argument has been used by **Descartes**, **Leibniz**, and **Spinoza**, and by several 20th-century philosophers. **Kant** criticized the argument, saying that being or existence is not a **property** or **predicate**. The other three traditional arguments **are the argument from design;** the **cosmological argument**; and the **moral argument**.

ontology
Branch of philosophy concerned with the study of **being**. In the 20th century, the German philosopher Martin **Heidegger** distinguished between an 'ontological' enquiry (an enquiry into 'Being') and an 'ontic' enquiry (an enquiry into a specific kind of entity).

organicism
In political philosophy, a theory about the nature of the state, describing and explaining the state in terms of a living organism. The theory owes much to the ancient Greeks, especially Aristotle. Some organicists, notably **Hegel**, seem to hold that the state is a superperson, and an end to which its citizens are the means. Other organicists include **Rousseau**. Compare **mechanism**.

Origen (c. 185–c. 254)

Christian theologian, born in Alexandria, who compiled a vast synopsis of versions of the Old Testament, called the *Hexpla*. By drawing on Greek philosophy and on Scripture, Origen produced fancifully allegorical interpretations of the Bible that disturbed the more orthodox. For example, he held that the Fall occurred when spiritual beings became bored with the adoration of God and turned their attention to inferior things.

> **OUCH ...**
>
> The Palestinian historian Eusebius says that Origen castrated himself to ensure his celibacy, but since Origen disapproves of such actions in his biblical commentaries, this may be just malicious gossip.

original sin

See *sin*.

Ortega y Gasset, José (1883–1955)

Spanish philosopher and critic. In his best-known work, *The Revolt of the Masses* (1929), he depicted 20th-century society as dominated by the mediocrity of the masses, and argued for the vital role of intellectual elites in averting the slide into barbarism. He considered **communism** and **fascism** the cause of the downfall of Western civilization.

> ❝ We live at a time when man believes himself fabulously capable of creation, but he does not know what to create. ❞
>
> **José Ortega y Gasset**, *The Revolt of the Masses*

other, the

Term often used when discussing the relationship between the subject (the knower) and the object (the known) or in analysing the nature of knowledge, of morality, or of being or existence. Our sense of the otherness of things or people arises from each individual's sense of 'I' or first-person perspective on the world.

> **OTHER MINDS?**
>
> A particular problem in the philosophy of knowledge is that of 'other minds'. How can we be certain that other people have thoughts and feelings? And are these similar to our own? For example, how do I know that you experience the colour red in the same way as I do?

'ought' and 'is'

See *is/ought problem*.

pacifism
Belief that **violence**, even in self-defence, is unjustifiable under any conditions, and that arbitration is preferable to **war** as a means of solving disputes. **See also:** *Gandhi; Russell.*

Paine, Thomas (1737–1809)
English radical writer and political theorist, who advocated republicanism, **deism**, the abolition of slavery, and the emancipation of women. His most famous work, *The Rights of Man* (1791), defended the French Revolution against the attack of Edmund **Burke**, and extended **natural** rights to include the **rights** of the citizens to government provisions for their welfare.

'THESE ARE THE TIMES THAT TRY MEN'S SOULS'

Paine went to America in 1774, where he fought for the colonists in the American Revolution. In 1787 he returned to Britain, but in 1792 was indicted for treason and escaped to France, where he sat in the National Convention. Narrowly escaping the guillotine, he regained his seat after the fall of Robespierre. In 1802 he returned to the USA, where he died.

❝ My country is the world, and my religion is to do good. ❞

Thomas Paine, *The Rights of Man*

---

pantheism
Doctrine that regards all of reality as divine, and God as present in all of nature and the universe. In some forms of pantheism, such as **Stoicism**, God is not regarded as transcendent or separate from the material universe and the forces of nature, as he is in orthodox versions of the monotheistic religions. In other forms, such as **neo-Platonism**, God (or 'the One'), is the ultimate reality of which the physical world is a manifestation. Pantheistic philosophers include **Bruno, Spinoza, Fichte, Schelling,** and **Hegel**. Pantheism also influenced the nature poets of **Romanticism**, such as Wordsworth.

paradigm

All those factors, both scientific and sociological, that influence the research of the scientist. The term, first used by Thomas **Kuhn**, has subsequently spread to social studies and politics.

paradox

A statement that seems contradictory that nevertheless contains, or appears to contain, an element of truth.

- Some paradoxes, such as those used in the Bible, are literary devices that yoke together apparent contradictions to invite closer examination of received truths or prejudices: for example, 'Love your enemies'; 'The first shall be last and the last shall be first.'

- Other paradoxes – those beloved of philosophers – expose some failure in our language or modes of thinking: these include the **Achilles paradox** (one of several paradoxes credited to **Zeno of Elea**), **Goodman's paradox,** the paradox of the **heap,** the **liar paradox,** and **Russell's paradox.**

  See also: *category mistake.*

Parmenides (*c.* 510–450 BC)

Greek pre-Socratic philosopher, head of the **Eleatic School.** Against **Heraclitus's** doctrine of becoming, Parmenides advanced the view that nonexistence was impossible, that everything was permanently in a state of being. Despite evidence of the senses to the contrary, motion and change are illusory – in fact, logically impossible – because their existence would imply a contradiction. Parmenides saw speculation and reason as more important than the evidence of the senses.

> ❝ Never will this prevail, that what is not is. Restrain your thought from this road of enquiry. ❞
>
> **Parmenides**, quoted in Plato, *Sophist fragment*

Pascal, Blaise (1623–1662)

French philosopher and mathematician. He contributed to the development of hydraulics, calculus, and **probability**, and invented an early form of calculating machine. At the age of 31 he underwent a mystical experience, and thereafter devoted himself to religion. In *Lettres provinciales/Provincial Letters* (1656) he defended **Jansenism** against the Jesuits. In his Pensées (1670) he defined faith as 'God perceived by the heart, not by the reason', and declared 'The heart has its reasons, which reason knows nothing of.' This intuitionist approach influenced later philosophers such as **Rousseau**, **Bergson**, and some of the **existentialists.**

PASCAL'S WAGER

Pascal developed the mathematics of probability in relation to gambling games such as dice. In the *Pensées* he applied the idea of the wager to belief, holding that it is best for the sceptic to bet on the fact of God's existence, and behave accordingly, given that eternal punishment in hell is a possibility, no matter how small. If God does not exist, the sceptic will have lost nothing.

Peano, Giuseppe (1858–1932)

Italian mathematician who was a pioneer in symbolic logic. His concise logical definitions of natural numbers, using the axiomatic method, were devised in order to derive a complete system of notation for logic. Peano also applied the axiomatic method to other fields, such as geometry. Some of Peano's work was used by Bertrand **Russell**.

Peirce, C(harles) S(anders) (1839–1914)

US philosopher and logician, founder of **pragmatism**, which influenced his friend William **James** and others. Peirce argued that genuine conceptual distinctions must be correlated with some differences of practical effect. He wrote extensively on the logic of scientific enquiry, suggesting that truth could be conceived of as the object of an ultimate consensus.

❦ He [William James] is so concrete, so living; I, a mere table of contents, so abstract, a very snarl of twine. ❧

C S Peirce, quoted in J Passmore, *A Hundred Years of Philosophy*

Pelagius (c. 360–c. 420)

Romano-British theologian. His doctrine of Pelagianism taught that each person possesses **free will** (and hence the possibility of salvation), denying **Augustine's** doctrines of **predestination** and original **sin**. Cleared of heresy by a synod in Jerusalem 415, he was later condemned by the pope and the emperor.

perception

The process by which we become aware of things or facts – either within our bodies or without – through the senses. It is distinguished from sensation, which is the experience of the unprocessed sense data. Perception thus involves some degree of interpretation and conceptualizing, and is an aspect of **cognition**. Perception can also lead to errors of interpretation, as in some optical illusions.

PERCEPTION AND SENSATION

To illustrate the distinction between perception and sensation, one might take the example of a very young baby: the baby can see a table, but cannot perceive it, because it has no idea what a table is.

> ❦ It is the soul that sees; the outward eyes
> Present the object, but the mind descries. ❧
>
> **George Crabbe**, *The Lover's Journey*

Peripatetics
Name given to some of the disciples of **Aristotle**, and also to later Greek commentators on his work. They derive their name from the nickname *Peripatos* ('peripatetic school') given to the Lyceum in Athens, because Aristotle walked up and down there as he gave his lectures.

pessimism and optimism
Although in everyday usage these terms are usually applied to states of mind or the dispositions of individual personalities, in metaphysics they apply respectively to theories that this is the worst of all possible worlds or the best. The latter view was taken by **Leibniz**, and scathingly satirized by **Voltaire** in *Candide*. The pessimistic view is associated above all with **Schopenhauer**. On a less metaphysical plane, philosophical views on **human nature** and the meaning of **life** range through the pessimistic, the neutral, and the optimistic.

> ❦ The optimist proclaims that we live in the best of all possible worlds; and the pessimist fears this is true. ❧
>
> **James Branch Cabell**, *The Silver Stallion*

Petrarch (1304–1374)
Italian poet. In addition to being one of the greatest figures in Italian literature, he was leader of the revival of classical learning that was the root of Renaissance **humanism**. A passionate believer in the power of ancient literature to restore antique virtue, culture, and social order to a degraded age, he despised the logic-chopping of late **scholasticism**, and espoused the practical ethics of ancient Roman writers such as **Cicero** and **Seneca**. His

Remedies Against Good and Evil applies the teaching of **Stoicism** to life's ups and downs.

❧ To be able to say how much you love is to love but little. ❧

Petrarch, *To Laura in Death*, poem 16

---

phenomena and noumena
A distinction, originally made by **Plato**, between:
things that can be perceived through the senses, and things that are thought. For Plato, the latter category applied to the **Forms**. The distinction was taken up by **Kant**, who held that phenomena were things as they appear to us, as opposed to noumena, which are things as they are in themselves, not know-able through reason.

phenomenalism
Philosophical position that argues that statements about objects can be reduced to statements about what is perceived or perceivable. J S **Mill** defined material objects as 'permanent possibilities of sensation'. Phenomenalism is closely connected with certain forms of **empiricism.**

phenomenology
Philosophical perspective, founded by Edmund **Husserl**, that concentrates on phenomena as objects of perception (rather than as facts or occurrences that exist independently) in attempting to examine the ways people think about and interpret the world around them. In contrast to positivism or 'scientific' philosophy, phenomenology sees reality as essentially relative and subjective.

Phenomenology was enormously important in 20th-century philosophy, and practitioners included the existentialists Martin **Heidegger** and Jean-Paul **Sartre**, and Maurice **Merleau-Ponty**. It can be interpreted as a type of idealism. **See also:** *intentionality.*

philanthropy
Literally, love felt by an individual towards humankind. It is expressed through acts of generosity and charity and seeks to promote the greater hap-piness and prosperity of humanity. The notion of caring for more than oneself and one's immediate family is the basis for all civilizations. Philanthropy in the forms of charity and aid has sometimes been accused of perpetuating poverty and inequality by victimizing the recipients rather than encouraging self-help. **See also:** *altruism.*

Philo Judaeus (lived 1st century AD)
Jewish philosopher of Alexandria. He attempted to reconcile Judaism with the ideas of **Plato**

In AD 40 Philo undertook a mission to Caligula to protest against the Roman emperor's claim to divine honours.

and **Stoicism**, particularly regarding the concept of **logos**. He influenced **Ibn-Gabirol** among others.

philosopher kings

Term applied by later commentators to the 'guards' or 'guardians' in **Plato's** *Republic*. They comprise the ruling elite who, through their education, have knowledge of the **Forms**, especially the Form of the Good.

philosopher's stone

Hypothetical substance that can transform base metals into gold. The search for the philosopher's stone was a main theme of alchemy in the Middle Ages. The stone was also thought to give eternal life.

Philosophes

The leading intellectuals of pre-revolutionary 18th-century France, including **Diderot**, **Rousseau**, and **Voltaire**. Their role in further-ing the principles of the **Enlightenment** and extolling

The alchemist and his assistant.

the power of human reason made them question the structures of the *ancien régime*, and they were held responsible by some for influencing the revolutionaries of 1789.

philosophy

Systematic analysis and critical examination of fundamental problems such as the nature of reality, mind, perception, self, free will, causation, time and space, and moral judgements. The word is derived from the Greek for 'love of wisdom'.

Traditionally, philosophy has three branches:
- Metaphysics (the nature of **being** and reality).

- Epistemology (theory of **knowledge**).

- **Logic** (study of valid inference).

Modern philosophy also includes **ethics**, **aesthetics** (dealing with the nature of the arts, criticism, and **beauty**), **political theory**, the philosophy of **science**, and the philosophy of **religion**. There are also philosophical approaches to, and/or overlaps with, other subjects: **See also:** *artificial intelligence; cognitive science; computer science; history, philosophy of;*

language, philosophy of; law, philosophy of; linguistics and philosophy; mathematics; psychology and philosophy.

> ❝ I have tried too in my time to be a philosopher; but, I don't know how, cheerfulness was always breaking in. ❞
>
> **Oliver Edwards**, quoted in James Boswell, *Life of Johnson*

Pico della Mirandola, Count Giovanni (1463–1494)
Italian mystic philosopher. He studied Hebrew, Chaldean, and Arabic, showing particular interest in the **kabbala**. His attempt to reconcile the religious base of Christianity, Islam, and the ancient world earned him the disapproval of Pope Alexander VI. He was a leading member of the **Platonic Academy** in Florence.

Plato (c. 427–347 BC)
Greek philosopher. He was a pupil of **Socrates**, teacher of **Aristotle**, and founder of the **Academy** school of philosophy. Central to his teachings on such topics as metaphysics, ethics, and politics is the notion of **Forms**, which are located outside the everyday world – timeless, motionless, and absolutely real. Plato's philosophy has influenced Christianity and European culture, directly and through St **Augustine**, the **neo-Platonists**, and countless others.

The dialogues
Of Plato's work, some 30 dialogues survive, in which the principal figure is Socrates. The early dialogues employ the Socratic method, in which he asks questions and traps the students into contradicting themselves; for example, *Iron*, on poetry. Other dialogues include the *Symposium*, on love, *Phaedo*, on immortality, and *Apology and Crito*, on Socrates' trial and death. It is impossible to say whether Plato's Socrates is a faithful representative of the real man or an articulation of Plato's own thought.

Ideas and ideals
Plato's philosophy rejects scientific rationalism (establishing facts through experiment) in favour of arguments, because mind, not matter, is fundamental, and material objects are merely imperfect copies of abstract and eternal 'ideas' (the Forms). 'Platonic love' transcends the physical, and culminates in the 'love of wisdom' (the literal meaning of 'philosophy').

Plato's political philosophy is expounded in two treatises, *The Republic and The Laws*. In the former he imagines an ideal state ruled by **philosopher kings**. In the latter, he imagines a state governed by a set of laws rather than by the wisdom of individuals.

See also: *beauty; cave, Plato's; demiurge; ethics; good; knowledge; irony, Socratic; love; realism.*

> ❝ There is only one good, namely knowledge, and only one evil, namely ignorance. ❞
>
> **Plato**, *Dialogues*

Platonic Academy

Group of Renaissance scholars and philosophers in 15th-century Florence drawn together by an interest in the philosophy of **Plato**. They thought of themselves as a recreation of the original **Academy** founded by Plato in Athens. Their patron was Cosimo de' Medici, and the Platonic Academy played a central role in the development of Renaissance **neo-Platonism**.

The original impetus for the Academy came from the desire to reunite the Eastern and Western Churches, but its main preoccupation became the reconciliation of Christian and pagan philosophy. The method they used was mysticism rather than exact reasoning, and the allegorical approach derived more from medieval biblical commentary than from the approaches that were being developed for contemporary textual criticism (see **humanism**). Leading members included Marsilio **Ficino** and **Pico della Mirandola**.

Platonism

Tradition of thinking derived from **Plato**, particularly his theory of **Forms**. The Platonic tradition was at first centred in the **Academy** founded by Plato in Athens, which continued until the 1st century AD. From the 3rd century AD, the focus shifted to Alexandria, where Plotinus and others established **neo-Platonism**. Platonic thought was transmitted to the West in the early Middle Ages via the writings of St **Augustine**, **Boethius**, and others. In the later Middle Ages, the philosophers of **scholasticism** were more interested in Plato's pupil, Aristotle, but in the Renaissance interest was revived in Plato and neo-Platonism by the scholars of the Platonic **Academy** in Florence. The theories and methods of Plato have continued to engage philosophers in many different schools.

pleasure

See *happiness.*

Plotinus (AD 205–270)

Alexandrian-born Roman philosopher who was one of the main founders of **neo-Platonism**. He held that the mystical union with the One or Good can be achieved by intense moral and intellectual discipline. He imagined a hierarchy of levels:

- The source of all being is the One or Good, from which the various levels of reality emanate timelessly.
- The first level is the Divine Intellect (**nous**), in which the Ideas (Plato called them **Forms**) are living intelligences and archetypes of the things of the world of sense.
- The next level is the Soul, the active principle forming and ordering the visible universe. People can choose to live on the level of the lower Soul (Nature) or the higher Soul (Intellect).

pluralism

In philosophy, the belief that reality consists of several different elements, not just two – matter and mind – as in dualism, or one, as in monism.

In political theory, pluralism is the view that decision-making in contemporary liberal democracies should be the outcome of competition among several interest groups in a political system characterized by free elections, representative institutions, and open access to the organs of power. This concept is opposed by, for example, corporatism, in which power is centralized in the state and its principal elites (the Establishment).

political science

The study of politics and political life. Originally it concentrated on the state and how it was organized, but more recently it has come to include the analysis of all those institutions and groups that possess and exercise political power.

Many philosophers, including **Aristotle**, **Hobbes**, and **Rousseau**, have been concerned with defining the political institutions that are held necessary for a properly functioning civil society. Political science, however, differs from **political theory** (political philosophy) in being descriptive rather than prescriptive, more concerned with how political institutions actually function than with how they ought to function.

political theory

The philosophical questioning of the assumptions underlying political life; for example, the grounds on which an individual is obliged to obey the state.

Classical and medieval ideas

Political theory seems to have emerged with the classical Greek city-states, most notably in the work of **Plato** and **Aristotle**. Later developments in the classical world include **Stoicism** and the idea of **natural law**. In the Middle Ages, Christianity provided the ultimate sanction for the exercise of political power, articulated in the doctrine of the **divine right of kings.**

The early modern period

The Renaissance brought a secularization of political thinking, most notably in the work of **Machiavelli**, and, in the 17th century, in that of **Hobbes** and

Locke, who developed the idea of the **social contract**. Locke also discussed **natural rights** and **civil liberties**.

In the following century, these ideas influenced **Enlightenment** thinkers such as **Rousseau** and the American and French revolutionaries. A more cautious view of political change was proposed by **Burke**, regarded as one of the founders of modern **conservatism**, while **Bentham** developed the idea of 'utility' as the justification for political action.

The era of ideology
In the 19th century, Bentham's **utilitarianism** was modified by J S **Mill**, who propounded the principles of **liberalism**. The century also saw the development of theories of **anarchism** and **socialism**, and the emergence of modern **nationalism**. The concept of a historical dialectic was introduced by **Hegel**, and adapted to revolutionary ends by **Marx** and **Engels**, the founders of **communism**.

The 20th-century witnessed the growth of totalitarian ideologies: **fascism**, and communism as developed by **Lenin** and other rulers. Attempts were also been made to humanize orthodox **Marxism**. Classical liberal thinking evolved along two separate lines: one strand emphasized free-market **capitalism** and **individualism** (the view of most modern conservatives), while the other accepted the desirability of a degree of **collectivism** in the realm of economics and welfare, while emphasizing civil liberties (the view of most social and liberal democrats).

See also: *communitarianism; democracy; ideology; law, philosophy of; libertarianism; mechanism; organicism; political science; state; violence; war.*

Pomponazzi, Pietro (1462–1525)

Italian philosopher, known for his challenges to Catholic dogma. He argued:

- That the immortality of the **soul** cannot be rationally demonstrated (thus opposing **Aquinas**), although it can be accepted as a principle of faith.
- That a belief in **immortality** (in salvation and damnation) was not essential to morality, citing ancient **Stoicism** as an example.
- That many so-called supernatural events have a rational explanation.
- That the Christian doctrines of **free will** and **predestination** are rationally incompatible.

Pomponazzi's views were widely attacked, and in Venice his books were publicly burned. His defence was that there is a fundamental difference between religion on the one hand and philosophy (and science) on the other.

Popper, Karl (1902–1994)

Austrian-born British philosopher. His theory of 'falsificationism' states that although scientific generalizations based on **induction** from observation and experiment cannot be conclusively verified, they can be conclusively falsified by a counterinstance; therefore, science is not certain knowledge but a series of 'conjectures and refutations', approaching, though never reaching, a definitive truth.

In *The Open Society and its Enemies* (1945) Popper investigated the long history of attempts to formulate a theory of the state. Animated by a dislike of the views of **Freud** and **Marx**, Popper believed he could show that their hypotheses about hidden social and psychological processes were falsifiable. Popper opposed Wittgenstein's view that philosophical problems are merely pseudoproblems, but his own view of scientific practice has been criticized by T S **Kuhn** and others.

See also: *historicism; science, philosophy of.*

❝ Every solution of a problem raises new unsolved problems. ❞

Karl Popper, *Conjectures and Refutations*

---

positivism

Theory founded by Auguste **Comte** that confines genuine knowledge within the bounds of science and observation. It is thus related to both **materialism** and **empiricism**. On the basis of positivism, Comte constructed his 'Religion of Humanity', in which the object of adoration was the Great Being; that is, the personification of humanity as a whole. **See also:** *logical positivism.*

possible world

A consistent set of propositions describing a logically, if not physically, possible state of affairs. The term was invented by **Leibniz**, who argued that God chose to make real one world from an infinite range of possible worlds. Since God could only choose the best, our world is 'the best of all possible worlds'. This view was satirized by **Voltaire** in *Candide*.

In the 20th century, philosophers have used Leibniz's metaphysics as a set of logical doctrines, and the concept of possible worlds is now used as a tool in modal logic (the formal logic of possibility and necessity).

The concept can help to analyse the **ontological argument** of St Anselm, which aims to prove the necessary existence of God. It can also be used to explain terms like 'necessary truth' or 'contingent truth' (see **contingent and necessary**). A necessary truth, such as $2 + 2 = 4$, is one that is true in all possible worlds, whereas a contingent truth, such as 'Italy is a republic', is one that is true only in some possible worlds.

postmodernism

An assemblage of artistic styles and critical and philosophical approaches that became fashionable in the late 20th century. In artworks, architecture, and literature, postmodernism often involves playfulness, irony, and an eclectic mixture of styles, in contrast to the single-mindedness of the modernist movement in the arts in the earlier 20th century.

Influenced to a degree by **poststructuralism** and **deconstruction**, postmodernist writing, whether literary, critical or philosophical, tends to deploy an array of devices and viewpoints:

- Self-consciousness of the medium.
- A conception of the text as an internally referring system of signs rather than as a representation of the 'outside' world.
- **Intertextuality** and absence of 'closure'.
- Multiple perspectives and moral relativism.
- An awareness of the impossibility of final truth or meaning.

One of the leading theorists of postmodernism was Jean François **Lyotard**.

poststructuralism

Movement in 20th-century philosophy, cultural theory, and literary criticism that debates and contests the theoretical assumptions of **structuralism**, rejecting the conclusion that there are fundamental structures in language and cultural systems that provide a key to meaning.

Following the work of **Derrida**, poststructuralist critics point to the free play of meaning in the 'texts' constituted by sign systems, which are considered to be open to a multiplicity of interpretations. As a discipline of thought, poststructuralism draws heavily on traditional categories of rhetorical study, such as metaphor and metonymy. **See also:** *deconstruction*.

pragmatics

The field of **linguistics** that deals with language as behaviour, focusing on the users of language, and the contexts in which it is used. **See also:** *language, philosophy of.*

pragmatism

Philosophical tradition that interprets truth in terms of the practical effects of what is believed and, in particular, the usefulness of these effects. Thus the grand metaphysical schemes of European philosophy are rejected as irrelevant. Pragmatism, a version of **empiricism**, originated in the USA, where it was founded by C S **Peirce**.

The pragmatist approach was applied to science, where the 'truth' of a theory depends on whether it works or not (the **instrumentalism** of John **Dewey**). William **James** also applied the approach to ethical principles and religious beliefs, where the 'truth' of the principle or belief was measured

---

JAMES'S PRAGMATIST

For William James, a pragmatist is someone who 'turns away from abstraction and insufficiency, from verbal solutions, from bad a priori reasons, from fixed principles, closed systems, and pretended absolutes and origins. He turns towards concreteness and adequacy, towards facts, towards action ... It means the open air and possibilities of nature, as against ... dogma, artificiality, and the pretence of finality in truth.'

---

by its utility in a person's life (in terms of comfort, happiness, and so on). Many other philosophers, including Peirce himself, thought that this was stretching 'truth' too far. Nevertheless, pragmatism influenced many subsequent philosophers, including the later **Wittgenstein** and **Quine**.

praxis
Term originating from the Greek for 'action', applied by **Aristotle** to practical as opposed to theoretical reasoning. In Marxism, the term came to imply the convergence of action, theory, and social reality.

predestination
In Christian theology, the doctrine asserting that God has determined all events beforehand, including the ultimate salvation or damnation of the individual human soul. Today Christianity in general accepts that humanity has **free will**, though in some forms, such as **Calvinism** and **Jansenism**, salvation can only be attained by the gift of God.

The theory of predestination caused the early-5th-century controversy between St **Augustine**, who claimed the absolute determination of choice by God, and **Pelagius**, who upheld the doctrine of free will. **Luther** and Calvin adopted the Augustinian view at the Reformation, although in differing degrees, but Jacobus Arminius adopted the Pelagian standpoint. **See also:** determinism.

predicate and subject
Traditionally, the two main parts of a sentence. The subject is a noun (or noun phrase) and the predicate is a verb phrase. In the sentence 'The chicken crossed the road', the chicken is the subject and crossed the road is the predicate.

In logic, the predicate is that that which is affirmed or denied of the subject of a proposition. So not all sentences that satisfy the grammatical description are logical subject–predicate sentences. The system of formal or symbolic logic that examines such matters is known as predicate calculus. Compare propositional calculus (see proposition).

premise
Either of the two propositions of a **syllogism** from which the conclusion is drawn. The major premise contains the major term, which forms the **predicate** of the conclusion. The minor premise contains the minor term, which forms the subject of the conclusion.

pre-Socratic philosophy
The ideas of the usually speculative ancient Greek cosmologists who mainly preceded **Socrates** (469–399 BC). The pre-Socratics range from **Thales** (640–546 BC) to **Democritus** (c. 460–361 BC). The school is defined more by an outlook and a range of interests than by any chronological limit. Unlike Socrates and the **Sophists**, who were both primarily concerned with ethics and politics, the pre-Socratics were mainly concerned with the search for universal principles to explain the whole of nature, its origin, and human destiny.

Other pre-Socratics include **Pythagoras, Xenophanes, Parmenides, Zeno of Elea, Anaximander, Empedocles, Heraclitus, Diogenes,** and **Protagoras**. Only short passages from the works of the pre-Socratic philosophers have survived.

prime mover
See *first cause.*

prisoner's dilemma
A hypothetical scenario that was originated in the branch of mathematics known as game theory. In the scenario, two prisoners accused of a crime are isolated from each other, and are separately offered various deals and prospects of punishment.

According to the way the rules are set up, if both the prisoners choose one of the deals on the basis of apparently 'rational' self-interest, they both end up worse off than if they were to act apparently 'irrationally' and cooperated unselfishly.

It has been argued that the prisoner's dilemma provides a rational basis for making moral laws, although others have disputed this. The prisoner's dilemma has been applied to many fields, such as economics, international relations, and the evolution of animal behaviour.

probability
Likelihood, or chance, that an event will occur, often expressed as odds, or in mathematics, numerically as a fraction or decimal. Probability theory is the basis of the science of statistics.

In general, the probability that n particular events will happen out of a total of m possible events is n/m. A certainty has a probability of 1; an impossibility has a probability of 0. Empirical probability is defined as the number of successful events divided by the total possible number of events. In the **scientific method**, empirical probability is often viewed as grounds for reasonable **belief** (or otherwise) in linking a particular cause with a particular effect (see **causality**).

Proclus (AD *c.* 410–485)
Greek philosopher, who was head of the revived **Academy** in Athens. He was the last major pagan philosopher, and helped to refine **neo-Platonism**. Although he was opposed to Christianity, his unification of God and the Good in the ultimate reality of 'the One' influenced later Christian theology. His writings also influenced medieval and Renaissance **Platonism**.

> ### THE ORIGIN OF PROBABILITY THEORY
>
> Probability theory was developed by the French mathematicians Blaise Pascal and Pierre de Fermat in the 17th century, initially in response to a request to calculate the odds of being dealt various hands at cards.

progress
Forward movement or advance. Science progresses, providing more comprehensive theories about the world, and these theories can be tested. In the

The Great Exhibition of 1851 at Crystal Palace exemplifies the Victorian belief in progress.

humanities, assessment of progress involves interpretation and is therefore harder, though not necessarily any less rational. Metaphysical philosophies of **history** as a form of purposive evolution (such as in the works of **Hegel** and **Marx**) try to show that progress (variously defined) is inevitable, as it is in teleology (the belief that all change serves a purpose). **See also:** *life, meaning of.*

> 💧 All progress is based upon a universal innate desire on the part of every organism to live beyond its income. 💧
>
> **Samuel Butler,** *Note-Books*

property

In philosophy, a quality or an attribute of a thing. For **Aristotle**, the term had a more restricted sense: a property of a species (class of things) was something possessed by all of its members, but not an essential or defining characteristic of the species. Other philosophers have argued whether things exist apart from their properties; and whether properties are individual or general. **See also:** *essence.*

property

In law and political theory, the right to control the use of a thing (such as land, a building, a work of art, or a computer program). Property is never absolute, since any society places limits on an individual's property (such as the right to transfer that property to another). Different societies have held widely varying interpretations of the nature of property and the extent of the rights of the owner of that property.

- For **Plato**, an essential prerequisite for the guardians of his Republic was that they owned no property.

- **Aristotle** saw private property as an equally necessary prerequisite for political participation.

- The story of Creation in the Bible was interpreted variously as a state of original communism destroyed by the Fall, or as justifying the institution of private property, since Adam was granted dominion over all things in Eden.

- In the 17th century John **Locke** argued that property rights to a thing are acquired by expending labour on it, and that the right to own property is a **natural right.**

- The 18th-century Scottish economist Adam Smith saw property as a consequence of the transition of society from an initial state of hunting (in which property did not exist) to one of flock-rearing (which depended on property for its existence).

- Karl **Marx** contrasted a mythical age in which all property was held in common with the situation under capitalism, in which the only 'property' of the worker, labour, was appropriated by the capitalist.

See also: *anarchism; capitalism; communism; Proudhon; socialism.*

> ❛The first man to fence in a piece of land, saying 'This is mine,' and who found people simple enough to believe him, was the real founder of civil society. ❜
>
> **Jean-Jacques Rousseau**, *Discourse on the Origin and Bases of Inequality among Men*

proposition
In logic, the content of a sentence that asserts that something is either true or false. Propositional calculus is the system of formal or symbolic logic that analyses the truth or falsehood of compound propositions linked by logical connectives ('and', 'or', 'if', and so on). Compare predicate calculus (see **predicate and subject**). **See also:** *syllogism.*

Protagoras (*c.* 485–415 BC)
Greek Sophist philosopher. In his dictum that 'Man is the measure of all things', Protagoras was probably both denying that there is any objective truth, and criticizing the theory of the **Eleatic School** that reality is single and unchanging.

Proudhon, Pierre-Joseph (1809–1865)
French theorist of **anarchism**, who believed in peaceful rather than revolutionary change. He sat in the Constituent Assembly of 1848, was imprisoned for three years, and had to go into exile in Brussels. He published *What is Property?* (1840) and *Philosophy of Poverty* (1846).

> ❛Property is theft. ❜
>
> **Pierre-Joseph Proudhon**, *What is Property?*

psychoanalysis
Theory and treatment method for neuroses, developed by Sigmund **Freud** in the 1890s. Freud asserted that the impact of early childhood sexuality and experiences, stored in the **unconscious**, can lead to the development of adult emotional problems. The main treatment method involves the free association of ideas. Some of Freud's supporters broke away and formed their own schools of psychoanalysis, notably Alfred Adler in 1911 and Carl **Jung** in 1913.

ID, EGO, AND SUPEREGO

Freud proposed a model of human psychology based on the concept of the conflicting id, ego, and superego.

- The id is the mind's instinctual element, which demands pleasure and satisfaction.
- The ego is the conscious mind, which deals with the demands of the id and superego.
- The superego is the ethical element, which acts as a conscience and may produce feelings of guilt.

The conflicts between these three elements can be used to explain a range of neurotic symptoms.

Psychoanalysis and its underlying theories have been criticized on the grounds that they are untestable, and therefore cannot lay claim to being scientific. The question has been raised as to how we can tell whether the successful conclusion of an individual case is the result of the underlying theories, or the personality of the analyst. Other questions that have been raised include how we can know of the existence and nature of the unconscious, and whether unconscious wishes (which Freud held to be the motivators of much behaviour) are reasons or causes (see **reasons and causes**).

psychology

The systematic study of human and animal behaviour. The emergence of psychology as a discipline separate from philosophy is usually dated to the establishment of the first psychology laboratory in 1879 by Wilhelm Wundt at Leipzig, Germany. Approaches to psychology have included **introspection, behaviourism, psychoanalysis, Gestalt, and cognitive science**.

The ways that we think and interact with the world have long been of interest to philosophers. Topics that provide a degree of overlap between psychology and philosophy include **abstraction, cognition, consciousness, emotion, human nature, imagination, knowledge, language, memory, mind, mind–body problem, motives** (see **reasons and causes**), **perception, reasoning** (see **reason**), **sensation, the unconscious,** and **volition**.

Philosophers who have thought about how we think and other aspects of human behaviour have included **Plato, Aristotle, Descartes, Hobbes, Locke, Hume** (who was particularly interested in our mental habits), **Kant**, and William **James** (who was also a psychologist).

punishment

As punishment of crime involves the deprivation of an individual's **human rights**, liberal democracies have felt the need to **justify** it. Punishment may be seen simply as retribution, which is assumed to be – as an expression of **justice** – a good in itself, without reference to any other consequences. Alternatively, punishment may be regarded as having some wider good, such as deterrence or rehabilitation (the point of view of **utilitarianism**).

The administration of punishment (as of the **law** as a whole) has traditionally been regarded as a function of the state. In **social contract** theories, it is among the powers that free individuals grant to government. The sub-contracting of prison administration to private companies in recent years in both the USA and the UK has therefore caused considerable concern among upholders of **civil liberties**.

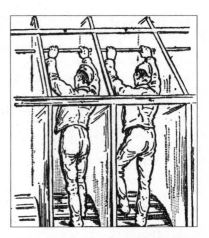

Prisoners on hard labour at the treadwheel in an English jail in the late 19th century. The prisoner had 15 minutes on, 5 minutes off the wheel until his time was finished for the day. The treadwheel was often used to grind flour for the prison.

CORPORAL AND CAPITAL PUNISHMENT

Those who support corporal and/or capital punishment usually regard justice as essentially retributive, and take the view that such punishments are **right** in themselves, although they may also offer utilitarian defences, such as deterrence (regarded as a **good**).

Those who argue against these forms of punishment argue primarily that they are wrong in themselves, and that state-sanctioned violence compromises the moral status of the state itself (these arguments may be linked to ideas of **natural law** and/or **civil liberties**). They may also argue in utilitarian terms, for example by denying the deterrence argument, and by avowing the brutalizing effects of such punishments on both the victims and the perpetrators.

Pyrrho
See *scepticism.*

Pythagoras (*c.* 580–500 BC)

Greek mathematician and philosopher, much of whose work concerned numbers, to which he assigned mystical properties. He is best known for Pythagoras' theorem. He founded a school and religious brotherhood in Croton, southern Italy, whose members became known as Pythagoreans, and whose tenets included **reincarnation**. It is not always possible to distinguish between Pythagoras' own achievements and those of his followers.

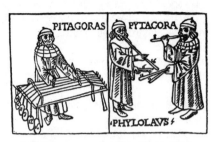

Among their many mathematical achievements, the Pythagoreans formulated the theory of proportion (ratio), and used it in their study of harmonics in stringed instruments. From this came the idea of the 'music of the spheres' and the belief that the universe could be understood in solely mathematical terms.

Pythagorus recognized a mathematical relationship between the length of a vibrating string, a column of air, or the size of a percussion instrument and the notes of a musical scale. Music belonged with the science of sound, and became part of the study of the cosmos.

❝ There is geometry in the humming of the strings. There is music in the spacings of the spheres. ❞

Pythagoras, quoted in Aristotle, *Metaphysics*

quantification

In logic, specification of quantity or number. There are two main quantifiers: the universal quantifier ('For all x ...') and the existential quantifier ('For at least one/some x ...'). Either of these quantifiers can be defined in terms of the other plus negation – just as 'some' can be defined as 'not all' in everyday speech.

THE QUANTIFIER SHIFT FALLACY

This is the fallacy of arguing from 'Every nice girl loves a sailor' to 'At least one sailor is loved by every nice girl'. The latter implies, but is not implied by, the former.

---

quantum mechanics or quantum theory

Branch of physics dealing with the interaction of matter and radiation, the structure of the atom, the motion of subatomic particles, and related phenomena. Just as Einstein's theory of **relativity** showed that **Newton's** laws of classical physics do not apply at the astronomical scale, so quantum mechanics (originated by Max Planck in 1900) shows that they do not apply at the atomic and subatomic level.

The world of quantum mechanics includes several features that undercut our conventional understanding of things like **matter, causality**, and **determinism**:

- Physical quantities that in classical physics range over a continuum of possible values are restricted in the quantum world to a range of possible discrete values.

- Particles such as electrons have wavelike properties, just as light and other electromagnetic radiation, generally seen as a wave phenomenon, can also in some ways be seen as composed of discrete particles (photons).

- Observing certain quantum events affects the outcome, and the **uncertainty principle** puts limits on the accuracy of certain measurements, making prediction impossible.

- When an atom gives out two photons, if we observe one photon of such a pair, the other photon (even if the two photons are billions of kilometres apart) instantly 'knows' that we have made an observation and adjusts its behaviour in certain ways. However, according to relativity, no information can travel faster than the speed of light.

Quine, Willard Van Orman (1908–)

US philosopher and logician with a highly scientific view of the world. He is often described as a nominalist because he believes that **universals** do not have any real existence outside of thought and language (see **nominalism**), and a pragmatist because he holds that our minds group together properties in the ways that are most useful for us (see **pragmatism**).

According to Quine, 'to be is to be the value of a variable' in a system of formal logic. By this, he means that we commit ourselves to the existence of something only when we can say that it has a quality or feature, and that existence itself is not a quality or feature.

QUINE'S THEORY OF TRANSLATION

Quine asserted that assured translation between two languages (or even within one language) is impossible in principle, because the designation of any two words or phrases as synonymous is impossible to justify completely.

---

rationalism

In philosophy, the view that self-evident **a priori** propositions (deduced by reason alone) are the sole basis of all **knowledge**. It is usually contrasted with **empiricism**, which argues that all knowledge must ultimately be derived from the senses. Rationalist philosophers include **Descartes**, **Leibniz**, and **Spinoza**.

  See also: *irrationalism*.

THEOLOGICAL RATIONALISM

In theology, rationalism is the belief that human reason rather than divine revelation is the correct means of ascertaining truth and regulating behaviour. This is one of the tenets of deism.

Rawls, John (1921–)

US philosopher. In *A Theory of Justice* (1971), he revived the concept of the **social contract** and its enforcement by civil disobedience. He argued that if we did not know which position we were to occupy in society, we would choose to live in a society in which there was equal liberty and the minimum of social and economic inequalities. His ideas represent one of the strands of modern **liberalism**, and have influenced left-of-centre parties throughout the world.

realism

In philosophy, the theory that **universals** (properties such as 'redness') have an existence independent of the human mind. Realists hold that the **essence** of things is objectively given in nature, and that our classifications are not arbitrary. As such, realism is contrasted with **nominalism**, the theory that universals are merely names or general terms.

More generally, realism is any philosophical theory that emphasizes the existence of some kind of things or objects, in contrast to theories that dispense with the things in question in favour of words, ideas, or logical constructions. In particular, the term stands for the theory that there is a reality quite independent of the mind. In this sense, realism is opposed to **idealism**, the theory that only minds and their contents exist.

reason

The human faculty that enables us to argue logically, to infer particulars from the general (**deduction**), and the general from the particular (**induction**). It is often contrasted with emotion and sometimes with **imagination**. It is also often contrasted with **faith**, although **Aquinas** held that the two were compatible. **See also:** *deism; Enlightenment; irrationalism; rationalism; Romanticism.*

❝ The sleep of reason brings forth monsters. ❞

Francisco de Goya, *title of print*

reasons and causes

When a reason is offered as the basis of an action, is it the same as a cause? The notion of **causality** implies the unavoidable necessity of the outcome (**determinism**), whereas offering a reason for an action is more akin to explaining a motive, and implies a degree of free will on the part of the actor. When we talk about a reason for a **belief**, we are offering a justification; **See also:** *certainty.*

reductio AD absurdum

Method of proof in which it is initially assumed that the proposition that it is desired to prove is not true. If it can then be shown that this assumption leads logically to a contradiction or 'absurdity', it will have been proved that the original proposition must be true.

reductionism

Broadly speaking, the method of explaining things in terms of their simplest and/or smallest constituents. It is often contrasted with **holism**. In metaphysics, monism – asserting that there is no distinction between mind/spirit and matter – is a form of reductionism.

In science, reductionism has been highly successful, for example in particle physics. However, the **quantum mechanics** required to describe phenomena at this scale is not sensibly applicable to most events in the 'everyday' world, where the classical mechanics of Isaac **Newton** still provides the best practical means of description and prediction.

❝ Science is built of facts the way a house is built of bricks; but the accumulation of facts is no more science than a pile of bricks is a house. ❞

Henri Poincaré, *La Science et l'hypothèse*

Claims that all human behaviour can be explained purely in terms of evolutionary genetics, or that **mind** or **consciousness** can be completely explained in terms of neurophysiology, have also been criticized as reductionist over-simplifications of the issues.

Reid, Thomas (1710–1796)
Scottish mathematician and philosopher. His *Enquiry into the Human Mind on the Principles of Common Sense* (1764) attempted to counter the sceptical conclusions of David **Hume**. He believed that the existence of the material world and the human soul is self-evident 'by the consent of ages and nations, of the learned and unlearned'. **See also:** *common sense.*

reification
Alleged social process whereby relations between human beings are transformed into impersonal relations between things. **Lukács** analysed this process as characteristic of capitalist society. Later **Marxists** have developed this analysis, thus extending Marx's early critique of **alienation**.

reincarnation
Belief that after death the human **soul** or the spirit of a plant or animal may live again in another human or animal. Alternative terms are 'transmigration' and 'metempsychosis'. The belief is part of the teachings of many religions and philosophies; for example, ancient Egyptian and Greek (the philosophies of **Pythagoras** and **Plato**), Buddhism, Hinduism, Jainism, Sikhism, certain Christian heresies (such as the Cathars), and theosophy. The question arises as to how meaningful a concept it is, when there is no consciousness of a previous existence.

relativism
Philosophical position that denies the possibility of objective truth (for example, regarding moral issues, or knowledge more generally) independent of some specific social or historical context or conceptual framework. It is sometimes compared to **absolutism**.

relativity
In physics, the theory of the relative rather than absolute character of motion, mass, and time, and the interdependence of **matter, time,** and **space**. The theory was developed by Albert Einstein in two parts: the special theory (1905) and the general theory (1916). Among the conclusions of relativity are:

- Nothing can go faster than the speed of light, which is independent of the speed of its source.

- An object moving rapidly past the observer will appear to be both shorter and more massive than when it is at rest (that is, at rest relative to the observer).

> ❝ Nature, and Nature's laws lay hid in night:
> God said, *Let Newton be!* and all was light. ❞
>
> **Alexander Pope**, 'Epitaph for Sir Isaac Newton'

- A clock moving rapidly past the observer will appear to be running slower than when it is at rest. (This and the previous phenomenon only become appreciable at speeds approaching that of light.)
- Space and time are a continuum, and **space-time** is modified locally by the presence of a body with mass.
- Energy and mass are equivalent, as expressed in the equation $E = mc^2$, where E is energy, m is mass, and c the speed of light in a vacuum.

The findings of relativity theory have been proved by experiment. They demonstrate that the classical physics of Isaac **Newton**, although applicable to the 'everyday' world, do not apply on the astronomical scale, just as **quantum mechanics** supersedes Newtonian mechanics on the atomic and subatomic scale.

> ❝ It did not last: the Devil howling 'Ho!
> Let Einstein be!' restored the status quo. ❞
>
> **J C Squire**, 'Answer to Pope's Epitaph on Sir Isaac Newton'

religion, philosophy of
The philosophy of religion as practised today largely concentrates on the Western monotheistic religions, Christianity in particular. Central concerns include:

- The nature of **God**, and the relation of God to humanity.
- Whether the existence or God can be demonstrated.
- Analysis of the language of traditional **theology**.
- Considerations of the nature of **faith, evil, free will, predestination**, and other concepts.
- The relationship between religion, **morality,** and **ethics**.

Significant influences on modern philosophers of religion have included linguistic philosophy (see **linguistics** and **philosophy**) and **existentialism**. **See also:** *deism; fideism; natural theology; pantheism; religion, science, and philosophy; theology.*

religion, science, and philosophy
The history of the relationship between philosophy, religion and science is a tangled one, especially as, until the Renaissance at least, science was considered a part of philosophy.

Ancient Greece and the Middle Ages

In **pre-Socratic philosophy**, attempts were made to suggest physical rather than supernatural explanations of the universe. However, both Plato (with his **demiurge**) and Aristotle (with his prime mover or first cause), suggested a divine explanation. **Neo-Platonism** proposed a hierarchy of levels of being, emanating from the One or Good. In medieval **scholasticism** attempts were made to incorporate Aristotelianism into **theology**, and to show that reason and faith are not incompatible.

The Scientific Revolution

At the Renaissance, the new spirit of **humanism**, and the discoveries of Copernicus that initiated the Scientific Revolution, brought about the beginnings of a change in attitudes towards religion. During the 17th century, and particularly in the 18th-century **Enlightenment**, traditional religious dogma was questioned, and the primacy of reason proclaimed, leading many thinkers to embrace *deism* (although few overtly adopted **atheism**).

The progress of science (most notably the advent of **Darwinism** in the mid-19th century) continued to undermine traditional religious explanations of the origin of the world and humanity. Nevertheless, the **idealism** of such philosophers as **Kant** nor **Hegel** continued alongside the **materialism** and **positivism** of the scientists and philosophers such as Karl **Marx**. Different perspectives, both highly influential on subsequent thinking about religion, are found in the writings of **Kierkegaard** and **Nietzsche**.

The 20th century

By the 20th century, many religious thinkers had conceded to science the causal account of life and the universe, and questions about God, faith, and so on, became a philosophical specialism (see **religion, philosophy of**). It is now generally agreed that science and religion are different areas of human experience (see, for example, **Wittgenstein's** idea of 'language-games').

Ironically, at the same time as this consensus was coming about, the scientific advances of the 20th century, such as **relativity** and **quantum mechanics**, appeared to undercut the rational, mechanistic and predictable model of the universe that had held sway since the time of Isaac **Newton**.

representation

In philosophy, a term with two distinct meanings. Firstly, in aesthetics, the idea that art (especially the visual arts and literature) represents the 'real' world goes back to Plato and Aristotle. Aristotle called this *mimesis* (imitation). This view of art is contrasted with views that a work of art is, for example, primarily an expression of inner feeling, or an internally coherent system of formal relations.

The second meaning refers to the relation between a picture, thought, word or sentence and what it represents. There has been considerable philosophical debate about whether pictorial representations are resemblances or not, and about exactly what kind of relation exists between a word, say, and what it represents (see, for example, **language, philosophy of; signs and symbols**).

right, the
Whether there is a distinction between the right and the **good** is a traditional problem of ethics. For some moral philosophers, the rightness of an action is intrinsic, and does not depend on any good that comes out of it (see **deontology**). In **utilitarianism** and other forms of consequentialism, the rightness of an action only depends on the resulting good. **See also:** *ends and means.*

rights
See *civil liberties; human rights; natural rights.*

Romanticism
Broad cultural and artistic movement that swept Europe in the late 18th and early 19th centuries, as a reaction against 18th-century Classicism and the **Enlightenment** emphasis on reason and science.

Inspired by **Rousseau's** views of the nobility of **nature**, the aesthetics of **Lessing**, and by contemporary political change and revolution in America and France, Romanticism asserted emotion and intuition over rationalism, the importance of the individual (especially the artist) over social conformity, and the exploration of natural and psychic wildernesses over Classical restraint.

Founders and aesthetic theorists of the movement included **Schiller** and the younger **Goethe**. In philosophy, the **idealism** of **Fichte**, **Schelling** and **Hegel** sought to find a spiritual unity in reality, graspable only by 'reason' in its highest form, as distinct from everyday 'understanding'. The English Romantic poet S T Coleridge borrowed this distinction when he compared **imagination** with 'fancy'. **Pantheism** was another component in Romantic philosophy, and is also found in the nature poetry of William Wordsworth and others.

ROMANTICISM AND POLITICS

In the political sphere, Romanticism became associated with both nationalism and liberalism, in the context of the efforts of various European peoples to free themselves from the rule of foreign empires and establish constitutional governments. The revolutionary hero is a recurrent theme in Romantic art and literature, epitomized by the poet Lord Byron, who died of malaria while fighting for Greek independence from the Ottoman Empire.

Rousseau, Jean-Jacques (1712–1778)

Swiss-born French social and political philosopher. He developed the idea of the **social contract**, and his political theories influenced the French Revolution. He believed that a pure state of nature could still be found in the behaviour of animals, children, and 'noble savages', and that it was civilized society that corrupted people (see **human nature**). These ideas influenced **Romanticism**.

Jean-Jacques Rousseau, from a print published in 1779.

In *Social Contract* (1762) Rousseau argued that government is justified only if sovereignty stays with the people. He thereby rejected representative democracy in favour of direct democracy (in which all issues are submitted to the electorate for a decision), and stated that a government could be legitimately overthrown if it failed to express the general will of the people. His novel *Emile* (1762) was written as an example of how to elicit the unspoiled nature and abilities of children, based on natural development and the power of example.

Rousseau's ideas were condemned by philosophers, the clergy, and the public, and he lived in exile in Britain for a year, being helped by David **Hume** until they fell out. Rousseau was one of the **Encyclopédistes**, but later rejected the values of the **Enlightenment**.

> ❝ Man is born free, and everywhere he is in chains. ❞
>
> **Jean-Jacques Rousseau**, *Social Contract*

Russell, Bertrand (1872–1970)

English philosopher, mathematician, and peace campaigner. He contributed to the development of modern mathematical logic, helped to found the tradition of **analytic philosophy,** and wrote about social issues.

Russell's work on mathematical logic was influenced by that of Gottlob Frege, but in 1902 he discovered that **Frege's** system could not cope with **Russell's paradox**. His first major publication was *Principia Mathematica*

(1910–13; with A N **Whitehead**), in which he attempted to show that mathematics could be reduced to a branch of logic.

Russell also made important contributions to epistemology and the philosophy of **language**, and developed **logical atomism**; some of this work was influenced by his pupil Ludwig **Wittgenstein**. Russell's other publications include *The Problems of Philosophy* (1912), and *A History of Western Philosophy* (1946). He was awarded the Nobel Prize for Literature in 1950.

> ❢ Three passions, simple but overwhelmingly strong, have governed my life: the longing for love, the search for knowledge, and unbearable pity for the suffering of mankind. ❢
>
> **Bertrand Russell**, *Autobiography*, Prologue

Russell's paradox
Paradox relating to **set theory** devised by Bertrand **Russell** in 1902, and which illustrated a fatal flaw in Gottlob **Frege's** system of mathematical logic. It revolves round the question of whether the set of all sets that are not members of themselves is a member of itself. Whichever way the question is answered, there is a contradiction.

Ryle, Gilbert (1900–1976)
British philosopher. His *The Concept of Mind* (1949) set out to show that the distinction between an inner and an outer world in philosophy and psychology cannot be sustained. He ridiculed the **mind–body** dualism of **Descartes** as the doctrine of 'the Ghost in the Machine'.

Saint-Simon, Henri de (1760–1825)

French political theorist who was an early advocate of **socialism**. He fought in the American Revolution and was imprisoned during the French Revolution. In works such as *The Industrial System* (1821) he advocated a society run by industrialists, in which the spiritual direction of society would be undertaken by scientists and engineers. In *New Christianity* (1825) – which precipitated a break with his collaborator August **Comte** – he proposed that the aim of religion was to guide society towards the ending of poverty.

Santayana, George (1863–1952)

Spanish-born US philosopher and critic. He rejected both religious supernaturalism and the metaphysical idealism of the 19th-century German philosophers in favour of **naturalism**, in which everything has a natural basis. Humans are considered as natural objects in the material world, and belief in the external world is based on 'animal faith'. His books, noted for their literary quality, include *The Life of Reason* (1905–06), volumes of poetry; and the best-selling novel *The Last Puritan* (1935).

⟨ The body is an instrument, the mind its function, the witness and reward of its operation. ⟩

George Santayana, *The Life of Reason*

Sartre, Jean-Paul (1905–1980)

French philosopher. Influenced by **Heidegger** and **phenomenology**, he became a leading proponent of **existentialism**, whose tenets he expressed in many novels and plays such as *Nausea* (1937) and *Huis clos/In Camera* (1944). His first major philosophical work, *Being and Nothingness* (1943), sets out a radical doctrine of human freedom. In the later *Critique of Dialectical Reason* (1960) he tried to produce a fusion of existentialism and **Marxism**.

Sartre refused the Nobel Prize for Literature in 1964 for 'personal reasons', but allegedly changed his mind later, saying he wanted it for the money.

Sartre was the long-time companion of the feminist writer Simone de **Beauvoir**. During World War II he was a prisoner of war for nine months, and on his return from Germany joined the Resistance. With Albert **Camus** he edited the left-wing newspaper *Combat* (1944–47), and also edited the existentialist journal *Les Temps modernes* ('modern times').

In *Being and Nothingness* Sartre put forward the theory that people have to create their own destiny without relying on powers higher than themselves. Awareness of this freedom takes the form of anxiety (**anguish**), and people therefore attempt to flee from awareness into what he terms *mauvaise foi* (**bad faith**). In the play *Les Mains sales/Crime passionel* (1948) he attacked aspects of communism while remaining generally sympathetic. In his later work Sartre became more sensitive to the social constraints on people's actions.

> ❝ I am condemned to be free. ❞
>
> **Jean-Paul Sartre**, *Being and Nothingness*

Saussure, Ferdinand de (1857–1913)

Swiss pioneer of modern linguistics and the originator of **structuralism**. Saussure saw language as both a unified and shared social system (*langue*) and as individual and idiosyncratic speech (*parole*). He also proposed that language can be described in 'synchronic' terms (as a system at a particular time) and in 'diachronic' terms (as changing through time).

scepticism

Philosophical view that absolute knowledge of things is ultimately unobtainable, hence the only proper attitude is to suspend judgement. Its origins lay in the teachings of the Greek philosopher Pyrrho (*c.* 360–*c.* 270 BC), who maintained that peace of mind lay in renouncing all claims to knowledge. It was taken up in a less extreme form by the Greek **Academy** in the 3rd and 2nd centuries BC. The Academic Sceptics claimed that although truth is finally unknowable, a balance of probabilities can be used for coming to decisions. The thinking of the ancient Sceptics was summarized in the 2nd–3rd century AD by **Sextus Empiricus**.

Scepticism was revived at the Renaissance, and given an impetus by the emergence of science and the spirit of questioning of medieval God-centred explanations. **Descartes** deployed a radical scepticism in questioning the reliability of any knowledge derived through the senses, but nevertheless stated that the role of philosophy was to defeat scepticism. However, the progress of experimental science continued to undermine **a priori** assumptions about the world, and this was reflected in British philosophical empiricism, which was sceptical of Cartesian **rationalism**. The **empirical** tradition culminated in the extreme scepticism of David **Hume**, who explored the limitations of human understanding. **See also:** *solipsism.*

Schelling, Friedrich (1775–1854)

German philosopher, whose views on nature and art influenced **Romanticism**. He developed a 'philosophy of identity', in which subject and object are seen as united in the **absolute**. Schelling began as a follower of **Fichte**, but moved away from subjective **idealism**, which treats the external world as essentially immaterial. His early philosophy influenced **Hegel**, but his later work criticizes Hegel, arguing that being necessarily precedes thought.

Schiller, Friedrich (1759–1805)

German dramatist, poet, historian, and philosopher, one of the central figures of **Romanticism** and a close friend of **Goethe**. Much of his literary work concerns the aspiration for political freedom and the avoidance of mediocrity. In philosophy he was influenced by **Kant**, and developed a form of **idealism**. His philosophical writing largely concerns art and aesthetics.

> ❝ Against stupidity the gods themselves struggle in vain. ❞
>
> **Friedrich von Schiller**, *The Maid of Orleans*

Schlick, Moritz (1882–1936)

German philosopher, physicist, adherent of **logical positivism**, and founder of the **Vienna Circle**. Under the influence of the early **Wittgenstein**, Schlick concluded that all philosophical problems arise from the inadequacy of language. He held that the task of philosophy is to clarify the question in dispute: if the question cannot be ascertained in principle by scientific methods, then the question is meaningless. He based **meaning** on the possibility of immediate sense-experience. The inaccessibility of this private experience of meaning led Wittgenstein to his later 'use' theory of meaning.

Schlick was assassinated in 1936 by a demented student, an event that hastened the break-up of the Vienna Circle.

scholasticism

The theological and philosophical systems and methods taught in the schools of medieval Europe, especially in the 12th–14th centuries. Scholasticism tried to integrate orthodox Christian teaching with the philosophy of **Aristotle**, and, to a lesser extend, **Plato**. The scholastic method involved surveying different opinions and the reasons given for them, and then attempting solutions of the problems raised, using logic and dialectic. **Erigena**, the 9th-century Platonist, is sometimes regarded as an early scholastic. But scholasticism properly began at the end of the 11th century, and in the 12th century the foundation of universities in Bologna, Paris, Oxford, and Cambridge, and the recovery of ancient Greek texts via the philosophers of the Arab world, stimulated scholasticism. The most notable scholastic philosophers, or 'schoolmen' as they were called, included:

- Late 11th century: Roscellinus, a supporter of **nominalism**, and **Anselm**, a supporter of **realism**, who disputed the nature of **universals**.
- 12th century: William of Champeaux, Peter **Abelard**, the English monk Alexander of Hales (died 1245), **Albertus Magnus**, and Peter Lombard.
- 13th century: Thomas **Aquinas** and **Duns Scotus**.
- 14th century: William of **Occam**.

See also: *neo-Thomism.*

Schopenhauer, Arthur (1788–1860)

German philosopher. His *The World as Will and Idea* (1818), inspired by **Kant** and ancient Hindu philosophy, expounded an atheistic and pessimistic world view: an irrational will is considered as the inner principle of the world, producing an ever-frustrated cycle of desire, of which the only escape is aesthetic contemplation or absorption into nothingness.

Having postulated a world of suffering and disappointment, Schopenhauer based his ethics on compassion. His notion of an irrational force at work in human beings strongly influenced both **Nietzsche** and **Freud**. The theory also struck a responsive chord in the composer Richard Wagner, the German novelist Thomas Mann, and the English writer Thomas Hardy.

> ❦ Belief is like love; it cannot be compelled. ❧
>
> **Arthur Schopenhauer**, *Essays and Aphorisms*

science, philosophy of

Systematic study of how science works (or should work), the extent of its ability to gain access to the truth about the material world, and of the concepts used in scientific enquiry, such as the **laws of nature, causality**, **probability, explanation,** and **induction** (reasoning from the particular to the general).

Philosophers of science also consider the nature of scientific systems. Some hold that scientific systems are abstract systems that we fit to the world, as we might choose between Euclidean and non-Euclidean geometries.

From the time of **Hume** it has been recognized that induction from observation cannot give explanations based on logic. In the 20th century **Popper** has described the scientific method as a rigorous experimental testing of a scientist's idea or **hypothesis**. The origin and role of these ideas, and their interdependence with observation, have been examined, for example, by T S **Kuhn**, who places them in a historical and sociological setting. The sociology of science investigates how scientific theories and laws are produced, and questions the possibility of objectivity in any scientific endeavour.

See also: *Goodman's paradox; conventionalism; instrumentalism; knowledge; Mach, Ernst; Pierce, C S; science and ethics.*

> ❛ Science may be described as the art of systematic oversimplification. ❜
>
> **Karl Popper**, remark, August 1982

THE SOCIAL SCIENCES

One area of contemporary debate is whether the social sciences (including anthropology, economics, psychology, and sociology) are actually sciences; that is, whether the study of human beings is capable of scientific precision or prediction in the same way as natural science is seen to be.

---

science and ethics

There are various ways in which scientists may be involved directly in ethical issues, for example:

- Embarking on a particular field of research, such as genetic engineering.
- Human embryo research.
- The use of animals in research, weighed against the good the research may do.
- The whole field of **medical ethics.**
- Research in fields that may have military uses.

Nevertheless, some scientists claim that science is ethically neutral, and it is the uses of science that politicians and industrialists decide on that may result in good or evil.

science, religion, and philosophy

See *religion, science, and philosophy.*

scientific method

The belief that in science experimentation and observation, properly understood and applied, can avoid the influence of cultural and social values and so build up a picture of a reality independent of the observer.

Techniques and mechanical devices that improve the reliability of measurements may seem to support this theory; but the realization that observations of subatomic particles influence their behaviour has undermined the view that objectivity is possible in science (see **uncertainty principle**).

The model of scientific method now generally accepted involves the use of observation and experiment to test a **hypothesis**, an idea regarding some phenomenon. The hypothesis itself is largely due to the creative imagination of the scientist who proposes it, although to a degree determined by and constrained within his or her social, cultural, historical, and intellectual context.

If the hypothesis is backed up by the empirical data, then it may be elevated into a **theory**, although this involves **induction**, which is not a *logically* certain process. However, scientists generally accept probability beyond reasonable doubt. Factors involved in establishing this probability include the ability of the hypothesis to make testable predictions, the repeatability of experiments, and the statistical significance of their results.

See also: *empiricism; Goodman's paradox; Kuhn; law of nature; Popper; religion, science, and philosophy; science, philosophy of.*

❝ A scientific hypothesis is elegant and exciting insofar as it contradicts common sense. ❞

Charles Lyell, attributed remark, quoted in
Stephen Jay Gould, *Ever Since Darwin*

Scruton, Roger (1944–)

British philosopher and right-wing social critic. His work on aesthetics seeks to link the subject to ethics. Advocating the political theories of Edmund **Burke** in such books as *The Meaning of Conservatism* (1980), he influenced the free-market movements in eastern Europe.

❝ The spirit of reform has been too much concerned with private "rights", and not enough concerned with the public order that makes them possible. ❞

Roger Scruton, *The Meaning of Conservatism*

---

self

The individual as an experiencing being, the subject of contemplation, the object of **introspection**, and the agent of thought and action.

Personality and ego are commonly used synonyms, though they do not have exactly the same meaning;

- The personality is more outwardly observable (by others, that is).

- The ego (at least in **psychoanalysis**) contains unconscious elements that the self does not recognize.

See also: *consciousness; emotion; imagination; memory; reason; solipsism; time; volition.*

semantics

Branch of linguistics dealing with the meaning of words and sentences. Semantics asks how we can use language to express things about the real world, and how the meanings of linguistic expressions can reflect people's thoughts.

Linguistic meaning has been studied for thousands of years. **Plato** believed that words or phrases related directly to the actual objects they pick out. **Aristotle** suggested that relationships between words and the world are indirect, mediated by social convention. More recently, the 'conceptualist' view of linguistic meaning has held that there is an indirect relationship between words and things, mediated by thoughts in the mind. **See** *language, philosophy of; thinking and language.*

semiology or semiotics

The study of the function of **signs and symbols** in human communication, both in language and by various nonlinguistic means. Beginning with **Saussure's** notion that no word or other sign (the signifier) is intrinsically linked with its meaning (the signified), it was developed by **Lévi-Strauss** and **Barthes,** among others. Semiotics has combined with **structuralism** in order to explore the 'production' of meaning in language and other sign systems, and has emphasized the conventional nature of this production.

Seneca, Lucius Annaeus

(*c.* 4 BC–AD 65)

Roman philosopher and playwright. His treatises and essays are known for their advocacy of Stoicism. His tragedies

Seneca committing suicide in his bath, having fallen out with Nero.

were accepted as classical models by 16th-century dramatists. He was tutor to the future emperor Nero, but lost favour after Nero's accession to the throne and was ordered to commit suicide.

sensation
The direct experience of the external world brought to us by our senses. This experience is said to consist of 'sense data'. Sensation is contrasted with **perception**, which involves some degree of interpretation and conceptualizing of the sense data. The reliability of sensation as a means of acquiring **knowledge** has long been a subject of controversy among philosophers. **Descartes** took an extremely sceptical view, while **empiricism** upholds the validity of sense impressions. See also: *sensationalism*.

sensationalism or sensationism
In philosophy, the doctrine originated by **Locke** that all our knowledge rests ultimately on sense data, or sensations, which are received by us free from any element of interpretation or judgement.

set theory
Mathematical and logical method originated by Georg **Cantor**.

- A set or class is any collection of defined things (elements), provided the elements are distinct and that there is a rule to decide whether an element is a member of a set.

- Various symbols are used to denote the relations between elements and sets, and between sets.

- Sets themselves are of different types, for example, finite, infinite, empty, and so on.

It was **Russell's paradox**, drawing on set theory, that showed the fatal flaw in **Frege's** attempt to put mathematics on a logical basis. Russell himself, with A N **Whitehead**, attempted to demonstrate that mathematics is reducible to the logic of sets.

Sextus Empiricus (c. 160–c. 210 AD)
Greek physician and philosopher. He was an exponent of **scepticism** of an agnostic, not a dogmatic, kind – that is, he rejected the view that knowledge was demonstrably impossible, and he insisted on keeping an open mind on this as on other questions. Sextus' work is a valuable source for the history of philosophy, because of his impartiality in presenting the arguments of his opponents.

Shaftesbury, Earl of (1671–1713)
English philosopher, author of *Characteristics of Men, Manners, Opinions, and Times* (1711) and other ethical speculations. His education was partially directed by John **Locke**. Influenced by the **Cambridge Platonists**, he believed

that humans are born with a natural love of virtue, a position opposed to that of Thomas **Hobbes**. This idea of a 'moral sense' was later developed by Francis **Hutcheson**. His advocacy of **deism** was also influential.

Sidgwick, Henry (1838–1900)

British philosopher. He held that the basic moral principle (which is not reducible to non-moral terms) rests on our intuitive grasp that we ought to aim at pleasure. However, the pleasure of others is as important as one's own, which gives Sidgwick's account a utilitarian complexion (see **utilitarianism**). The problem then is to reconcile the conflicting demands of one's own and other people's pleasure.

signs and symbols

Definitions of these two terms vary. For example:

- Sometimes they are regarded as synonymous.

- C S **Pierce** distinguished 'natural signs' (for example, a runny nose is a sign of a cold); invented signs that have some resemblance to the thing signed, and which he called 'icons'; and 'symbols', which are invented signs that do not have any resemblance to the thing signed, and whose use is understood entirely by convention.

- Other thinkers have regarded the distinction as being the other way round. Signs, such as = and others in mathematics, have an arbitrary relationship to the thing referred to, whereas symbols (such as the Christian cross) have some intrinsic relationship with what is referred to.

- Signs may also be thought of as denoting a single meaning, while symbols connote a range of meanings (see **connotation and denotation**).

- Words may be regarded as signs in the sense of their arbitrary relationship with what is referred to, but words may also be used as symbols, particularly in literary contexts, in terms of embodying a range of associated ideas. The way that words 'mean' is, however, complex (see **language, philosophy of; semantics**).

The study of signs and symbols is called **semiology**.

sin

Transgression of the will of God or the gods, as revealed in the moral code laid down by a particular religion. Such transgressions may either involve the commission of a forbidden act, or the omission to do something one ought to do. In Roman Catholic theology, a distinction is made between 'mortal sins', which, if unforgiven, result in damnation, and 'venial sins', which are less serious. This distinction was denied by the Protestant reformers, who saw all sin as mortal.

Christian theology further divides sin into material sin and formal sin. Material sin is any transgression of the divine will or law; material sins

---

ORIGINAL SIN

In Christian belief, humanity has been in a state of 'original sin' since Adam and Eve's disobedience in the Garden of Eden and is therefore in need of redemption through the crucifixion of Jesus. The concept of original sin informs the Christian view of **human nature**, and has also indirectly influenced some of the more authoritarian theorists of political conservatism.

---

become formal sins when they are deliberately and knowingly committed. Only formal sins involve guilt. **See also:** *evil; morality.*

situationism
In ethics, the doctrine that any action may be good or bad depending on its context or situation. Situationists argue that no moral rule can apply in all situations, and that what may be wrong in most cases may be right if the end is sufficiently good. In general, situationists believe moral attitudes are more important than moral rules. One of the key texts of situationism is *Joseph Fletcher's Situation Ethics* (1966). Situationism has been most influential in Christian moral theology, where its proponents have argued that an intensely thankful and loving attitude will result in good actions. **See also:** *ends and means.*

social contract
The idea that government authority derives originally from an agreement between ruler and ruled in which the former agrees to provide order in return for obedience from the latter. Social contract theory originated in the 17th century, in opposition to the doctrine of the **divine right of kings**. It has been used to support both absolutism (**Hobbes**) and democracy (**Locke** and **Rousseau**).

Social contract theory has survived a period of disrepute during the 1950s and early 1960s, and versions have been incorporated in the work of modern political theorists such as John **Rawls**. **See also:** *state.*

social Darwinism
An influential but contentious social theory, extrapolated originally by Herbert **Spencer** from the work of Charles Darwin (see **Darwinism**), which claimed to offer a scientific justification for late 19th-century *laissez-faire* capitalism (the principle of unrestricted freedom in commerce).

Popularized – particularly in the USA – by academics and by entrepreneurs such as Andrew Carnegie, social Darwinism was used to legitimize competitive **individualism** and a market economy unregulated by government. It argued that only the strong and resourceful businesses and individuals would thrive in a free environment ('the survival of the fittest', in Spencer's words). Social Darwinism is regarded as a classic case of the naturalistic fallacy – the derivation of values from factual premises (see **is/ought problem**).

socialism

Political theory and movement aiming to establish a classless society by substituting public for private ownership of the means of production, distribution, and exchange. It is generally internationalist in outlook, opposing narrow **nationalism**. The term has been used to describe positions as widely apart as **anarchism**, **communism**, and **social democracy**.

Socialist ideas appeared in classical times, in early Christianity, and among later Christian sects such as the Anabaptists and Diggers. In the 18th and early 19th centuries, systematic socialist aims were put forward by Jean-Jacques **Rousseau**, Henri de **Saint-Simon**, François Fourier, and Robert Owen, among others. These schemes were largely utopian in nature (see utopianism). In the mid-19th century Karl **Marx** and Friedrich **Engels**, the founders of communism, claimed to be putting socialism on a scientific basis.

The late 19th and early 20th centuries saw a division in the socialist movement. Some, such as **Lenin**, continued to emphasize the original revolutionary significance of Marx's teachings, leading to the creation of communist parties. Many trade unionists (up until World War I) supported the syndicalism of Georges **Sorel**. Others reacted against Marxism, leading to the formation of social **democratic** parties espousing evolutionary change.

SOCIAL DEMOCRACY

Social democratic parties today (for example, the Social Democratic Party in Germany and the Labour Party in the UK) uphold the ideals of liberal **democracy**, and a blend of **individualism** and **collectivism**. They generally believe in:

- A mixed economy, in which free-enterprise activity is moderated by regulation.
- A degree of state economic intervention.
- Government provision of education, welfare, health care, and so on.

---

social sciences

See *science, philosophy of; anthropology; psychology.*

society, civil
See *civil society*.

Socrates (*c.* 469–399 BC)
Greek philosopher, resident in Athens. He wrote nothing, but was immortalized in the dialogues of his pupil **Plato**. In contrast to the emphasis on cosmology in **pre-Socratic philosophy**, Socrates turned his attention particularly to ethics, and his methods are sometimes regarded as the foundation of logic.

In his desire to combat the **scepticism** of the **Sophists**, Socrates asserted the possibility of genuine knowledge. In ethics, he put forward the view that the good person never knowingly does wrong. True knowledge emerges through dialogue and systematic

Socrates on trial for 'corrupting youth' and 'impiety'. He was sentenced to death by drinking hemlock.

questioning, and an abandoning of uncritical claims to knowledge. **See also:** *irony, Socratic; Socratic method.*

THE CUP OF HEMLOCK

The effect of Socrates' teaching was disruptive since he opposed tyranny. Accused in 399 on charges of impiety and corruption of youth, he was condemned by the Athenian authorities to die by drinking hemlock, which he is said to have taken willingly.

❦ Nothing can harm a good man, either in life or after death. ❧

Socrates, quoted in Plato, *Apology*

Socratic method
Method of teaching used by **Socrates**, in which he aimed to guide pupils to clear thinking on ethics and politics by asking questions and then exposing their inconsistencies in cross-examination. This method was effective against the **Sophists**. **See also:** *irony, Socratic.*

solipsism

A view that maintains that the **self** is the only thing that can be known to exist. It is an extreme form of **scepticism**. The solipsist sees himself or herself as the only individual in existence, assuming other people to be a reflection of his or her own consciousness. Part of the method of **Descartes** was to assert that the only rational certainty was Cogito, ergo sum ('I think, therefore I am'), but Descartes went beyond this solipsistic conclusion, using it as a basis to rebuild human knowledge. **See also:** *other, the (other minds); idealism.*

Sophist

In ancient Greece, originally a 'wise man', but in the 5th-century BC the terms was applied to any of a group of itinerant lecturers on culture, rhetoric, and politics. Sceptical about the possibility of achieving genuine knowledge, they applied bogus reasoning and were concerned with winning arguments rather than establishing the truth. **Plato** regarded them as dishonest, and recounts **Socrates'** successful defeat of them in argument. Since then, 'sophistry' has come to mean fallacious reasoning. In the 2nd century AD the term was linked to the art of public speaking.

Sorel, Georges (1847–1922)

French philosopher who believed that **socialism** could only come about through a general strike. This was the basis of the ideology known as 'syndicalism', which was influential among trade unionists up to World War I. Sorel's theory of the need for a 'myth' to sway the body of the people was adopted by **fascism**.

soul

According to many religions, an intangible part of a human being that survives the death of the physical body. In contrast, **Aristotle** regarded the soul as the form of the living creature, not as a substance separable from it. However, for **Plato**, the soul is immaterial, and only united with the body during life. This is also the view of Judaism, Christianity, and Islam, which all teach that at the end of the world each soul will be judged and assigned to heaven or hell on its merits (compare **reincarnation**).

Although philosophers today do not by and large concern themselves with the theological aspects of the soul, the dualism proposed by **Descartes** between the mind (which he identified with the soul) on the one hand, and the physical body on the other, is at the basis of the **mind–body problem**.

❝ The ghost in the machine. ❞

Gilbert Ryle, *The Concept of Mind*

space and space-time

In everyday life, we think of space in a variety of ways. For example:

- Space consists of three dimensions, is theoretically infinite in all directions, and is the same throughout.
- No object is able to occupy the space of another object.
- Space may alternatively be regarded as the emptiness between particles of matter, a vacuum (as in 'outer space').
- Space and time are separable, and can be measured independently.

However, since around the beginning of the 20th century, physicists have cast doubt on some of these assumptions.

This is partly owing to discoveries about the nature of **matter**. Matter is made up of atoms, and atoms themselves are largely empty space, with the nucleus and electrons only occupying a tiny fraction of the whole. Subatomic particles sometimes behave as waves, and some types are continually passing through the Earth without any impact.

The other major discovery that affects our ideas of space is Albert Einstein's theory of **relativity**. At speeds approaching that of light (relative to the observer), the dimensions of objects are altered, and time is dilated. Space as a three-dimensional entity is replaced by space-time, a continuum in which time is the fourth dimension. Space-time is the location in which all events occur. Space-time is distorted by the presence of material bodies, an effect that we observe as gravity. This has repercussions on the idea of the 'evenness' and infinite nature of space.

Spencer, Herbert (1820–1903)

Self-taught English philosopher, who was a railway engineer before becoming a journalist. He founded **social Darwinism**, and coined the phrase 'survival of the fittest'. In *Social Statics* (1851) he expounded his *laissez-faire* views on social and political issues. In 1862 he began his ten-volume *System of Synthetic Philosophy*, in which he extended Charles Darwin's theory of evolution (**Darwinism**) to the entire field of human knowledge, including ethics and sociology. He is regarded as the prime exponent of the naturalistic fallacy (see **is/ought problem**), and mistakenly interpreted evolution by natural selection as purposive and progressive (see **teleology**).

> ❝ Progress ... is not an accident, but a necessity ...
> It is part of nature. ❞
> **Herbert Spencer**, *Social Statics*

Spinoza, Benedict de or Baruch (1632–1677)

Dutch philosopher, a lens-grinder by trade. He believed in a rationalistic

pantheism that owed much to **Descartes's** mathematical appreciation of the universe.

Spinoza regarded mind and matter as two modes of an infinite substance that he called God or Nature. He held that the highest good was 'knowledge of the union existing between the mind and the whole of Nature', and that intuition, proceeding from reason, brings about the 'intellectual love of God'.

In ethics he held that good and evil are relative, and that human action is motivated by self-preservation. In political theory he developed a more liberal version of Thomas **Hobbes's** social contract.

Spinoza was excommunicated by the Jewish community in Amsterdam on charges of heretical thought and practice in 1656. His main work is *Ethics* (1677), but the only one of his works published during his life was *A Treatise on Religious and Political Philosophy* (1670), which was attacked by Christians as an instrument 'forged in hell by a renegade Jew and the devil'. In the century after his death Spinoza was largely ignored as a dangerous atheist, but was rediscovered by **Goethe, Lessing**, and others, and had a major influence on **Hegel**.

> ❝ Virtue is nothing else but action in accordance with the laws of one's own nature. ❞
>
> **Benedict de Spinoza**, *Ethics*

state

Territory that forms its own domestic and foreign policy, acting through laws that are typically decided by a government and carried out, by force if necessary, by agents of that government.

The classic definition of a state is given by R M MacIver in *The Modern State* (1926): 'An association which, acting through law as promulgated by a government endowed to this end with coercive power, maintains within a community territorially demarcated the universal external conditions of social order.' There are four essential elements in this definition:

- That people have formed an association to create and preserve social order.
- That the community comprising the state is clearly defined in territorial terms.
- That the government representing the people acts according to promulgated laws.
- That the government has power to enforce these laws.

It can be argued that growth of regional international bodies such as the European Union means that states no longer enjoy absolute sovereignty. In

addition, the growth of globalization means that considerable power is in the hands of multinational companies, not answerable to any particular state.
See also: *social contract.*

Stoicism
Greek school of philosophy, founded about 300 BC by Zeno of Citium (*c.* 335–262 BC). The name is derived from the porch (Greek *stoa*) in Athens where Zeno taught. The Stoics were pantheistic materialists (see **pantheism; materialism**) who believed that happiness lay in accepting the law of the universe. They believed that the reason behind the organization of the universe should also inform human behaviour. They developed a system of practical ethics, and encouraged a calm acceptance of both good and ill fortune.

The early Stoics emphasized human brotherhood, denounced slavery, and were internationalist. In the 3rd and 2nd centuries BC, Stoics took a prominent part in Greek and Roman revolutionary movements. After the 1st century BC Stoicism became the philosophy of the Roman ruling class and lost its revolutionary significance; instead there was an increasing stress on the importance of duty. Outstanding Stoics of this period were **Seneca**, **Epictetus**, and **Marcus Aurelius.** The ethical approach of Stoicism has continued to be influential. **See also:** *Petrarch.*

> ❦ If you can meet with triumph and disaster
> And treat those two imposters just the same …
> Yours is the Earth and everything that's in it,
> And – which is more – you'll be a Man my son! ❧
>
> **Rudyard Kipling** *'If'*

Strawson, Peter (1919–)
English philosopher who studied the distortions that logical systems impose on ordinary language. He also analysed the ways in which we distinguish individual things, concluding that the location of things in space and time is fundamental to all the various ways in which we distinguish individuals of any kind. He called his approach 'descriptive metaphysics' and he identified **Kant** as a fellow practitioner. **See also:** *language, philosophy of.*

structuralism
20th-century philosophical movement that has influenced such areas as linguistics, anthropology, and literary criticism. Inspired by the work of **Saussure**, structuralists believe that objects should be analysed as systems of relations, rather than as positive entities.

Saussure proposed that language is a system of arbitrary signs, meaning that there is no intrinsic link between the 'signifier' (the sound or mark) and the 'signified' (the concept it represents). Hence any linguistic term can only be defined by its differences from other terms. His ideas were taken further by Roman Jakobson (1896–1982) and the Prague school of linguistics, and were extended into a general method for the social sciences by **Lévi-Strauss**.

Barthes took the lead in applying the ideas of structuralism to literary criticism, arguing that the critic should identify the structures within a text that determine its possible meanings, independently of any reference to the real. This approach is radicalized in Barthes's later work and in the practice of **deconstruction**, pioneered by **Derrida**. Here the text comes to be viewed as a 'decentred' play of structures, lacking any ultimately determinable meaning. **See also:** *postmodernism; poststructuralism; semiology.*

Suárez, Francisco (1548–1617)
Spanish philosopher, considered to be the greatest Jesuit theologian. He tried to reconcile **Aquinas's** view of the Redemption as the final cause of the Incarnation with that of **Duns Scotus**. He also attacked the doctrine of a **divine right of kings**.

subconscious
See *unconscious.*

subject
See *predicate and subject.*

subjective
See *objective and subjective.*

sublime, the
In the arts, the quality of being awe-inspiring or possessing grandeur. In the 18th century it became an aesthetic category, when '**beauty**' no longer seemed adequate to express the spiritual and emotional impact of art or nature. The search for the sublime was apparent in a predilection for wild landscapes in painting, and in the new genre of the Gothic novel. The notion anticipated **Romanticism**.

suicide
The act of intentionally killing oneself. In Classical Greece and Rome it was sometimes thought of as a noble act, as it has traditionally been regarded in Japan. However, Judaism, Christianity, and Islam all condemn it.

Aquinas put forward three arguments against suicide:

- Suicide is contrary to the **natural law**, in that 'everything naturally keeps itself in being'.

- Suicide injures the community to which every person belongs.

- Suicide sins against God, because life is God's gift.

Hume argued that suicide might sometimes be justifiable, either for the good of the individual concerned or of society. Nevertheless, it was not until 1961 that suicide ceased to be a criminal offence in English law. For assisted suicide, **see** *euthanasia.*

superman
See *Nietzsche*.

syllogism
A form of argument using **deduction** devised by **Aristotle** in his work on **logic**. It establishes the conditions under which a valid conclusion follows or does not follow from given **premises**.

A syllogism is made up of three **propositions** (two premises and a conclusion), and has the general structure:

- All *x* are *y*.
- All *y* are z.
- Therefore all *x* are *z*.

The propositions themselves can belong to any of the following 'forms':

- All *x* are y.
- No *x* are y.
- Some *x* are y.
- Some *x* are not y.

The following is an example of a valid syllogism:

- All men are mortal.
- Socrates is a man.
- Therefore Socrates is mortal.

In a valid syllogism, one cannot assert the premises and deny the conclusion. Propositions themselves can be analysed in terms of **predicate** and **subject**.

symbol
See *signs and symbols*.

symbolic logic
See *logic*.

syndicalism
See *Sorel, Georges*.

syntactics
A term with three meanings:

- The branch of grammar that deals with syntax, which is the relationship between words, as opposed to the form of individual words (morphology).
- The branch of mathematics dealing with the number of ways of putting things together, such as permutations, combinations, and so on.
- The branch of **semiology** dealing with the formal relations and properties of signs.

synthetic
Term employed by **Kant** to describe a judgement in which the **predicate** is not contained within the subject. For example, 'The flower is blue' is synthetic, since every flower is not blue. It is the converse of **analytic**.

taste
In art, the ability to judge the quality of a work of art. A person who consistently enjoys the tawdry and the second-rate is said to have 'bad taste' whereas those who admire only the best display 'good taste'. Since taste is nowadays regarded as essentially subjective, the term is useful only as a means of instigating critical debate.

teleology
The view that there is a purpose to, and a design behind, life and the universe (see, for example, **argument from design**). Teleology views developments and changes in organisms or systems as being due to the purposes or design served by them.

This belief that all change is purposive has been very influential in metaphysical thought from **Aristotle** and **Stoicism** in ancient Greece through Christian theology (see **eschatology**) to **Hegel** in the 19th century. A notable example of teleology is the misinterpretation of **Darwinism** by Herbert Spencer and others, who have tried to see evolution as **progress**.

Teleology has been opposed by, among others, **Epicurus**, **Lucretius**, **Descartes**, **Hobbes**, and Francis **Bacon**, all of whom argued that evolution and change are purposeless.

Thales (c. 624–c. 547 BC)
Greek pre-Socratic philosopher and scientist. He lived in Miletus in Asia Minor. He made advances in geometry, predicted an eclipse of the Sun in 585 BC, and, as an advocate of philosophical **materialism**, theorized that water was the first principle of all things. He explained such events as earthquakes in terms of natural phenomena, rather than in the usual terms of activity by the gods. He is also said to have introduced the notion of proof by **deduction**.

THALES AND THE OLIVES

Aristotle records that, when he was reproached for being impractical, Thales, having predicted that weather conditions the next year would be conducive to a large olive harvest, bought up all the olive presses in Miletus and exploited his monopoly to make a large profit.

theism
Belief in the existence of gods, but more specifically in that of a single personal **God**, at once immanent (active) in the created world and transcendent (separate) from it. **See also:** *agnosticism; atheism; deism; pantheism.*

theodicy
In Christian theology, defence of the justice of God and investigation of the problem of **evil**. It is a subdivision of **natural theology**. The term was introduced by **Leibniz** in 1710.

theology
Study of God or gods, either by reasoned deduction from the natural world (**natural theology**) or through divine revelation (revealed theology), as in the scriptures of Christianity, Islam, or other religions. One way or another, theology throughout its history has been influenced by philosophical approaches and methods.

Other branches of theology include:

- Comparative religion (the study of the similarities and differences between faiths).
- **Eschatology** (the study of the hypothetical end of the world and afterlife).
- Exegesis, the critical study of a particular religion's scriptures.
- Historical theology, the study of the evolution of doctrine.

Theological attitudes towards other faiths range from exclusivism (that one's own religion is correct and all the others wrong) to the more modern dialogue theology (promoting awareness of other religions) and relativism (arguing that different religions are separate paths to a similar goal).

See also: *Anselm; Aquinas; argument from design; Augustine; Barth; Buber; Calvinism; cosmological argument; deism; dogma; Erasmus; faith; fideism; free will; Jansenism; Luther; Maimonides; moral argument; neo-Thomism; ontological argument; pantheism; predestination; religion, philosophy of; religion, science, and philosophy; scholasticism; sin; soul; theism; theodicy.*

theorem
Mathematical proposition that can be deduced by logic from a set of **axioms** (basic facts that are taken to be true without proof). Advanced mathematics consists almost entirely of theorems and proofs, but even at a simple level theorems are important.

theory
In science, a set of ideas, concepts, principles, or methods used to explain a wide set of observed facts. Among the major theories of science are

relativity, **quantum mechanics**, and **evolution** (see **Darwinism**). **See also:** *scientific method.*

thing-in-itself

Technical term (German *Ding-an-sich*) in the philosophy of **Kant**, employed to denote the unknowable source of the sensory component of our experience. Later thinkers, including **Fichte** and **Hegel**, denied the coherence of this concept.

thinking and language

Can we think without language? For some kinds of thinking, probably not. Reasoning would generally seem to require language, if we also count formal systems such as symbolic logic and mathematics as 'languages'.

However, induction (reasoning from the particular to the general) would appear not always to require language. For example, a laboratory rat can be trained to generalize from a few happy or unhappy experiences, and presumably does not say to itself in rat language, 'I'd better not touch that yellow button, because all the other yellow buttons I've touched have given me a nasty shock.' Other kinds of thoughts are also language-free, such as thinking of a mountain scene, or running a tune through one's head. **See also:** *perception.*

> ❧ Miditation [sic] is a gift confined to unknown philosophers an' cows. Others don't begin to think till they begin to talk or write. ❧
>
> **Finley Peter Dunne**, *Mr Dooley's Philosophy*

Thomas Aquinas, St

See *Aquinas, St Thomas.*

Thomism

The method and approach of **Thomas Aquinas**. **See also:** *neo-Thomism.*

Thoreau, Henry David (1817–1862)

US author. Like his friend **Emerson**, he was a proponent of **transcendentalism**, and his vigorous defence of **individualism** was highly influential. His famous *Walden, or Life in the Woods* (1854), based on his two-year experiment living the simple life by Walden Pond, stimulated the back-to-nature movement. His essay 'Civil Disobedience' (1849), prompted by his refusal to pay taxes, advocated peaceful resistance to unjust laws, and has continued to have a wide impact.

> ❝ Every man is the builder of a temple, called his body, to the god he worships ... We are all sculptors and painters, and our material is our own flesh and blood and bones. ❞
>
> **Henry David Thoreau**, *Walden*, 'Higher Laws'

thought experiments

Imagined scenarios used by philosophers and scientists to explore various concepts. Examples include the 'Chinese room' (see *artificial intelligence*), 'Schrödinger's cat' (an illustration of the **uncertainty principle** in which a cat is both dead and alive until someone looks at it), the twin experiment (see **time**), and various gruesome situations in which brains are transplanted into other bodies to test the idea of **self**, personal identity, and so on.

time

The continuous passage of existence, conventionally recorded by division into hours, minutes, and seconds. Time is the dimension in which **change** takes place. It moves in one direction, in that some processes, such as death and decay, are irreversible.

Relative time

It was long thought by scientists that time was absolute, uniform in the rate of its passage, and measurable separately from three-dimensional space. But the theory of relativity shows that time is not absolute. At speeds approaching that of light (**relative** to the observer), time is significantly dilated. Time becomes part of the four-dimensional **space-time** continuum, which is distorted by the presence of material bodies, an effect that we observe as gravity. Thus time can no longer be measured separately from space.

The experience of time

Our own experience of time is often subjective. If we have little to do, time can seem to run much more slowly than when we are busy. Then there is the question of 'now'. The present instant is always infinitely small, yet we do not experience it in this way. Our **consciousness** is always aware of the presence of the past (via **memory**), and is constantly anticipating the future. This is part of what constitutes our sense of personal identity. In addition, the whole way that we think and act is rooted in the notion of **causality**, the awareness of one thing leading to another in the course of time.

TIME TRAVEL?

According to relativity, if one twin were to travel from Earth in a very fast spaceship, and returned some time later, he would have aged less than his Earth-bound twin. Travelling back in time is also theoretically possible. The question arises as to whether someone travelling back in time can change the future, for example, by killing his or her own grandparents. This seems logically impossible, but the time traveller may affect the future, for example by introducing his grandfather to his grandmother prior to their marriage.

toleration

The acceptance of other people's views, values, and beliefs. It is usually grounded in **relativism**, the view that there is no absolute truth. Historically in Europe, toleration for long meant toleration of other people's religions. The issue became a burning one (literally) from the time of the Reformation. It was advocated by the thinkers of the **Enlightenment**, but it was not until the 19th century that religious toleration became widespread. Toleration is a major component of **liberalism**, and **civil liberties** are now largely con-

The Massacre of St Bartholomew, the slaughter of Huguenots (Protestants) in France in 1572. About 25,000 people are believed to have been killed.

sidered as extending to toleration of race, ethnicity, gender, and sexual orientation. **See also:** *freedom.*

> ❧ I disapprove of what you say, but I will defend to the death your right to say it. ❧
>
> **Voltaire**, attributed remark

transcendentalism

Philosophy inaugurated in the 18th century by **Kant**. As opposed to metaphysics in the traditional sense, transcendental philosophy is concerned with the conditions of possibility of experience, rather than the nature of being. It seeks to show the necessary structure of our 'point of view' on the world. The nature of experience depends on the processes of reason, and only by critically examining these can we attain knowledge of the nature of reality. Introduced to Britain, transcendentalism influenced the writers Samuel Taylor Coleridge and Thomas Carlyle.

NEW ENGLAND TRANSCENDENTALISM

The 'New England Transcendentalists', who included **Emerson** and **Thoreau**, believed in the unity of nature, the inborn goodness of humanity, and the value of intuition as the path to knowledge, and in deciding moral issues. They were influenced by Coleridge's and Carlyle's versions of Kant, and also by **neo-Platonism**, and various mystical writers such as Jakob **Boehme**.

---

truth

The question 'What is truth?' is one that has engaged philosophers from the time of the ancient Greeks. It is one that is associated with questions as to what constitutes **belief, certainty**, and **knowledge**.

- Truth may be objective or subjective (see **objective and subjective**).
- Some have asserted that there are absolute truths, others that truth can only ever be relative (compare **absolutism** and **relativism**).
- Some argue that truth only comes through **a priori** reasoning, while others argue that truth can be gleaned from experience (compare **rationalism** and **empiricism**, and also **deduction** and **induction**).

Logic provides certain rules for establishing the truth or falsehood of a statement or proposition. The traditional tool is the **syllogism**, but in formal or symbolic logic there is propositional calculus and predicate calculus (see **proposition** and **predicate and subject**). Philosophers of language have examined the relationships between truth and meaning (see **language, philosophy of** and **liar paradox**). **See also:** *verifiability*.

Philosophers have also examined the notion of truth in terms of the relations between propositions and other things.

- In the 'correspondence theory', the truth or falsity of a proposition depends on it having a relation of correspondence with a fact. The theory verges on tautology, and has been criticized for its circularity.

- In the 'coherence theory', the truth or falsity of proposition depends on it having a relation of coherence or consistency with other propositions. This theory has been criticized for its relativism.

- In the 'pragmatic theory', the truth of an idea is tested by how *useful* it is in dealing with the world, for example in predicting (see **pragmatism** and **instrumentalism**), but this is still a form of relativism.

> ❝ There is no permanent absolute unchangeable truth; what we should pursue is the most convenient arrangement of our ideas. ❞
>
> **Samuel Butler**, *Note-Books*

Turing, Alan (1912–1954)

English mathematician and logician. In 1936 he described a 'universal computing machine' that could theoretically be programmed to solve any problem capable of solution by an algorithm. This concept, now called the 'Turing machine', foreshadowed the digital computer. He is believed to have been the first to suggest (in 1950) the possibility of machine learning, and devised the 'Turing test' for **artificial intelligence**.

During World War II, Turing was a leading figure in the Ultra project that cracked the German Enigma cipher, so giving the Allies an immense military advantage.

übermensch
See *Nietzsche*.

uncertainty principle or indeterminacy principle
In **quantum mechanics**, the principle that it is impossible to know with unlimited accuracy both the position and momentum of a particle; the more accurately the one is determined, the more uncertainty there is in the other. The principle also applies to other pairs, such as time and energy. The principle was established by German physicist Werner Heisenberg (1901–76), and has undermined both the notion of **causality** and the view that the **scientific method** can be completely objective.

> ❝ Heisenberg probably rules OK. ❞
>
> **Graffito**, London, early 1970s

unconscious
In **psychoanalysis**, a reservoir within one's mental state that contains elements and experiences of which one is unaware, but which may to some extent be brought into preconscious and conscious awareness, or inferred from aspects of behaviour.

A related concept in psychoanalysis is that of 'resistance', a process by which unconscious elements are forcibly kept out of the conscious awareness by an active repressive force. Psychoanalysis places much importance on the influence of painful and unpleasant experiences that, although forgotten, continue to have a detrimental influence on the mind.

> ❝ My unconscious knows more about the consciousness of the psychologist than his consciousness knows about my unconscious. ❞
>
> **Karl Kraus**, in *Die Fackel*, 18 January 1917

universal
In philosophy, a property that is instantiated by all the individual things of a specific class: for example, all red things instantiate 'redness'. Many

philosophical debates have centred on the status of universals, including the medieval debate between **nominalism** and **realism**. **See also:** *essence; form.*

utilitarianism

Theory of ethics outlined by Jeremy **Bentham** and developed by J S **Mill**. According to utilitarianism, an action is morally right if it has consequences that lead to happiness, and wrong if it brings about the reverse. Thus society should aim for the greatest happiness of the greatest number. The theory has been very influential, particularly in social policy.

Utilitarianism has been criticized by some moral philosophers for equating the good (a moral term) with a descriptive term (**happiness**), regarded as an example of the naturalistic fallacy (see **is/ought problem**). It has been criticized by others for identifying the rightness of an action with the good that results from it (see **right, the**). **See also:** *consequentialism; ends and means; felicific calculus; punishment.*

utopianism

The wish or attempt to create an ideal social and political system. The term originates from Sir Thomas Moore's book *Utopia* (1516), which pictured a perfect society in order to satirize the shortcomings of existing institutions. Many thinkers have drawn up outlines of the ideal society (see **political theory**).

Attempts at creating utopian communities have often taken the form of communes. In the early 19th century cooperative communities were suggested by, for example, the French socialist François Fourier and attempted by Robert Owen in Scotland and the USA. Henri de Saint-Simon also had utopian ideas, as in *New Christianity* (1825).

CRITICS OF UTOPIA

Utopia is the Greek word for 'nowhere', and utopianism has often carried the connotation of impossibility. **Socialism, communism**, and **anarchism** have all been criticized for their utopianism in this sense, largely by those who hold a negative view of **human nature** (as in **conservatism**). Others believe that utopian ideologies tend to result in totalitarianism (the view of **liberalism**). The latter category includes writers who have imagined 'dystopias' (the reverse of a utopia), such as Aldous Huxley in *Brave New World* (1932) and George Orwell in *Nineteen Eighty Four* (1949).

validity

In logic, a property of inferences or arguments, which are valid if the conclusion follows necessarily (by **deduction**) from the premises, as in a **syllogism**. The premises may be false, but if they are true the conclusion must be true.

value

The property of something that attracts commendation, or that makes it desirable.

- In ethics, value is often associated with the **good** or the **right**. Some moral philosophers think of it as an intrinsic property of actions, while others think it measurable only in terms of outcomes. The value of life, both as an absolute in itself, and in terms of its quality, is also variously discussed (see **life, meaning of** and **violence**).

- In aesthetics, value is often associated with **beauty**, or some other aesthetic property. Traditionally the main argument has been between those who believe in some kind of objective value, and those who believe value in art is subjective.

- In economics, the theory of value is of central importance. The 18th-century Scottish economist Adam Smith distinguished between value in use or utility, and value in exchange. Smith and other classical economists regarded the value in exchange as related to the labour required to produce the product. Karl **Marx** also developed the labour theory of value. In neoclassical economics, value is simply the price a product can command in the market.

> ❛ [A cynic] A man who knows the price of everything and the value of nothing. ❜
>
> **Oscar Wilde**, Lady Windermere's Fan

value judgement

Assessment involving some moral, aesthetic, ideological, or theoretical interpretation of superiority or inferiority. There are long-standing debates about whether value judgements, especially in ethics, can ever be objective. Discussion continues about whether the social sciences can be free of value judgements – and, if so, whether this means that objective truth is impossible in the social sciences. Similar questions have also been asked about the physical sciences (see **science, philosophy of**). **See also:** *is/ought problem; naturalism; taste.*

verifiability

In logic and philosophy, the feature of a **proposition** that enables us to check that it is true. A verifiable proposition has to be **contingent**; that is, it must be possible that it is false.

In the 20th century, adherents of **logical positivism** and **empiricism**, seeking to dismiss metaphysics and theology as nonsense, made verifiability into a theory of meaning that requires meaningful propositions to have a method of verification. Since few statements are conclusively verifiable, A J **Ayer** and others sought to defend 'weak' verifiability in which provision of evidence would suffice. **See also:** *language, philosophy of.*

Vico, Giambattista (1668–1744)

Italian philosopher, considered the founder of the modern philosophy of **history**. His cyclical theory of history was put forward in *New Science* (1725). Vico argued that we can understand history more adequately than nature, since it is we who have made it. He believed that the study of language, ritual, and myth is a way of understanding earlier societies – a departure from the traditional ways of conceiving of history either as a collection of biographies or as preordained by God's will.

VICO'S CYCLE OF HISTORY

Vico postulated that society passes through a cycle of four phases:
- The divine, or theocratic, when people are governed by their awe of the supernatural.
- The aristocratic, or 'heroic' (as exemplified in Homer and *Beowulf*).
- The democratic and individualistic.
- Chaos, a fall into confusion that startles people back into supernatural reverence.

Vienna Circle

Group of philosophers in Vienna, Austria, in the 1920s and 1930s, who advocated **logical positivism**. The group, which was highly influential, included Rudolf **Carnap**, and centred on Moritz **Schlick**, professor of philosophy at the University of Vienna, and dispersed after he was assassinated in 1936.

violence

Is violence, including killing, ever justified? Adherents of radical pacifism would say no, in all circumstances. But there are a range of contexts in which violence occurs, from violence between individuals to violent punishment, and from an uprising against an oppressive regime to war between states. In these different contexts, a range of arguments have been proffered.

Violence and the law

In most societies, violence perpetrated by one individual against another individual is generally condemned by the law, and punished. However, self-defence, if limited to 'reasonable force', is often regarded as a mitigating circumstance. Some forms of violence, notably violent sports such as boxing, are legal in many countries, although subject to tight regulation.

Issues such as abortion and euthanasia are variously interpreted, the arguments often taking the form of a dispute between ideas of individual rights and ideas such as the 'sanctity of life'. For issues relating to corporal and capital punishment, see punishment. **See also:** *law, philosophy of.*

Political violence

Various political theorists have discussed the right of citizens to change their government, by force if no other option is open, if the government breaches the social contract. For Locke, such an occasion arises when the government fails to uphold the rights of the citizens, and this argument was used by both the American and French revolutionaries. For Marx and his followers, the revolutionary overthrow of capitalism is not only desirable, but inevitable.

Some Marxists have deployed the concept of the 'structural violence' of the state to justify armed resistance or revolution; such structural violence is seen as implicit in state institutions, such as police and armed forces, used to maintain social injustice, itself regarded as a form of violence.

See also: *war.*

> ❝ Civilization is nothing more than the effort to reduce the use of force to the last resort. ❞
>
> **José Ortega y Gasset**, *Revolt of the Masses*

virtue

Originally, ability or efficiency, often involving moral worth. In classical Greek it is used especially to refer to 'manly' qualities. Christian teaching distinguishes the 'cardinal virtues' of prudence, temperance, fortitude, and justice, from the 'theological virtues' of faith, hope, and love (or charity), which St Paul gives as the basis of Christian life. **See also:** *good; right, the; sin.*

vitalism

The idea that living organisms derive their characteristic properties from a universal life force. This view is associated particularly with **Bergson**.

volition

In philosophical psychology and the philosophy of mind, the act of willing. Different interpretations of volition are offered in relation to the **mind–body problem**:

- Philosophers who hold that mind and body are different substances (dualists) tend to hold that volitions cause actions.
- Those who hold that mind and body are fundamentally one substance (monists) tend to hold that volitions are inseparable from actions.

See also: *free will.*

Voltaire (1694–1778)

Pen name of François-Marie Arouet, French philosopher and writer. One of the *Philosophes*, he is often regarded as the embodiment of the **Enlightenment**, and was one of the *Encyclopédistes*. He wrote histories, books of political analysis and philosophy, essays on science and literature, plays, poetry, and the satirical fable *Candide* (1759), his best-known work. He was a leading proponent of **deism**.

Voltaire's *Lettres philosophiques/Philosophical Letters* (1733) are essays in favour of English ways, thought, and political practice, particularly in relation to religious and political toleration. In *Candide*, as well as satirizing social and political evils, Voltaire mocks the philosophical position of **Leibniz** that this is 'the best of all **possible worlds**'.

Voltaire and his circle.

Voltaire's other works include the satirical tale *Zadig* (1748) and *Dictionnaire philosophique/Philosophical Dictionary* (1764). He was often forced to flee from his enemies and was twice imprisoned. From 1751 to 1753 he stayed at the court of Frederick the Great of Prussia, who had long been an admirer, but the association ended in deep enmity.

> ❝ People use thought only to justify their injustices, and they use words only to disguise their thoughts. ❞
>
> **Voltaire**, *'Dialogue du Chapon ed de la Poularde'*

war

War has been supplied with a variety of justifications. The theory of 'just war' was first developed by the Catholic Church in the Middle Ages. Christians were expected to be the defenders, not the aggressors, and have just cause for action. Only a legitimate authority could undertake war.

The defensive criterion has continued to be used, and the violent infringement of another state's sovereignty has often been regarded as a justification for the military intervention of third parties. Religion, ideology, ethnic 'superiority', and the defence of the state against internal revolt or secession have also often been cited as 'just causes'. Such causes have often led to the bloodiest of conflicts, as the violence often extends to civilians on a major scale.

Increasingly the international community regards large-scale violence against civilians as a justification for third-party military intervention on humanitarian grounds. However, sceptics point out that such interventions occur inconsistently, and sometimes suspect underlying motives of self-interest.

See also: *pacifism; violence.*

Warnock, Mary (1924–)

English philosopher and educationist. In philosophy she has written on the ethics of **existentialism**, and on topics such as memory and imagination. She is known to a wider public through her participation in a number of important committees of inquiry, including issues relating to **science and ethics**, such as animal experiments and human fertilization and embryology.

Watson, J(ohn) B(roadus)

See *behaviourism.*

Weber, Max (1864–1920)

German sociologist, one of the founders of modern sociology. He emphasized cultural and political factors as key influences on economic development and individual behaviour. Weber argued for a scientific and value-free approach to sociological research (see value **judgement** and sci-ence, philosophy of**), yet highlighted the importance of meaning and consciousness in understanding social action. His ideas continue to stimulate thought on social stratification, power, organizations, law, and religion.

Whitehead, A(lfred) N(orth) (1861–1947)

English philosopher and mathematician. Whitehead collaborated with Bertrand **Russell** on *Principia Mathematica* (1910–13) in which, inspired by the work of **Peano**, they attempted to deduce mathematics from logic in a general and fundamental way. He went on deal with the philosophy of science in such works as *Principles of Natural Knowledge* (1919) and *The Concept of Nature* (1920), and later turned to metaphysics, in such works as *Science and the Modern World* (1925) and *Process and Reality* (1929).

> ❢ It is a safe rule to apply that, when a mathematical or philosophical author writes with a misty profundity, he is talking nonsense. ❣
>
> **A N Whitehead**, *An Introduction to Mathematics*

will
See *free will; volition; Nietzsche; Schopenhauer.*

William of Occam
See *Occam, William of.*

wisdom
Intellectual and moral understanding applied to the way one lives and acts. The word 'philosophy' itself is derived from the Greek for 'love of wisdom'.

- For Plato, knowledge of the **Forms** would produce wise rulers in the form of philosopher-kings.
- **Aristotle** held that **happiness** or self-fulfilment lies in the use of reason, both in thought and as a guide to virtuous living.
- **Stoicism** advocated that we accept all that occurs with equanimity.

The **Cyrenaics, Epicureanism**, and the **Cynics** also had practical advice to give on the wisest ways to lead one's life, but since Classical times Western philosophy has tended to avoid the question.

> ❢ Knowledge is proud that he has learn'd so much;
> Wisdom is humble that he knows no more. ❣
>
> **William Cowper**, *The Task*

Wittgenstein, Ludwig (1889–1951)
Austrian philosopher, one of the most influential on English-speaking philosophers in the 20th century, particularly in relation to the philosophy of **language**. He was born in Vienna, where he trained as an engineer, then studied at Cambridge, where Bertrand **Russell** was one of his teachers, and where he himself taught in the 1930s and 1940s.

Wittgenstein's *Tractatus Logico-Philosophicus* (1922) postulated the 'picture theory' of language: that words represent things according to established conventions. He held that it must be possible to break down a sentence into 'atomic propositions' whose elements stand for elements of the real world (see **logical atomism**).

Wittgenstein subsequently rejected the picture theory, and developed the quite different idea that usage was more important than convention. In this later anthropological view of language, words are used according to different rules in a variety of human activities – different 'language games' are played with them. The traditional philosophical problems arise through the assumption that words (like 'exist' in the sentence 'Physical objects do not really exist') carry a fixed meaning with them, independent of context. His work from this later period, notably *Philosophical Investigations* (1953), was published posthumously.

> ❝ My German engineer, I think is a fool. He thinks nothing empirical is knowable – I asked him to admit that there was not a rhinoceros in the room, but he wouldn't. ❞
>
> **Bertrand Russell**, on Ludwig Wittgenstein, in a letter, 1911

WITTGENSTEIN THE APHORIST

Wittgenstein's Tractatus is famous for its aphorisms, including:

- 'Everything that can be said can be said clearly.'
- 'It is not how things are in the world that is mystical, but that it exists.'
- 'The limits of my language mean the limits of my world.'
- 'The world is everything that is the case.'
- 'Whereof one cannot speak, thereof one must be silent.'

Wollstonecraft, Mary (1759–1797)

British writer, a pioneer of feminism. She was a member of a group of radical intellectuals called the English Jacobins. Her book *A Vindication of the Rights of Women* (1792) demanded equal educational opportunities for women. She married William **Godwin** in 1797 and died giving birth to a daughter, Mary (later Mary Shelley).

> ❝ I do not wish them [women] to have power over men; but over themselves. ❞
>
> **Mary Wollstonecraft**, *Vindication of the Rights of Woman*

Xenophanes (*c.* 560–*c.* 470 BC)

Greek poet and pre-Socratic philosopher. He attacked the immoral and humanlike gods depicted by the poet Homer, holding that there is only one deity, 'in no way like men in body or in thought'. He speculated that stars were ignited clouds, and that everything was mud since fossils of sea creatures were found inland. His outlook was generally undogmatic, because 'seeming is wrought over all things'. Considerable fragments of his elegies and of his poem *On Nature* have survived.

Zeno of Citium (*c.* 335–262 BC)

Greek founder of the Stoic school of philosophy in Athens, about 300 BC. *See* **Stoicism**.

Zeno of Elea (*c.* 490–*c.* 430 BC)

Greek pre-Socratic philosopher of the **Eleatic School**. He pointed out several paradoxes that raised 'modern' problems of space and time. For example, motion is an illusion, since an arrow in flight must occupy a determinate space at each instant, and therefore must be at rest. Another example is the **Achilles paradox**.

❝ What is moving is moving neither in the place in which it is nor in the place in which it is not. ❞

Zeno of Elea, quoted in Diogenes Laertius, *Lives of the Philosophers*

Appendix

CHRONOLOGICAL LIST OF PHILOSOPHERS

Particularly major figures are in capital letters.

c. 624–c. 547 BC	Thales
c. 610–c. 546 BC	Anaximander
died c. 528 BC	Anaximenes
c. 580–500 BC	Pythagoras
c. 560–c. 470 BC	Xenophanes
c. 544–c. 483 BC	Heraclitus
c. 510–450 BC	Parmenides
c. 500–428 BC	Anaxagoras
c. 493–433 BC	Empedocles
5th century BC	Leucippus
c. 490–c. 430 BC	Zeno of Elea
c. 485–415 BC	Protagoras
c. 469–399 BC	SOCRATES
c. 460–c. 370 BC	Democritus
c. 444–c. 366 BC	Antisthenes
c. 435–356 BC	Aristippus
c. 427–347 BC	PLATO
c. 412–c. 323 BC	Diogenes the Cynic
c. 410–337 BC	Speusippus; succeeded Plato as head of the Academy
396–314 BC	Xenocrates; head of the Academy
384–322 BC	ARISTOTLE
c. 360–c. 270 BC	Pyrrho, founder of scepticism
341–270 BC	Epicurus
c. 335–262 BC	Zeno of Citium; founder of Stoicism
c. 315–248 BC	Arcesilaus, head of the Academy
c. 280–207 BC	Chrysippus, head of the school of Stoicism in Athens
214–129 BC	Carneades, head of the Academy
c. 130–c. 68 BC	Antiochus of Ascalon, exponent of Platonism
106–43 BC	Cicero
c. 99–55 BC	Lucretius
c. 4 BC–AD 65	Seneca
1st century AD	Philo Judaeus
c. AD 55–135	Epictetus
2nd century AD	Celsus; adherent of Platonism, later attacked by Origen
121–180	Marcus Aurelius
c. 160–c. 210 AD	Sextus Empiricus
c. 185–c. 254	Origen
205–270	Plotinus
3rd century AD	Diogenes Laertius
216–276	Mani, founder of Manichaeism
c. 232–c. 305	Porphyry; edited works of Plotinus, and wrote commentaries on Plato and Aristotle
c. 250–c. 325	Iamblichus; exponent of neo-Platonism
354–430	St Augustine of Hippo
c. 360–c. 420	Pelagius
c. 370–c. 415	Hypatia
c. 410–485	Proclus
480–524	Boethius
c. 490–c. 570	Philoponus; attacked Aristotelian science from Christian standpoint
9th century	al-Kindi
c. 815–c. 877	Erigena
c. 870–950	al-Farabi
979–1037	Avicenna
c. 1020–c. 1057	Ibn Gabirol
c. 1033–1109	St Anselm of Canterbury
c. 1050–c. 1122	Roscellinus; one of the founders of scholasticism
1079–1142	Peter Abelard

c. 1080–1140	Judah Halevi	1632–1704	John LOCKE
1126–1198	Averroës	1638–1715	Nicolas Malebranche
1135–1204	Moses Maimonides	1642–1727	Newton
c. 1169–1253	Robert Grosseteste	1646–1716	LEIBNIZ
c. 1170–1245	Alexander of Hales; exponent of scholasticism	1647–1706	Pierre Bayle
		1668–1744	Giambattista Vico
1200–1280	Albertus Magnus	1670–1772	John Toland; advocate of deism, then pantheism
c. 1214–1294	Roger Bacon		
1225–1274	St Thomas AQUINAS	1671–1713	Earl of Shaftesbury
c. 1265–c. 1308	Duns Scotus	1675–1729	Samuel Clarke; debated with Leibniz
1265–1321	Dante		
c. 1297–c. 1358	Jean Buridan; scholastic philosopher	1685–1753	BERKELEY
		1689–1755	Montesquieu
c. 1300–1349	William of Occam	1694–1746	Francis Hutcheson
1304–1374	Petrarch	1694–1778	VOLTAIRE
1401–1464	Nicholas of Cusa	1703–1758	Jonathan Edwards; upheld Calvinist version of predestination
c. 1407–1457	Lorenzo Valla; advanced Renaissance humanism		
1433–1499	Marsilio Ficino	1710–1796	Thomas Reid
1462–1525	Pietro Pomponazzi	1711–1776	David HUME
1463–1494	Pico della Mirandola	1712–1778	ROUSSEAU
1469–1527	Machiavelli	1713–1784	Diderot
c. 1469–1536	Erasmus	1715–1771	Claude Adrien Helvetius; his ideas anticipated utilitarianism
1483–1546	Luther		
1509–1564	John Calvin; founder of Calvinism		
		1715–1780	Etienne Bonnot de Condillac; Encyclopédiste
1530–1596	Jean Bodin		
1533–1592	Montaigne	1717–1783	Jean le Rond d'Alembert; mathematician and Encyclopédiste
1548–1600	Giordano Bruno		
1548–1617	Francisco Sua{acute}rez		
1561–1626	Francis Bacon	1723–1791	Richard Price; argued against naturalism in ethics
1564–1642	Galileo		
1575–1624	Jakob Boehme	1723–1789	Baron d'Holbach; atheist philosopher of the Enlightenment
1583–1645	Hugo Grotius		
1583–1648	Herbert of Cherbury; early advocate of deism		
		1724–1804	KANT
1585–1638	Cornelius Jansen, founder of Jansenism	1729–1781	Gotthold Lessing
		1729–1786	Moses Mendelssohn
1588–1679	Thomas HOBBES	1729–1797	Edmund Burke
1592–1655	Pierre Gassendi; revived atomism of Democritus and Lucretius	1737–1809	Thomas Paine
		1743–1826	Thomas Jefferson
		1744–1803	Johann Gottfried von Herder; held the belief that thinking and language are inseparable
1596–1650	DESCARTES		
1617–1688	Ralph Cudworth; leading member of the Cambridge Platonists		
		1748–1832	Jeremy BENTHAM
1623–1662	Pascal	1749–1832	Goethe
c. 1625–1669	Arnold Geulincx	1756–1836	William Godwin
1632–1677	SPINOZA	1759–1797	Mary Wollstonecraft

1759–1805	Schiller	1856–1939	FREUD
1760–1825	Saint-Simon	1857–1913	Ferdinand de SAUSSURE
1762–1814	Fichte	1858–1917	Emile Durkheim
1766–1824	Maine de Biran; argued that the will is the source of human freedom	1858–1932	Giuseppe Peano
		1859–1938	HUSSERL
		1859–1941	Bergson
1770–1831	HEGEL	1859–1952	John Dewey
1773–1836	Mill, James; advocate of utilitarianism, and father of J S Mill	1861–1916	Pierre Duhem; physicist and philosopher of science
		1861–1947	A N Whitehead
1775–1854	Friedrich Schelling	1862–1943	David Hilbert
1788–1856	William Hamilton	1863–1952	Santayana
1788–1860	SCHOPENHAUER	1864–1920	Max Weber
1798–1857	Auguste Comte	1866–1925	John McTaggart Ellis McTaggart; neo-Hegelian exponent of idealism
1803–1882	Emerson		
1804–1872	Ludwig Feuerbach		
1806–1871	Augustus De Morgan	1866–1952	Benedetto Croce
1806–1873	J S MILL	1869–1948	Gandhi
1809–1865	Pierre-Joseph Proudhon	1870–1924	Lenin
1813–1855	KIERKEGAARD	1872–1970	Bertrand RUSSELL
1814–1876	Bakunin	1873–1958	G E MOORE
1815–1864	George Boole	1874–1945	Ernst Cassirer; exponent of neo-Kantianism
1817–1862	Thoreau		
1818–1883	MARX	1875–1944	Giovanni Gentile
1820–1895	Engels	1875–1961	Jung
1820–1903	Herbert Spencer	1878–1965	Martin Buber
1833–1911	Wilhelm Dilthey	1881–1966	L E J Brouwer
1836–1882	Thomas Hill Green; follower of Kant and Hegel	1882–1936	Moritz Schlick
		1882–1945	Otto Neurath; member of Vienna Circle
1838–1900	Henry Sidgwick		
1838–1916	Franz Brentano	1882–1973	Jacques Maritain
1838–1916	Ernst Mach	1883–1955	José Ortega y Gasset
1839–1914	C S PEIRCE	1883–1969	Karl Jaspers
1842–1910	William James	1884–1962	Gaston Bachelard
1842–1918	Hermann Cohen; leading figure of neo-Kantianism	1884–1978	Etienne Gilson; exponent of neo-Thomism
1842–1921	Kropotkin	1885–1971	Georg Lukács
1844–1900	NIETZSCHE	1886–1968	Karl Barth
1845–1918	Georg Cantor	1889–1943	R G Collingwood
1846–1924	F H Bradley	1889–1951	WITTGENSTEIN
1847–1922	Georges Sorel	1889–1973	Gabriel Marcel
1848–1923	Bernard Bosanquet	1889–1976	HEIDEGGER
1848–1925	Gottlob Frege	1891–1937	Antonio Gramsci
1853–1920	Alexius Meinong; his philosophical psychology influenced Moore and Russell	1891–1953	Hans Reichenbach; developed 'logical empiricism' to broaden logical positivism
1855–1916	Josiah Royce; advocate of absolute idealism	1891–1970	Rudolf Carnap
		1892–1940	Walter Benjamin

1895–1985	Suzanne Langer	1913–1960	Albert Camus
1898–1979	Marcuse	1914–	Stuart Hampshire
1899–1992	Friedrich Hayek	1915–1980	Roland BARTHES
1900–	Hans-Georg Gadamer; hermeneutic philosopher	1917–	Donald Davidson; theorist of mind and language
1900–1976	Gilbert Ryle	1918–1990	Louis Althusser
1901–1981	Lacan	1919–	Richard M Hare; influential
1902–1994	Karl Popper		moral philosopher
1903–1969	Theodor Adorno	1919–	Peter Strawson
1905–1980	SARTRE	1921–	John Rawls
1906–	Nelson Goodman; originator of Goodman's paradox	1922–1996	Thomas Kuhn
		1924–	Mary Warnock
1906–	Emmanuel Levinas; extended phenomenology to ethics	1924–1994	Paul K Feyerabend; sceptical philosopher of science
1906–1975	Hannah Arendt	1924–1998	Jean François Lyotard
1906–1978	Kurt Gödel	1925–	Gilles Deleuze; exponent of
1907–1991	Gregory Vlastos; proponent of a radical egalitarianism		poststructuralism
		1925–	Michael Dummet; opponent
1908–	Lévi-Strauss		of realism
1908–	Quine	1926–1984	Michel Foucault
1908–1961	Merleau-Ponty	1928–	Noam CHOMSKY
1908–1986	Simone de Beauvoir	1929–	Jean Baudrillard
1909–1943	Simone Weil; political activist and mystic; proponent of Christian Platonism	1929–	Jürgen Habermas
		1930–	DERRIDA
		1932–	Umberto Eco
		1932–	John R Searle; influential philosopher of language and mind
1909–1997	Isaiah Berlin		
1910–1989	A J Ayer		
1911–1960	J L Austin	1938–	Robert Nozick
1912–1954	Alan Turing	1941–	Julia Kristeva; feminist and
1913–	Paul Ricoeur; attempted to resolve differences in linguistic, hermeneutic, and critical-theory approaches		semiologist
		1944–	Roger Scruton

SIGNIFICANT EVENTS IN THE HISTORY OF PHILOSOPHY

6th century BC	Beginning of pre-Socratic philosophy	later 5th century BC	Socrates teaching in Athens
	Beginnings of philosophical materialism	c. 400 BC	Foundation of Cynic and Cyrenaic schools
	Beginnings of democracy in ancient Athens	c. 387 BC	Plato founds his Academy
		355 BC	Aristotle founds the 'peripatetic school' at the Lyceum in Athens
mid-6th century	Foundation of school at Croton by Pythagoras	later 4th century BC	Foundation of scepticism and Epicureanism
early 5th century BC	Eleatic School	c. 300 BC	Foundation of Stoicism
5th century BC	Sophists	3rd–1st centuries BC	Greek schools continue to flourish

79 BC	Closure of Academy in Athens
1st century AD	Philo Judaeus attempts to reconcile Judaism with Platonism and Stoicism
	Stoicism becomes philosophy of Roman ruling class
	Origins of hermeticism.
2nd century AD	Beginnings of Gnosticism
3rd century AD	Beginning of neo-Platonism and Manichaeism
4th century AD	Revival of Academy
4th–5th century	Christian theology developed by St Augustine
529	Closure of Academy and other pagan schools by Emperor Justinian
9th century	Islamic scholars begin to study and preserve ancient Greek philosophy
	Erigena attempts to reconcile Christianity with neo-Platonism
11th–14th centuries	Scholasticism attempts to incorporate Aristotelianism into Christian doctrine
late 11th century	Beginning of debate between nominalism and realism
	Origin of ontological argument
13th–16th centuries	Kabbalistic writing at its height (see kabbala)
13th century	Experimental science developed by Roger Bacon
1259–64	Aquinas, *Summa contra gentiles*; argues that reason and faith are compatible
1306–08	Dante, *The Banquet*
early 14th century	Principle of 'Occam's razor'
mid-14th century	Beginnings of Renaissance humanism in work of Petrarch and others
1462	Foundation of Platonic Academy in Florence
1511	Erasmus, *The Praise of Folly*
1513	Machiavelli, *The Prince*
1516	Thomas More, *Utopia*
1517	Luther initiates Protestant Reformation

1543	Copernicus, *De revolutionibus orbium coelestium*; demonstrates how Earth orbits the Sun, and initiates Scientific Revolution
1580–88	Montaigne, *Essais*
1605	Francis Bacon, *The Advancement of Learning*
1620s	Origins of deism
1632	Galileo, *Dialogues on the Two Chief Systems of the World*
1637	Descartes, *Discourse on Method*
1641	Descartes, *Meditations on the First Philosophy*
mid-17th century	Cambridge Platonists
1651	Hobbes, *Leviathan*; origin of social contract theory
1677	Posthumous publication of Spinoza, *Ethics*
1680	Sir Robert Filmer, *Patriarcha*; espouses the divine right of kings
1687	Newton, *Principia*
1690	Locke, *Essay Concerning Human Understanding*
	Locke, *Two Treatises on Government*
c. 1690–1790	The Enlightenment
c. 1710	Beginnings of idealism in early work of Berkeley
1714	Leibniz, *The Monadology*
1725	Vico, *New Science*; origin of modern philosophy of history
1733	Voltaire, *Philosophical Letters*; introduces ideas of Locke and Newton to France
1739–40	Hume, *Treatise of Human Nature*
1748	Montesquieu, *The Spirit of the Laws*
1751	Hume, *Enquiry Concerning the Principles of Morals*
1751–77	The Encyclopédistes at work
1759	Voltaire, *Candide*
1762	Rousseau, *Social Contract*
1776	American Declaration of Independence influenced by Enlightenment ideas
1780	Bentham, *Principles of Morals*

	and Legislation (published 1789); lays foundation of utilitarianism
late 18th century	Origins of modern socialism
1781	Kant, *Critique of Pure Reason*
1788	Kant, *Critique of Practical Reason*
1789	French Revolutionaries influenced by Enlightenment ideas
c. 1790	Beginnings of modern conservatism in writings of Edmund Burke
1790	Kant, *Critique of Judgement*
late 18th century	Beginnings of Romanticism
1791	Paine, *The Rights of Man*
1792	Wollstonecraft, *A Vindication of the Rights of Women* marks beginning of modern feminism.
1793	Godwin, *Enquiry Concerning Political Justice*; founds modern theory of anarchism
c. 1800	Nationalism begins to spread in Europe
1807	Hegel, *The Phenomenology of Mind*
1817	Hegel, *Encyclopedia of the Philosophical Sciences*
1818	Schopenhauer, *The World as Will and Idea*
1821	Hegel, *The Philosophy of Right* Saint-Simon, *The Industrial System*; early text of socialism
c. 1830	Beginning of positivism
1830s	Development of New England Transcendentalism
1840s	Beginnings of existentialism in writings of Kierkegaard
1840	Proudhon, *What is Property?*; influential text of anarchism
1848	Marx and Engels, *Communist Manifesto*; marks foundation of modern communism
1858	Evolution by natural selection (Darwinism) first proposed
1859	Mill, *On Liberty*; classic text of liberalism
1860s	Beginnings of social Darwinism
1862	Coinage of the term nihilism

1863	J S Mill, *Utilitarianism*
c. 1865–1920s	Neo-Kantianism
1867–95	Marx, *Das Kapital*
1869	J S Mill, *On the Subjection of Women*
1869	Coinage of the term agnosticism
later 19th century	Beginnings of pragmatism
1872–89	Nietzsche publishes his main works
1879	Establishment of psychology as an experimental science
after 1879	Beginning of neo-Thomism
1890	James, *Principles of Psychology*
1890s	Foundation of psychoanalysis
1900	Freud, *The Interpretation of Dreams* Foundation of quantum mechanics
c. 1900	Beginning of analytic philosophy
1902	Frege's attempt to put mathematics on a logical foundation ended by Russell's paradox Kropotkin, *Mutual Aid* Lenin, *What is to be Done?*
1903	Moore, *Principia Ethica*
1905	Einstein's special theory of relativity
1905–06	Santayana, *The Life of Reason*
1907	James, *Pragmatism*
c. 1910	Beginnings of Gestalt psychology
1910–13	Russell and Whitehead, *Principia Mathematica*
1912	Jung, *Psychology of the Unconscious*; provokes rift with Freud
1913	Husserl, *Phenomenological Philosophy*; foundation of phenomenology
1916	Einstein's general theory of relativity Posthumous publication of Saussure, *Course in General Linguistics*; foundation of structuralism
1919	J B Watson applies behaviourism to human psychology

Beginnings of fascism

1920s–30s High point of logical positivism and Vienna Circle

1922 Wittgenstein, *Tractatus Logico-Philosophicus*

1923 Foundation of Frankfurt School
Lukács, *History and Class Consciousness*

1927 Heidegger, *Being and Time*; key text of existentialism
Uncertainty principle discovered by Werner Heisenberg

1929 Ortega y Gasset, *The Revolt of the Masses*

1930s Beginning of emotivism

1931 Gödel proves that mathematics can never be totally consistent and totally complete

1936 Ayer, *Language, Truth and Logic*
Turing propounds theoretical basis of modern computing

1942 Langer, *Philosophy in a New Key*

1943 Sartre, *Being and Nothingness*

1945 Popper, *The Open Society and its Enemies*

1949 Beauvoir, *The Second Sex*

Ryle, *The Concept of Mind*

1950 Alan Turing proposes idea of artificial intelligence

1950s Development of semiology

1953 Wittgenstein, *Philosophical Investigations* (posthumous publication)

1957 Barthes, *Mythologies*; marks beginning of deconstruction

1960s Beginning of poststructuralism

1960 Sartre, *Critique of Dialectical Reason*

1962 Kuhn, *The Structure of Scientific Revolutions*

1964 Marcuse, *One-Dimensional Man*

1966 Lacan, *Ecrits/Writings*

1967 Derrida, *Of Grammatology*

1970s Beginning of postmodernism

1971 Rawls, *A Theory of Justice*

1974 Nozick, *Anarchy, State and Utopia*; influential text of modern libertarianism

1980 Scruton, *The Meaning of Conservatism*